DATE

Creating Chinese Ethnicity

Creating Chinese Ethnicity

SUBEI PEOPLE IN

SHANGHAI, 1850–1980

Emily Honig

YALE UNIVERSITY PRESS

NEW HAVEN AND LONDON

Published with assistance from China Publication Subventions and from the
Frederick W. Hilles Publications Fund of Yale University.
Grateful acknowledgment is made to the following for permission to reprint:
University of California Press for material from *Chinese History in Economic
Perspective,* edited by Thomas Rawski and Lillian Li, ©1992 The Regents of the
University of California; Institute of East Asian Studies for material from
Shanghai Sojourners, edited by Frederic E. Wakeman and Wen-hsin Yeh, China
Research Monograph, no. 40 (Berkeley: University of California, 1992);
University of California at Los Angeles for material from *Modern China* (July
1989); Westview Press for material from *Unofficial China,* edited by Perry Link
et al. (Boulder: Westview Press).

Designed by Jill Breitbarth and set in Bembo type by
Tseng Information Systems, Inc., Durham, North Carolina.
Printed in the United States of America by BookCrafters, Inc., Chelsea,
Michigan

A catalogue record for this book is available from the British Library.

The paper in this book meets the guidelines for permanence and durability of
the Committee on Production Guidelines for Book Longevity of the Council
on Library Resources.

10 9 8 7 6 5 4 3 2 1

Library of Congress Cataloging-in-Publication Data
Honig, Emily.
    Creating Chinese ethnicity : Subei people in Shanghai, 1850–1980 /
Emily Honig.
        p.   cm.
    Includes bibliographical references (p.   ) and index.
    ISBN 0-300-05105-0 (alk. paper)
      1. Ethnology—China—Shanghai—History.   2. Outcasts—China—
Shanghai—History.   3. Shanghai (China)—Ethnic relations.
    I. Title.
DS796.S29H66   1992
305.8′00951132—dc20   92-6055
                                                                CIP

For Rosa and Maya

CONTENTS

MAPS

PREFACE

This book about ethnic identities in Shanghai has its origins in El Paso, Texas. I first went to El Paso in 1977, with two friends, to conduct oral histories of Chicanas who had been involved in a strike at the Farah Manufacturing Company from 1972 to 1974. Impressed by the solidarities formed among Chicana workers during the strike, we were initially chagrined to learn that the strike was also characterized by divisions and antagonisms between Chicanas and Mexicanas. These divisions, we discovered when we returned to conduct further interviews in 1978 and 1979, compounded the meaning of ethnicity in a border city such as El Paso.

The women we had interviewed and befriended in El Paso, as well as our attempts to unravel their solidarities and frictions, were very fresh in my mind when I went to Shanghai, in 1979, to spend two years researching the history of women cotton mill workers. Perhaps unconsciously, issues that had absorbed me in El Paso influenced my research, for it is hardly coincidental that divisions among women workers in Shanghai (particularly between women from the northern and southern parts of Jiangsu Province) became a prominent theme of that study. The Yangzi River seemed to divide Jiangsu in ways that recalled, for me at least, the division represented by the Rio Grande as it separated El Paso from neighboring Ciudad Juárez on the Mexican side of the border. From the first hint, in Shanghai, of divisions based on local origins, I pressed in interviews and in my reading of documentary sources to explore what they meant in the lives of women workers and their implications for the development of class consciousness and political organization.

Yet within the context of studying the history of women workers a fundamental question remained unanswerable, and that concerned the origins of the division between people from the two parts of Jiangsu, and more particularly, the origins of the inferior status of natives of northern Jiangsu—Subei people. Two realizations made me interested in pursuing this question: first, that the division was not confined to the cotton mills but in fact structured social and economic hierarchies throughout Shanghai; second, that the division—as well as the prejudice against Subei natives—persisted throughout the decades after the socialist revolution of 1949. This book began, then, as an attempt to analyze the origins of prejudice in Shanghai. I imagined, initially, that I was constructing a history of Shanghai's "underclass": Subei people.

The extreme paucity of data about Subei people nearly caused me to abort this project on several occasions. But what pushed me closest to abandoning it was the startling realization—reached only after I had been working for several years—that no clear definition of *Subei* or *Subei people* existed. All along I had assumed, as did most of my sources and informants, that it was obvious who a Subei person was. When I began to probe, however, I discovered that Subei was not an objective, clearly defined place, but rather represented a belief in the homogeneity of a particular region. Depending on whom one asked, that region could include all of northern Jiangsu or only certain parts; it could include areas in the neighboring provinces of Shandong and Anhui as well as some districts in southern Jiangsu. It could be defined by geography, language, or economics—but each of these produced very different, if not contradictory, definitions. My subject, it seemed, as well as the credibility of my sources, was dissolving before my very eyes.

Instead of terminating my study, this unsettling realization eventually transformed it. From then on I was no longer trying to assemble a straightforward history of Subei people in Shanghai, but rather to examine the process through which the category Subei people was constructed and the function it played. And as I began to see native place identities (such as that of Subei people) as socially constructed categories, I also began to consider the ways in which they assumed ethnic meanings. It became increasingly clear to me that in Shanghai, at least, local origins defined social relationships that in U.S. history have been considered ethnic, an analysis never previously applied to China, perhaps because of the shared Han identity of the overwhelming majority of the population. Ultimately, then, this became not a study of the making of Shanghai's underclass, but rather one concerning the creation of Chinese ethnicity.

This book does not pretend to be a complete history of Subei people in Shanghai; nor is it arranged chronologically. Instead, each chapter examines the arenas in which Subei ethnicity was formed and contested. Following an introduction, three chapters focus on elite constructions of the social category Subei people. Chapter 2 explores the variety of meanings attached to *Subei* and analyzes its creation as a social category in response to the arrival of immigrants from northern Jiangsu in Jiangnan and Shanghai. The formation of a Subei immigrant community in Shanghai and the attempts of Shanghai authorities to marginalize that community are the subject of chapter 3. Chapter 4 focuses on the work experience of Subei people in Shanghai, analyzing how the labor market both produced and was shaped by ethnicity. Chapter 5 shifts our perspective to that of northern Jiangsu natives themselves, exploring how they constructed their own identity in Shanghai, contesting and resisting the generic Subei identity formulated by the elite. The single historic moment when the status of Subei people became the subject of public debate, when the social category was hardened and challenged in unprecedented ways, was the Japanese attack on Shanghai in 1932, and this is the subject of chapter 6. While the first chapters all focus on the late imperial and Republican periods, chapter 7 deals with the persistence and renegotiation of Subei ethnicity in the decades after 1949, and chapter 8 concludes the book with reflections on the ethnic dimensions of native place identity.

My aim of questioning social categories whose meanings have previously been taken for granted creates a problem of terminology: how to refer to the people whose history I am describing. Throughout this book I shall use the term *Subei* to refer to northern Jiangsu, a core area from the Yangzi to the old Huai River bed, and *Subei people* or *Subei ren* to refer to its residents. When I use the expression *Subei,* I mean the people who were called Subei folk in Shanghai, regardless of their exact place of origin. I do this in the hope that *Subei* will be understood as a complex noun—as both a real and imagined place, as both an actual and socially constructed category.

Jiangbei, not *Subei*, is the term most commonly used in Shanghai to refer to northern Jiangsu. In fact, a number of Shanghai residents looked at me quizzically when informed that I was studying Subei people; once they heard the term *Jiangbei*, however, my subject was clear. I use *Subei* because

Jiangbei has become a pejorative word in Shanghai, even though it might not have been so before 1949. To use the term *Jiangbei ren* throughout the book would have been equivalent to referring to African-Americans as niggers throughout a history of their experience in the United States.

ACKNOWLEDGMENTS

I am indebted to numerous friends and colleagues for their contributions to this project, and most important, for encouraging me to persist. I am grateful to Lisa Rofel, in particular, for helping me see the more exciting intellectual possibilities at the moments I was most convinced that my subject had slipped away. Diana Wylie spent many a run in New Haven listening to and offering criticisms of my most preliminary thoughts about native place ethnicity. As I began to write, Christina Gilmartin, Carmalita Hinton, Gail Hershatter, and Marilyn Young as well as Lisa Rofel devoted major portions of our Saturday marathon sessions to discussions of my work. They read and commented on, sentence by sentence, more versions of the chapters of this book than any of us could possibly care to remember.

Many others have contributed to this project. Elizabeth Perry and Susan Mann were not only extremely generous in sharing their own data about Shanghai workers, but offered detailed comments on the entire manuscript as well. I am also grateful to Deborah Davis, Jonathan Spence, and Kathryn Bernhardt for reading and commenting on a final draft of the book. David Montgomery was an endless source of comparative examples. Over the years, numerous colleagues have spent dinners, lunches, or conference sessions discussing ideas and suggesting sources about Subei people: Marston Anderson, Beatrice Bartlett, Joseph Esherick, Harold Kahn, James Lee, Thomas Rawski, Helen Siu, Wang Shaoguang, Lyman Van Slyke, Frederic Wakeman, Jr., Jeffrey Wasserstrom, Ellen Widmer, and Judith Zeitlin. Valerie Hansen, by sharing her experience conducting research about the Song dynasty, helped put my problems of data in perspective. Micaela diLeonardo generously shared her expertise in the anthropological literature about ethnicity.

Were it not for the generous assistance of numerous individuals in Shanghai, however, there would never have been a manuscript, or even ideas, for friends and colleagues in the United States to critique. I am first and foremost indebted to all of the Subei natives in Shanghai who agreed to be interviewed. The Shanghai Academy of Social Sciences sponsored my research, and the staff of its Foreign Affairs Office, particularly Zhao Nianguo, often went to great lengths to arrange interviews. I am grateful to Xiao Wenyan, Ma Xiuyin, and members of the Shanghai Huai Opera

Troupe for an unforgettable trip to Subei. During my time in Shanghai, Deng Yuzhi, Xu Xinwu, Xue Suzhen, and Chen Zengnian provided critical support and assistance for my research.

A number of fellowships made it possible for me to conduct this research. These include grants from the National Endowment for the Humanities, the Wang Institute for Chinese Studies, the Yale Center for International and Area Studies, and the Griswold Fund at Yale University. These grants enabled me to take advantage of invaluable research assistance from Zhao Xiaojian, Shen Xiaohong, and Liang Kan. At Yale University Press, Charles Grench was a source of moral support and of the occasional nudging one expects from an editor; Lawrence Kenney provided careful manuscript editing. The thoughtful review of the manuscript for the Press by Jerry Dennerline forced me to refine my analysis.

Several people contributed to this project in less direct, but nonetheless meaningful ways. I would like to thank Liza Fiol-Matta and Louise Murray for an apartment in New York City's West Village to spend a week pondering conclusions to this study; Edith Hurd for a house with a view of San Francisco in which to do the final revisions; Rosa and Maya Polan for play and story-telling; and Licia Fiol-Matta for expanding my intellectual and geographic imagination. Finally, from the time we both went to El Paso in 1977 through numerous research trips to China, Gail Hershatter has been a tireless and tough critic, as well as an ever-dependable friend.

Creating Chinese Ethnicity

I

INTRODUCTION

This book explores the history of the most despised group of people in China's largest city, Shanghai. It is the story of how local origins, not race, religion, or nationality, came to define identities that are ethnic in the context of China as surely as African-American and Chicano, Polish and Italian identities have been considered ethnic in the United States. This book about Subei (also called Jiangbei) people, individuals whose families were originally from the part of Jiangsu Province north of the Yangzi River, concerns the social construction and meaning of native place ethnicity in China.

Since the late nineteenth century, being a Subei person in Shanghai has meant being poor. Mostly refugees from floods, famine, or war in their home districts, Subei people did the jobs in Shanghai that were the least lucrative and least desirable. They dominated the ranks of unskilled laborers —rickshaw pullers, dockworkers, construction workers, night soil haulers and garbage collectors, barbers, and bathhouse attendants. Most Subei people resided in the slums on the city's periphery, where they built shacks from reeds, cardboard, and whatever scrap materials they could find.

Partly because of their poverty, Subei people were the objects of prejudice and discrimination. They were laughed at for wearing tasteless, gaudy red and green garments, shunned for the smell of garlic on their breath, and ridiculed for speaking Subei dialect. Subei culture, considered a symbol of sophistication through the mid-Qing dynasty, by the late nineteenth century came to be regarded as low-class and despicable. And from the early twentieth century, calling someone a Subei swine meant that the person, even if not actually from Subei, was poor, ignorant, dirty, and unsophisticated.

Even today, "Subei swine" remains one of the most common curses in Shanghai local dialect: people are said to be "dirty like a Subei person," "ignorant like a Subei person," and even "sexually promiscuous like a Subei person." The districts in which most Subei people live are considered rough and dangerous, and parents warn their children against entering them. University graduates dread the prospect of being assigned to teach in schools in Subei districts, where students reputedly have poor motivation. Finally, no one wants to marry Subei people. When young people, including those whose families are from Subei, go about the business of finding a marriage partner, they almost always specify that the person *not* be of Subei origins.

So tenacious is the prejudice against Subei people that it has been transported, recreated, and ascribed new meanings by Shanghainese who have emigrated. For example, an elderly woman whose family had enjoyed considerable wealth in pre-Liberation Shanghai explained that whenever she wants to complain about the behavior of Puerto Ricans or African-Americans while riding the subways in New York, where she has lived for many years, she refers to them as Subei people. In this way she believes she averts the possibility of being called racist and being attacked.

Prejudice against Subei people, so obvious and so readily admitted to by Shanghai residents, has been largely invisible to Western observers and historians of Shanghai. More concerned with inequalities and antagonisms based on class or gender differences, they have overlooked those defined by native place identity.[1] Yet in the immigrant city of Shanghai, native place identity structured social hierarchy and gave shape to popular senses of pride as well as prejudice. This book aims not merely to analyze the historical experience of one immigrant community, Subei people, but, more important, to suggest bases of identity, prejudice, and social conflict that have been central to China's urban residents and that in a Chinese context may constitute ethnicity.

The experience of Subei people in Shanghai immediately brings to mind cross-cultural comparisons with groups whose ethnic identity is rarely doubted. At first glance, the poverty of Subei people and the prejudice against them seem reminiscent of the experience of such racial minorities in the United States as African-Americans, Chicanos, Puerto Ricans, and Asian-Americans. Unlike these groups, however, Subei people were not physically distinct from the rest of the Shanghai population, almost all of whom were Han Chinese. Although the elite may have treated Subei people *as if* they belonged to a different race, they in fact could be distinguished only by dialect.

White immigrants to the United States, for example, the Irish who fled the potato famine in the early nineteenth century, might offer a closer analogy. In cities of New England, as in the English cities of London, Manchester, and Liverpool, Irish immigrants lived in separate neighborhoods, were looked down on, and did jobs that natives were unwilling to do.[2] Yet the Irish, though they shared with Subei people an identity based on migration, possessed an ethnicity defined largely by nationality: they came from a country with cultural traditions and a history undeniably different from that of their new home. Furthermore, determining who was Irish was not problematic: the Irish were, quite simply, people from Ireland.

Not so for Subei people. They were not migrants from across national boundaries, and Subei was not a place with an obvious or straightforward definition. The name *Subei* referred to neither a city, prefecture, nor province, but to a region whose boundaries and coherence were debatable. Thus, more than to ethnic groups in the United States defined by race or national origins, their experience is analogous to those defined by regional difference, such groups as the Appalachian "hillbillies" who settled in northern cities and southwestern "Okies" who migrated to California.

Superficially at least, Subei people might well be called the Okies of Shanghai. Like Subei people, the Okies came from an area whose regional coherence was articulated only in response to the arrival of its migrants elsewhere. The region was not defined by the boundaries of Oklahoma, as the name implies, but included parts of Texas, Arkansas, and Missouri as well. No one imagined these four states as constituting a region until thousands of their natives, the famed dust bowl migrants of the 1930s, resettled in California's Central Valley. As immigrants they performed tasks in agricultural production that California natives were unwilling to do and that had been previously performed by Mexican migrants. Although Okies, like the natives, were white, they were treated as a "despised and alien social group." Calling someone an Okie, like calling someone a *Jiangbei lao* (old Jiangbei), became a popular derogatory expression, implying backwardness, poverty, and inferiority. Finally, although Okies were a recognized ethnic group in California, Okie ethnicity was not an identity initially created by the migrants themselves but was instead the product of their relationship to native Californians.[3] Likewise, Subei ethnicity was not based on heritage but was created in Shanghai.

In spite of the similarities between the experience of the Okies in California and that of Subei people in Shanghai, the analogy remains imperfect. The Okie identity was, according to the historian James Gregory, bound to class; the name *Okie* essentially a metaphor for low-class. Migrants from Oklahoma and other southwestern states who secured respectable jobs in Los Angeles and San Francisco, or even in the Central Valley, were not looked down on or accused of being Okies. The Okie stereotype, Gregory tells us, "was never meant for all Southwesterners."

> Middle-class newcomers encountered little resentment or disesteem. Even in the midst of the anti-migrant campaign most were accorded the same basic respect as other whites of their economic station. The Okie stereotype was not in the first instance a matter of regional prejudice. . . . Class was the essential dividing line. The Okie outgroup included people who were not Southwesterners, and the socially respectable ingroup included some who were.[4]

A person's local origins were far less important than his or her occupation; regional difference became salient only to distinguish the white poor from the white rich.

In Shanghai, however, the relationship between class and native place identity was far more complex. On the one hand, the distinction between Jiangnan and Subei natives was based largely on class difference. The expression *Subei ren* (or Jiangbei lao) was clearly a metaphor for low-class, the noun to identify poor, stigmatized people. Class, in Shanghai, was constituted through native place identities, and the construction of native place identities was part of a discourse about class. Furthermore, it was precisely because those identities were so inextricably linked to class that they assumed ethnic dimensions.

On the other hand, the creation of the social category Subei people was not strictly a class phenomenon; the importance of one's local origins was never subordinate to one's occupation. Try as some Subei natives did to disguise their origins, their identity could not be transcended by class mobility. Wealthy landlords fleeing land reform in the 1940s were as likely to be insulted and looked down on as Subei swines as were poor peasants fleeing natural disasters. Even in Shanghai today, it is not only the sons and daughters of workers of Subei origins who are shunned as marriage partners, but also the sons and daughters of officials of Subei origins. In other words, in Shanghai something more than class was and is at stake. Ethnicity may well overlap with and reinforce class divisions, but it is not reducible to class.

Identifying what is at stake in Shanghai requires a consideration of Chinese comparisons, only some of which have been described as ethnic. In fact, those groups that have been most commonly described as ethnic in China are perhaps least relevant to understanding the experience of Subei people in Shanghai. Studies of Chinese ethnicity frequently focus on national minorities: non-Han groups such as the Miao, Yi, Uighurs,. Mongols, and Tibetans, who altogether represent less than 10 percent of China's population. Although a number of recent studies show that the ethnic identity of these groups is no straightforward proposition,[5] their racial and cultural distinction from the Han majority is not disputed. Most live in border areas and therefore are not central to notions of ethnicity in interior or coastal provinces. In other words, if the development of ethnic-like relationships throughout China depended on the existence of non-Han minorities, little or no ethnicity would be found. A major point of this study is to demonstrate how ethnic identities can be constituted among Han peoples themselves.

More analogous to Subei people than the national minorities are a variety of Han peoples who, through most of the Qing dynasty at least, were considered déclassé and subject to discrimination. Such groups as the *duomin* (literally, "fallen people") in Zhejiang, the "musician households" of Shanxi and Shaanxi, and the "boat people" of Guangdong were relegated to a status entirely different from—and beneath—the rest of the Han population. They were not allowed to participate in the examination system, they were registered separately from commoners (*liangmin*), and their women were not allowed to bind their feet and thereby gain respectability and status.[6] Like Subei people in Shanghai, members of these groups were all Han, yet their déclassé status was defined strictly by occupation.

Even more analogous to Subei people are an infinite variety of migrant communities throughout China, the members of which are also all Han. The most obvious comparison is to the Hakkas (whose name—*kejia* in Mandarin—literally means "guest people") of southeastern China. Like Subei people, Hakkas were an immigrant population, distinguished from natives (*bendi ren*) primarily by dialect. And like Subei people, they were often the objects of prejudice, described as poor, uneducated, country bumpkins, uncivilized, and even non-Chinese barbarians. As opposed to Subei people in Shanghai, however, the Hakkas had no coherent place of origin: their ancestors are believed to have left Henan in the fourth century; the majority, though, are descendants of Tang dynasty migrants from Fujian. Certain regions of southeastern China, particularly Guangdong, became almost exclusively Hakka communities.[7] Hakkas identified themselves as different from and superior to their Cantonese neighbors: they saw themselves as the descendants of Song dynasty officials, while native Cantonese, in contrast, were allegedly descendants of aboriginal barbarians.[8]

Less obvious than the Hakkas are immigrant populations in other parts of China. For example, during the Ming and Qing dynasties, migrants from Fujian and northern Guangdong settled on the mountainsides of Jiangxi. Despite the heterogeneity of these immigrants, natives viewed them all as belonging to the uniform category shed people or guest people and called them by these derogatory names. Natives' antagonism toward these shed people was based on their relative poverty as well as on differences in dialect and cultural practices.[9] Jiangxi natives were themselves on the move during the Qing. When large numbers of them settled in Hunan, conflict between them and Hunan natives became rampant. So as to distinguish themselves from the despised Jiangxi immigrants, Hunanese thought of them as non-Han tribesmen, though eventually these so-called barbarians overwhelmed the natives economically, as they came to dominate the growing commercial sector.[10]

The point is not that the shed people in Jiangxi or the Jiangxi barbarians in Hunan were inherently ethnic, a question not addressed by those who have studied them. Rather, both cases suggest the ways in which the experience of Subei people in Shanghai belongs to a larger history of antagonistic relations between immigrant and native populations throughout China.[11]

Immigration within China gave rise to the concept of native place identity (jiguan). Historically, Chinese have always distinguished their place of birth from their native place, the latter referring to the home of their ancestors. For official documents as well as for identifying oneself to others, local origins have been at least as significant as one's birthplace. "The concept of native place was a critical component of personal identity in traditional China," observes Bryna Goodman in her study of native place organization and consciousness in Shanghai. "[It] was generally the first matter of inquiry among strangers, the first characteristic recorded about a person (after name and pseudonyms), and the first fact to be ascertained regarding individuals coming before the law."[12]

Native place identity, however, is a malleable construction: an individual can determine which generation's home to claim as his or her native place; moreover, native place might refer to a particular village, district, city, or province. Central as it is to one's identity, then, describing one's native place is not a straightforward proposition.

Historians and anthropologists have long recognized the centrality of native place identity to Chinese conceptions of self and community. Ho Ping-ti's study of guilds was one of the first to call attention to the importance of native place in China; native place identities and hometown bonds are implicit in G. William Skinner's study of mobility strategies: of how localities cultivated specific human talents that were then exported across China—the Shanxi bankers, Ningbo entrepreneurs, and so on.[13] Likewise, Susan Mann analyzes the ways in which, drawing on native place ties, Ningbo natives in Shanghai were able to build a powerful community.[14] James Cole, too, chronicles the reliance on native place ties by Shaoxing natives away from home.[15] More recently, Susan Naquin and Evelyn Rawski, in their history of eighteenth-century China, observe that "native place was the principle most often invoked as grounds for affiliation and assistance by men who left their homes to work in an alien environment."[16] Although the role of native place ties does not figure prominently in David Strand's study of Beijing, he describes factions among workers based on native place, identifies the important role that native place associations continued to play in the 1920s, and suggests the ways in which native place connections sometimes provided a base for power in urban politics.[17]

The most extensive analysis of native place ties in an urban environment is William Rowe's richly detailed study of the central China treaty port city Hankou. Although concluding that "the prevailing mood of the city was cosmopolitan,"[18] he nevertheless emphasizes the persistence of localism in urban development. Rowe describes the importance of hometown bonds in securing jobs, financial help in time of need, and defense in daily street brawls. Commercial cliques, worker recruitment, and leisure activities were often organized around native place ties. Residence, too, reflected the persistence of localism: certain districts of Hankou were so dominated by people from a particular native place that they resembled ethnic enclaves. Despite the emergence of new, urban institutions, native place associations played a central role in the social and political life of Hankou residents. The prominence of native place identities led Rowe to conclude that "geographically determined subethnic distinctions . . . constituted the most important distinguishing feature between individual Chinese in the late imperial period."[19]

While recognizing the importance of native place identity in defining social relations, Rowe's study and the others treat it in a literal way. They do not examine how it intersects and is enmeshed with notions of class and culture and embodies meanings more comprehensive and variable than the place-name itself. What it means to identify as a Ningbo or Shanxi person is not problematized or understood as the product of social construction.

More dynamic ways of analyzing the meaning of native place identity in

China are suggested by recent anthropological studies of ethnicity in non-Chinese contexts. While not offering clear-cut answers as to when native place identity becomes "ethnic," these studies propose ways of thinking about social groups that, when applied to China, suggest analyses of native place identity far more complex than those presented in previous examinations. Sylvia Yanagisako's study of Japanese-Americans in Seattle, Karen Blu's of the Lumbee Indians in North Carolina, and James Clifford's of Native Americans on Cape Cod all move us from focusing on the literal to explore symbolic, socially constructed identities.[20] The new scholarship argues for understanding ethnicity not as a singular identity, but as a system of relationships. Identities form, that is, only in relation or contradistinction to other identities in particular local and historical contexts.

Ethnicity, however, is not simply a set of relationships. The new scholarship also highlights ethnicity as a historical process. Rather than taking social categories—African-Americans, the Irish, Okies, Subei people—articulated by residents of any particular locale as a given, it challenges us to explore the process by which these categories were created and by which their meanings change. Instead of considering a "common heritage" or "sense of peoplehood," phrases commonly invoked in definitions of ethnicity, as static beliefs brought by immigrants to their new home, these scholars argue that we should see them as ideas or even myths created as a result of migration. As William Yancey, Eugene Ericksen, and Richard N. Juliani concluded in their influential article "Emergent Ethnicity," "The assumption of a common heritage as the essential aspect of ethnicity is erroneous. Ethnicity may have relatively little to do with Europe, Asia or Africa, but much more to do with the exigencies of survival and the structure of opportunity in this country."[21]

The point, then, is not to determine when and if native place identity in China passes some litmus test for ethnicity. Instead, if we allow that it may be ethnic, we can then look at it in a way that highlights a range of previously indiscernible social relationships and historical processes. We can also, by viewing native place identity as continuously in the process of being created and given new meanings, understand social, economic, and cultural aspects of Chinese urban history in entirely new ways. The relationship of native place identities to notions of class and to the contested terrain of urban culture suddenly becomes apparent.

What exactly, the reader may well wonder, is meant by *ethnicity*? Few subjects have been as contentiously debated by anthropologists, and it would be foolhardy to propose a definition without acknowledging those debates.[22] What is more, while this book draws on debates about ethnicity, it also aims to contribute to them by examining a form of ethnicity—

one defined by native place—that has been largely ignored. One of the purposes of this book—by examining a situation in which the clues most familiar to us as markers of ethnicity, for example, race and nationality, are absent—is thus to challenge readers to think about ethnicity in new ways.

Some observations about the meaning of ethnicity may be instructive nevertheless. First, ethnicity is not an objective thing, such as blood ties, but rather a process. More specifically, it involves the creation, invocation, and manipulation of notions of cultural distinctiveness to establish self/other dichotomies among people in a shared political and economic system. Language, race, religion, historical experience, and geographic origins are among the myriad attributes that may be drawn on to create such boundaries. But it must be underlined that what constitutes a different or distinct language, religion, race, history, or place of origin is entirely malleable. No feature inherently represents an ethnic marker. "A particular attribute," the anthropologist Lee Drummond points out, "such as physical appearance, dress, speech, mode of livelihood, or religion, has ethnic significance, or marking, only by virtue of the system of meanings in which it is embedded." [23]

This leads to a second observation about the meaning of ethnicity: no group of people is inherently or immutably ethnic. The Irish, for example, were obviously not ethnic in Ireland but only became so when they migrated to the United States. The same is true for African-Americans and almost every other group of people who have been considered ethnic throughout American history. Likewise, Subei people were not a people in Subei; they only became Subei people in Shanghai. Ethnicity, in other words, depends upon context.

A third observation about the meaning of ethnicity concerns agency, or who does the defining of social categories. Ethnic identity, as the anthropologist Ruth Mandel points out, may be articulated by people seeking to identify as a "collective solidarity group." Such solidarity may be expressed to resist stigmatization or discrimination, to demand political and economic rights, as well as to assert pride in a group's heritage. However, Mandel rightly insists, the sense of "boundedness" may just as well be "extrinsically determined, for example, for purposes of subordination and domination." [24] It is this latter phenomenon that predominates in the construction of Subei ethnicity in Shanghai.

A fourth observation about the meaning of ethnicity concerns its relationship to class. While a society may be structured by class and not ethnicity and vice versa, in many cases the two seem to intersect or even to represent different names for the same group of people. Although both are rooted in structures of inequality, class is defined by one's place in the production process, whereas ethnicity is defined by distinctions based on origins. Neither can be reduced to the other, yet the two often overlap, just as beliefs about ethnic difference are often used, if not created, to explain or rationalize occupational hierarchies.

I use the term *ethnicity* in this book both cautiously and deliberately. I use it with caution because ethnicity is a concept that does not exist in China. It is most often translated there as *minzu*, a term that most literally means "nationalities" or "minorities" and that refers only to non-Han peoples.[25] The subject I am writing about is a phenomenon that has no name in Chinese. Moreover, even Western anthropologists have rarely extended it to encompass regional, as opposed to national, racial, religious, or tribal, identities. Yet I use *ethnicity* quite deliberately, for no other term is even approximately adequate to describe the function of the category Subei people in Shanghai's history. To refer simply to native place identity obscures the process of social construction as well as the relationships of dominance and subordination that are involved.

A number of scholars have invoked the terms *subethnic* and *quasi-ethnic* to describe social groups in China that are defined by local origins.[26] Calling native place identity in Shanghai subethnic is problematic, however, as it implies the existence of some more prominent and presumably more authentic type of ethnicity to which native place identities are subordinate. As Pamela Crossley poignantly argues,

> It may be that in the terminology of "subethnic" which has become conventional when describing ethnicity among the *han* we are looking at yet another legacy of sinology. That is, as the *han* have only one admissible "language"—and the languages of China become "dialects" in sinological idolect—so they can only be one "people," and variations among that people become not "ethnic," but "subethnic." Certainly the greater meaning of "ethnic" handily includes cultural variations among people who on one level all consider themselves *han* yet on another evince recognizable ethnic consciousness. The intrusion of "subethnic" seems not only unwarranted but possibly misleading, for historically it is surely true that the geographical and cultural entity of China is a totality of convergently and divergently related localisms.[27]

Ascribing the term *ethnic* to groups defined by local origins does in fact have precedent in studies of China. Its applicability was first suggested by G. William Skinner in his analysis of urban systems in Qing China. "The pattern of economic specialization by native place that prevailed in late imperial cities," he proposed, can be profitably analyzed in terms of an ethnic division of labor. There is no difficulty whatsoever in viewing the "colonies" of extra-regional traders in Chinese cities as ethnic minorities. . . . Anhwei merchants in Chungking, Ningpo merchants in Peking, Hokkien merchants in Hankow, Ningpo merchants in Canton, Shansi merchants in Foochow—all spoke languages unintelligible to the natives and practiced customs that appeared outlandish at best. But if recent studies of ethnicity have taught us anything, it is that ethnic solidarity is no simple function of cultural distinctiveness; slight accents and even minor mannerisms may serve as ethnic markers if either side finds it advantageous to maintain or erect ethnic boundaries.[28]

This analysis has been applied in several case studies, although in somewhat limited ways. Both David Ownby and Stevan Harrell, for example, describe divisions between migrants to Taiwan from different localities in southeast China in the late Qing as ethnic.[29] Hill Gates analyzes the process through which relationships between mainlanders and native Taiwanese became ethnic in the decades following World War II.[30] Finally, C. Fred Blake, analyzing the social structure of a market town in the New Territories outside Hong Kong, insists upon the term *ethnic* to describe group identities defined largely by native place.[31] My study of Subei people draws on these works, extending geographically a conceptual framework that has heretofore been confined to studies of Taiwan and Hong Kong.[32]

This brings us back to Shanghai, for this book is not about native place identity in general, but about one specific group. Neither is it about Subei people in general, but rather about their particular experience in Shanghai. (Indeed, the category Subei people did not exist outside of Shanghai and Jiangnan—individuals from the area that Shanghainese called Subei who lived in cities such as Beijing and Hankou were not thought of as Subei people.) It is about the meaning of native place, but also about the making of Shanghai history.

When a specific native place group such as Subei people is the focus of study, we see how, in Shanghai, social and economic relations were defined largely by local origins. This should not be entirely surprising, for pre-1949 Shanghai was a city of immigrants. "Shanghai is a hybrid place which mixes up people from all over China," noted the authors of the Shanghai local gazetteer in 1907. "The numbers of outsiders surpass the natives."[33] Statistics confirm this impression: in 1885, immigrants represented some 85 percent of the city's population; in 1930, 78 percent (the lowest the figure ever dropped); and in 1949, 84.9 percent.[34]

Local origins structured much of Shanghai's social and economic land-

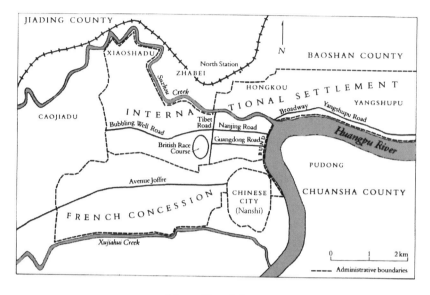

Map 1. Shanghai, 1919

scape. The enclaves of various foreign populations—the unmistakably French, British, Russian, and Japanese districts—were paralleled by neighborhoods dominated by immigrants from particular regions of China. Ningbo people, for instance, concentrated in the French Concession and in the northern part of the South City (Nanshi) along the Huangpu River; Cantonese mainly settled in Hongkou or along Guangdong Road, near the large shipyards where many were employed; natives of northern Jiangsu were found mostly in shack settlements on the outskirts of the foreign concessions[35] (see map 1).

From the mid-nineteenth century, when the city's development as a commercial and industrial metropolis began, laborers, merchants, and entrepreneurs in Shanghai came mostly from three areas: Guangdong, Jiangnan (the Ningbo-Shaoxing region of Zhejiang and the Wuxi-Changzhou area of Jiangsu), and northern Jiangsu (called Subei) (see map 2). Which of these areas one hailed from was critical in shaping work opportunities, residential patterns, cultural activities, and social status. Hierarchy was structured largely according to local origins: the elite was composed primarily of people from Guangdong and Jiangnan, and the unskilled service sector was staffed mostly by migrants from Subei. Even though not all migrants from Ningbo were wealthy and not all those from Subei poor, identity as a Ningbo native connoted wealth and urbanity as certainly as a Subei identity was associated with poverty and ignorance.

Social conflict, too, was often based on native place antagonisms. Previ-

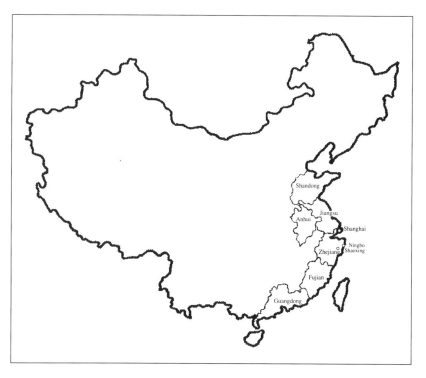

Map 2. Outline map of China, showing eastern provinces

ous scholarship has observed the pronounced rivalry between Cántonese and Ningbo natives in the mid-nineteenth century.[36] Yet conflict between Subei and Jiangnan natives, by far the most salient native place cleavage in Shanghai from the late nineteenth century on, has been largely ignored. Moreover, the economic, social, cultural, and sometimes even political history of Shanghai is in no small part the working out of this conflict in a colonial setting. Understanding social organization as well as the relationship between class and native place identity in the immigrant city of Shanghai requires analysis of the antagonism between these two largest immigrant groups.

The creation and naming of social categories in Shanghai also reflected the centrality of native place identity. Given Shanghai's immigrant population, it is not surprising that local origins defined some of the major social groups (the Shanghai *bang,* or clique, the Ningbo bang, and the Subei bang) much as in the United States individuals and ethnic groups are often defined by national origins. But, as mentioned above, how one's place of origin is defined is not always a straightforward proposition. An American from China may be Chinese-American or Asian-American; one from

Mexico, Mexican-American, Chicano, or Hispanic. Conflicts over these choices, over how minority groups define themselves as opposed to how they are defined by the elite, attest to the fact that more than names per se are at stake. That people from northern Jiangsu did not usually accept the name *Subei* imposed by the Jiangnan elite suggests the analogous conflicts that pervaded Shanghai's history.

Finally, focusing on Subei people forces us to understand Shanghai identity and Shanghai culture in new ways. Claims to both were heavily contested. The struggle of Jiangnan immigrants to claim Shanghai identity as theirs depended largely on the belief in the existence of a despised group of Subei people—a belief that has been central throughout Shanghai's development as a modern, industrial center. Shanghai identity can be understood only in contradistinction to the other against which it defined itself, and Subei people represented that other.

While the experience of Subei people sheds light on previously invisible aspects of Shanghai history, certain facets of Shanghai's development are central to analyzing the formation of the social category Subei people. The large percentage of the population composed of immigrants has already been observed. Equally important, although for reasons less immediately apparent, is Shanghai's status as a treaty port. From the signing of the Treaty of Nanjing at the end of the Opium War in 1842, foreign merchants and missionaries flocked to Shanghai. By the early twentieth century, the original Chinese city was geographically marginal to the International Settlement, composed of the British and American concessions, and French Concession.

The alleged poverty and backwardness of Subei people were therefore measured not simply by the standards of a Chinese elite, but by a foreign one as well. British buildings along the Bund and the villas in "Frenchtown" magnified the dilapidation of the shack settlements in which Subei people lived. European fashions highlighted the alleged raggedness of Subei people's clothes. Trams and automobiles initially imported from abroad dramatized the backwardness of rickshaws pulled by many Subei natives.

Foreign political, economic, and social domination of Shanghai affected the construction of the category Subei people in other ways as well. First, foreign development of industry in Shanghai had a profound effect on the Jiangsu rural economy. It intensified the division of the province at the Yangzi River, such that southern and northern Jiangsu came to represent, respectively, wealth and poverty. Had Shanghai not been a treaty port, there might well have been no place called Subei. Second, foreign investment structured the Shanghai labor market, so that certain jobs were defined as high-status by dint of belonging to the modern sector, and what was modern was defined largely by foreigners. The low-status nature ascribed to jobs associated with Subei people must be understood in the context of a foreign-controlled economy. Finally, the Jiangnan elite that played such a crucial role in constructing the category Subei people, or Subei ren, was itself in a subordinate position. Its claim to a Shanghai identity was defined largely by an association with—if only an aspiration to emulate—foreigners. Subei people, in contrast, were backward because they lacked not simply urbanity but knowledge of Western ways as well.

Colonialism provided more than a context for the development of the category Subei ren. Foreigners were sometimes active agents in the construction of that category. In the 1930s, for example, Japanese invaders employed Subei people, thereby contributing to the popular perception of Subei people as despised collaborators. Throughout the first half of the twentieth century, the foreign-controlled Shanghai Municipal Council continually struggled to eliminate the shack settlements in which Subei people lived and to reduce the prolific number of rickshaws that they pulled. It was foreigners who imposed beliefs concerning what a modern city should be, and Subei people were perceived as a blemish on that ideal.

The history of Subei people, then, is not simply that of Shanghai's poverty-stricken underclass, but also that of the process, consequences, and meaning of urbanization, immigration, and industrialization in China's major treaty port city. It exemplifies how, by drawing on anthropological theories of ethnicity, we may understand the experience of a particular migrant community in entirely new ways and in addition recognize forms of inequality and prejudice in Shanghai that were previously invisible.

Little has been written about Subei people. Unlike intellectuals, peasants, women, or even factory workers and prostitutes, Subei people have rarely been recognized as a distinct social group and therefore have not been the subject of surveys, investigations, and reports. Besides, although some of their occupations, rickshaw pulling, for example, were often investigated, many others, such as working in barbershops and bathhouses, hauling night soil, and peddling vegetables, were rarely written about. Even census takers did not count the number of Subei people in Shanghai, making it impossible to know the exact percentage of the population they constituted at any given time.

Of the thousands of books and articles in periodicals concerning social conditions in Shanghai before 1949, no more than two or three focus on the experience of Subei people. And like most nonelite groups, Subei people have written very little about themselves. Finally, even those sources that do provide scattered references to Subei people (and it is hundreds of such scattered, piecemeal references that form the core of this book) are problematic, for they never recognize that the identification of a person as Subei is debatable.

Despite these limitations, the outlines of the history of Subei people in Shanghai can be assembled, incomplete though they may be. Subei people must be sought between the lines: in studies of Shanghai's shack dwellers, gang organizations, and workers; in guidebooks, linguistic surveys, and publicity about local opera. They are perhaps most easily found in local newspapers, which before 1949 invariably specified the native place of individuals about whom they were reporting. Those factory records and records of native place associations representing districts in northern Jiangsu that are accessible provide invaluable data.

Without oral history interviews, however, this book would have been impossible. I conducted formal interviews with a large number of Subei people in Shanghai during 1986 and 1988, primarily to document their work experience. Often, however, the inadvertent comments or even the ways people behaved were as revealing and significant as the information they shared. For instance, members of the Shanghai Huai Opera Troupe were overjoyed at the prospect of being accompanied by a foreign scholar on the first leg of their two-month performing tour through Subei. My presence promised to make entertaining what for them would have been an otherwise dreary trip—dreary because accommodations and food in Subei were far inferior to what they were accustomed to in Shanghai. The tour was necessary, though, because the Shanghai audience was not sufficiently large to support them. They had never before imagined being of interest to a foreigner and relished the opportunity to inquire about groups of performers in the United States whose status resembled theirs in Shanghai. Likewise, a group of sanitation department workers from Subei were so delighted to be of interest to a foreign scholar that they welcomed me to their work unit in Shanghai with heaping platters of fruits, nuts, and sweets in addition to the more common and simple cup of tea offered at units more confident of their respectability. A bathhouse pedicurist from Yangzhou arrived at an interview dressed in a Western suit, while his co-workers from Yancheng dressed in more ordinary workers' clothes; he thus underlined his attitude that though they were all from Subei, Yangzhou people were far more urbane and sophisticated. And many sessions that began as formal interviews turned into heated arguments among the interviewees about the nature and reasons for discrimination against Subei people in Shanghai. The anger and indignation expressed in these spontaneous debates told me far more about their attitudes than their responses to formal questions about what it meant to them to be from Subei.

Casual conversations were as important as formal interviews in exploring attitudes, both current and historic, toward Subei people. Since the status of Subei people, unlike that of the working class or national minorities after 1949, has never been a political issue almost no sensitivity, embarrassment, or shame censored people's derogatory comments. The mere mention of my research topic, for example, inevitably elicited impassioned expositions on the character defects of Subei people. Even conversations on topics unrelated to Subei people were likely to produce comments indicative of popular attitudes. Such was the case when a friend related to me the story of a teacher at her university who was allegedly involved in a number of extramarital affairs. "He was from Subei, of course," she observed, not knowing that Subei people were of special interest to me. Likewise, an American scholar struggling to board a bus was informed that *all* the people guilty of pushing and shoving on the Shanghai buses were from Subei. In another instance, when a Chinese train passenger betrayed his ignorance of the fact that Washington, D.C., is the capital of the United States, fellow passengers quickly explained to an American scholar riding the train that the man was from Subei and hence exceptionally ignorant. In still another exchange, following an interview of a Subei family in which it was revealed that the family members had domestic quarrels, the residence committee official accompanying an American sociologist explained, "That is why we don't want our children to become friends with Subei people—they seem nice on the surface, but underneath there are always these kinds of problems." In all these instances, comments about Subei people were spontaneous and unsolicited and therefore markedly useful as an index to popular prejudice.

In assembling through casual conversations, interviews, and documentary sources what can be known of the history of Subei people as an immigrant community, I aim to analyze the origins of the most virulent prejudice and discrimination in Shanghai. More broadly, I examine the relationship between local origins and social hierarchy and the implications of that relationship for the process and meaning of urbanization in China. Finally, in emphasizing the construction and meaning of social categories based on native places such as Subei, I hope to suggest new ways of thinking about the creation of ethnicity in Chinese history. Every ethnicity has a history and can be understood only by tracing that history in its most local dimensions. That, ultimately, is the endeavor of this book.

2

IN SEARCH OF SUBEI

Jiangbei people live in straw huts that are very cheap to build [and] there are often fires in their settlements. They eat food that is hardly better than garbage. . . . They are not very sanitary. They only change their clothes once every week or two. . . . Most men are rickshaw pullers, construction, dock, or transport workers. Most women are maids, servants, or work in silk filatures. One can say that they do the lowest strata of jobs. Jiangbei men are often in fights; the women are often raped. They have little legal protection because they are so ignorant.[1]

Subei people have been recognized as a major social category in Shanghai ever since the mid-nineteenth century, when Shanghai's population became composed primarily of immigrants. Most non-Subei people in Shanghai believed that despite economic, linguistic, and cultural differences among districts north of the Yangzi River, natives of northern Jiangsu shared a common identity and experience and therefore represented a homogeneous group, described by the categorical term *Subei ren* (or *Jiangbei ren*).

From the time Chinese newspapers began publication, Subei ren was one of the most common identities ascribed to individuals. People from north of the river were identified as generic Jiangbei ren or occasionally as someone "speaking with a Jiangbei accent." Likewise, accounts of "Jiangbei shack dwellers" and, at times of floods, "Jiangbei refugees" commonly appeared in the popular press. Some accounts, referring to the "Jiangbei bang" (clique), implied that Subei migrants represented not only a coherent, homogeneous group, but a united one as well.[2] Newspapers rarely identified someone as being a native of a specific Subei district, such as Yancheng, Yangzhou, or Huai'an. In contrast, individuals from Wuxi were invariably identified as "Wuxi ren," those from Ningbo as "Ningbo ren." They were never grouped under the rubric "Jiangnan ren," a category that existed only at the national level.

During the Republican period, social surveys, though rarely focusing on Subei people, frequently identified them as a category. Subei was one of the major native places attributed to workers in the survey of Shanghai labor published in the special labor issue of *New Youth Magazine* (1920) as well as in the more comprehensive study *Shanghai's Enterprises and Workers* (1939). Occasionally, articles appeared that dealt specifically with Subei people, deploring their plight in Shanghai. And workers interviewed about their experiences in Shanghai before 1949 recount with passion and certainty the characteristics, occupations, and residences of Subei people. Subei people, in short, were an unmistakable presence and social category in the Shanghai social landscape.

Who were these Subei people whom everyone seemed able to identify? The most obvious answer: people from Subei. That Subei was a place whose definition was understood is implicit in almost all the historic literature: news articles bore headlines about floods, famine, and war in Subei; rural surveys of Jiangsu invariably divided the province into Jiangnan and Subei, providing lengthy descriptions of an area called Subei. Clearly, a place called Subei existed. Nothing in the historic literature suggests its definition needed articulation and was anything less than obvious. Even in Shanghai today, ask any person for a definition of Subei, and he or she will answer so immediately and confidently that one would never suspect this was a question of any controversy. "Subei is northern Jiangsu," most people initially reply. "It is *all* of Jiangsu north of the Yangzi."

When more specific questions are asked, however, the definition of Subei becomes increasingly elusive. "Is the area north of the Huai River part of Subei?" Some say yes, others no. "What about areas on the northern bank of the Yangzi, such as Haimen and Nantong—are they part of Subei?" Again, a variety of answers are presented. The same is true for places on the southern bank of the Yangzi, such as Zhenjiang. Some Shanghai residents, as they begin to ponder the definition of Subei, insist that even Nanjing be included, while others suggest that parts of Shandong and Anhui belong to Subei as well. In other words, the more one presses, the more the certainty surrounding the definition of Subei dissolves. That confusion surrounds the definition of Subei is not surprising, for Subei is not a political construct with obvious, clearly delineated boundaries. Neither province nor county, it is a region for which no consistent definition exists, much like Appalachia in the United States.[3] The anthropologist Fei Xiaotong's observation that "as a regional concept, 'northern Jiangsu' is not very clearly defined" understates the problem.[4] The problem is that Subei is not an objective place but rather represents the belief in the geographic, cultural, linguistic, and economic homogeneity of a particular area.[5] Moreover, the belief in the homogeneity of northern Jiangsu is itself historically constructed: the idea of a place called Subei emerged only in the context of social and economic changes that culminated in the mid-nineteenth century.

Subei: The Place

Subei, most literally, is a geographic region, referring to the part of Jiangsu north of the Yangzi River (see map 3). As the name Subei implies, it is north (bei) Jiangsu (su). It is also referred to as Jiangbei—north (bei) of the river (jiang). This is a vast and varied area, including everything from Haimen and Nantong on the northern bank of the Yangzi River to Haizhou in the far north and Xuzhou at the distant northwestern edge of the province. The most northern area (the part of the province north of the Huai) is the most rugged, being dry and having a short growing season, one that supports winter wheat, millet, corn, peanuts, and sweet potatoes. The French geographer L. Richards described the area around Xuzhou as "in no wise different from that of the North of China. It is even less rich and has but sparse clumps of bamboos, while the willow, poplar and a few acacias are the only trees that afford a little verdure to this impoverished tract. The mulberry is scarce, and the country has neither rice nor the tea-plant. There are a few fruit trees and the fruit is excellent, especially the peaches."[6] A missionary report painted an even bleaker picture of this area:

> The northern section of the province [Jiangsu] from Shantung to the old basin of the Yellow River is economically least favored. The alkali soil characteristic of so much of this region seems much less productive than the black soil of southern Kiangsu. Areas subject to floods in summer bear only a single crop of winter wheat. Higher land produces wheat in winter, and "kaoliang," beans, peanuts, or

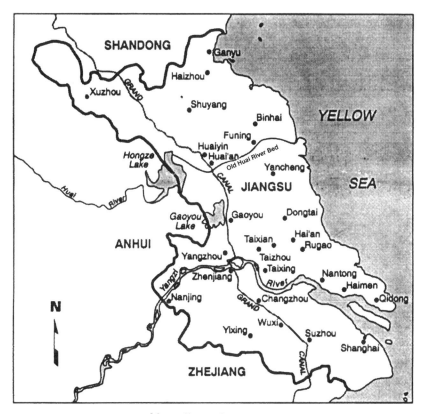

Map 3. Jiangsu Province, 1935

other crops in summer. Inquiry has brought out the fact that for a northern family to obtain the same support secured by the southern farmer from planting twenty mow (3 acres) of land, it must cultivate from forty to one hundred mow.

The people of this whole section are markedly plainer, poorer, and of a more rugged sturdy type than farther south. Their struggle for a living has been continuously hard, and the repeated famines have left small margins of food supply. The homes are plainer, with fewer furnishings, less ornamentation, and fewer comforts. The dress is almost wholly cotton rather than silk or wool. The manners of the people are more brusque and direct—"more like foreigners"—with much less of the formal politeness of the south.[7]

The area close to the Shandong border was known as a center of salt smuggling, banditry, and opium growing.[8] Its reputation as a breeding ground for criminals is typified by a report written in 1897 by the *North China*

Herald's correspondent in northern Jiangsu. "The season when highway-men are especially numerous and dangerous is upon us," he warned. "The kaoliang is in its prime, and being 7 or 8 feet high and very thick affords a most convenient ambush. It is unsafe to travel alone even in daylight over lonely roads."[9]

Moving southeast, to the area bordering the old Huai River bed, one finds a very different, though not undifferentiated, region. As the name of its major city, Yancheng (Salt City), suggests, part of this area consists of land reclaimed from the sea, suitable for little but producing salt and raising pigs. Farther inland the land is not so salty and hence can support cotton crops. Still farther west, the land, stretching south toward Yang-zhou and Taizhou, is broken by a series of lakes, marshes, rivers, and canals and is thus wet enough to grow rice. The area yet farther south, including Nantong, Qidong, Haimen, and Rugao, is a fertile peninsula on the northern bank of the Yangzi that was a major producer of the nationally famous Nantong (Tongzhou) cotton.

In spite of literal meanings and popular sensibilities that Subei includes all of Jiangsu north of the Yangzi and implicitly all the regions described above almost all historical geographers and students of the rural economy include only a portion of the northern area in Subei, though they disagree about which portion. For purposes of discussion, I shall refer to three general areas of Jiangsu north of the Yangzi: northern (north of the Huai), central (from the Huai south to Yangzhou), and southern (the area on the northern shore of the Yangzi).

Most Republican-era observers argue for a basic distinction between the northern and central areas—between the areas north and south of the old Huai River bed in Jiangsu. For example, both Wang Peitang and Li Changfu, writing in the 1930s, identified two radically different regions north of the Yangzi: one called Subei, the other Huaibei, the former closer to Jiangnan in its economy and culture, the latter closer to Anhui and Shandong. Wang observed that the Huai was the division between rice- and wheat-producing regions; people north of the Yangzi and south of the Huai, like residents of Jiangnan, depended primarily on rice. Housing styles, too, changed at the Huai: people north of the Huai constructed houses with mud and grass, while most people south of the Huai, like Jiangnan residents, had tile-roofed dwellings.[10] The insistence that Subei and Huaibei be distinguished is reflected in Communist organizing strategy in the 1940s: the part of Jiangsu north of the Yangzi was divided into two administrative regions, Central and Northern Jiangsu; the old Huai River bed served as the boundary.[11] In all these cases, the far northern Jiangsu districts of Xuzhou and Haizhou belong to Huaibei; Subei includes everything from Nantong and Haimen in the south, Yangzhou, Taizhou, and Gaoyou in the center, and Yancheng, Funing, and Huai'an in the north.

Many studies by Western scholars, though not addressing the definition of Subei, implicitly confirm this distinction between the parts of northern Jiangsu north and south of the Huai. In her study of the Yangzhou hinterland, for example, Antonia Finnane observes, "Climatically, the Huai river bed, occupied by the Yellow River for the greater part of the Qing dynasty, was a more important dividing line than the Yangtze, the areas to its north being differentiated from those to its south by levels of precipitation. This signified that it served as the border separating the Yangtze rice-wheat area from the winter wheat-kaoliang area." [12] She also shows that travel, transport, and communication between what she calls central and northern Jiangsu (divided by the Huai) were extremely difficult, whereas an abundance of waterways eased travel within central Jiangsu and between central and southern Jiangsu. [13] In her analysis, then, central and northern Jiangsu must be treated as two entirely different regions, not one homogeneous Subei. Likewise, Elizabeth Perry, in her study of peasant rebellion in north China, focuses on Huaibei, which by her definition represents the area between the Huai and the Yellow rivers, "the heart of China's so-called flood and famine region, an area noted for the harshness of both its geography and its people." Here, the part of Jiangsu north of the Huai is described as belonging to the same region as southwestern Shandong and northeastern Anhui and implicitly is distinguished from Jiangsu south of the Huai. [14] Finally, Joseph Esherick's study of the origins of the Boxer Uprising describes a region encompassing southwestern Shandong and the northernmost part of Jiangsu, implying that the part of Jiangsu north of the Huai belongs to a different region than the area to the south. [15]

Not all pre-1949 observers of the rural economy shared this understanding of Subei, however. Some treated the above two regions as a single, homogeneous unit. Chen Guofu, for example, in his recollections of governing Jiangsu Province in the 1930s, described conditions in Xuzhou in his discussion of Jiangbei. [16] Another writer not only included Xuzhou and Haizhou, but excluded the southern areas of Nantong and Haimen. By his definition, Subei included everything in Jiangsu north of Yangzhou, while the area south of Yangzhou yet north of the Yangzi belonged to Jiangnan. [17] A final geographic definition of Subei is implied by writers who exclude Yangzhou, suggesting it rightly belongs to Jiangnan. For example, Yi Junzuo, in his controversial *Xianhua Yangzhou* (Musings of Yangzhou), published in the mid-1930s, underlined a distinction between Yangzhou and Subei. After declaring that Yangzhou shares the climatic patterns of Jiangnan, he goes on to say that "the personality of Jiangbei people is doughty, whereas Yangzhou people are very peaceful. Although Yangzhou people are located in Jiangbei, they became 'Jiangnan-ized' from early on. From the Sui, they have represented the whole Jiangnan style. To say that Yangzhou is part of Jiangbei is totally absurd!"[18] Wang Shuhuai, author of a study of Jiangsu, concurs, portraying Yangzhou as almost identical to Jiangnan places. " 'People's customs in Yangzhou are entirely different from Huaibei," he observes. "There is tea, salt, cotton, and silk; people like commerce."[19] By these accounts, then, Subei begins only north of Yangzhou.

The importance of these descriptions of northern Jiangsu is not so much their accuracy, but their lack of consensus on what constitutes Subei. If no standard definition of Subei as a geographic region exists, and if what some writers think of as Subei is considered Huaibei by others, it becomes difficult to identify who are Subei people.

Geography, however, is not the only criterion employed in defining Subei. Language is equally important and equally elusive. In the absence of any physical or racial distinctions between Jiangnan and Subei natives, dialect becomes the only marker of a Subei person in Shanghai. In general, people in the northern and southern parts of Jiangsu speak dialects that belong to entirely different linguistic families and are mutually incomprehensible: Wu dialect predominates in the south, while variations of Yangzhou dialect are spoken in the north. Although the Yangzi River does represent a rough boundary between the two, no neat correlation between geographic and linguistic variations exists. The Wu dialect does not confine itself to districts south of the river any more than the so-called Subei dialects confine themselves to the north (see map 4). For example, in Piaoshui and Zhenjiang, both south of the Yangzi, northern dialects predominate.[20] A major survey of Jiangsu dialects conducted in 1960 included the Jiangnan districts of Nanjing, Jiangning, and Jurong along with Piaoshui and Zhenjiang, as belonging to the same dialect region as the Subei districts of Yangzhou, Yancheng, Funing, and Gaoyou.[21] Likewise, the Wu dialect predominates in Nantong, Qidong, Haimen, Jingjiang, and Rudong, all of which are north of the Yangzi.[22]

Sometimes the configuration is even more complex, as a given district may itself be divided into Wu and northern dialect areas. Such is the case in Jingjiang on the northern bank of the Yangzi, where according to one study a version of Wu dialect identical to that spoken in Changzhou, south of the river, predominates in five counties, while Jianghuai dialect is spoken in the others. This division is attributed to the peculiar historic development of Jingjiang: it was originally an island in the middle of the

Map 4. Jiangsu dialects

Yangzi whose residents were Wu-speaking Jiangnan people. During the Ming dynasty, a sandbar formed between the island and the northern bank of the Yangzi, and as the island gradually became linked to the northern shore Jianghuai-speaking people from north of the Yangzi came to inhabit the newly available land.[23]

According to linguistic criteria, then, the category Subei native would not include residents of all the areas north of the Yangzi; parts of Jingjiang, Nantong, Haimen, and Qidong would be Jiangnan. By the same token, natives of Zhenjiang, Piaoshui, and perhaps even Nanjing would be Subei ren. Some people who are geographically Subei ren are linguistically Jiangnan natives, while some geographically Jiangnan natives are marked as Subei ren by dint of speech. This complexity led the author of one study of Jiangsu to conclude that only people with a superficial view believe that "Jiangbei is simply north of the Yangzi and Jiangnan is south."[24]

In addition to the confusion surrounding the identity of people living on the banks of the Yangzi, linguistic criteria confirm and complicate the Subei/Huaibei dichotomy described above. Despite popular beliefs in a uniform Yangzhou-based "Subei dialect" spoken everywhere north of the Yangzi, the Huai in fact roughly differentiates two further dialect groups. North of the Huai, a version of Mandarin (*beifang guanhua*) similar to Shandong dialect, not Yangzhou dialect, predominates.[25] Language, in other words, offers no obvious, straightforward definition of Subei. It also helps explain why some people from Shandong are identified as Subei ren.

In addition to geography and language, culture is a third criterion often employed in defining Subei. A variety of aspects of cultural life underline the blurriness of the Jiangnan/Subei division as well as the diversity of northern Jiangsu. First, as suggested by linguistic patterns, the Yangzi did not always provide a neat boundary between so-called Jiangnan and Subei culture. For example, despite its location north of the Yangzi, many Jiangnan customs prevailed in Jingjiang. "Because it is close to Jiangnan," observed the author of one study of Jiangsu, "it is popular for women to have short hair and to wear a long dress (*qipao*)."[26] Similarly, the Wu speakers of Jingjiang, considering themselves superior to their neighboring Subei ren, celebrate festivals according to Jiangnan customs. For example, they worship ancestors for the ten days before the Tomb-Sweeping Day (*qingming jie*) and the Winter Solstice, as opposed to the Jianghuai speakers whose custom it is to worship ancestors only on the holiday itself. In addition, the Wu speakers, presumably to confirm their southern identity, persist in crossing the Yangzi to buy goods on the southern bank.[27]

The second disunity of northern Jiangsu highlighted by cultural life is the division between the area north and south of the Huai. The Huai, for example, was said to mark the boundary between areas where foot-binding was widely practiced and those where women had natural feet: north of the Huai women worked mostly within their homes, while south of it they worked in the fields.[28] Clothing styles changed at the Huai as well. North of the Huai clothes were made mostly of cotton. In the area between the Huai and the Yangzi, people wore both silk and cotton, so that, according to Wang Peitang, "they are closer to the customs of Jiangnan," where silk was more common.[29] Even personality types were said to change at the Huai. "People in Jiangnan are very civilized," according to Wang Shuhuai, "while in Huaibei (north of the Huai) they are coarse. But Jiangbei (between the Huai and the Yangzi) people are between civility and coarseness."[30]

Perhaps the most vivid example of cultural patterns that defy the notion of a homogeneous area north of the Yangzi is local opera, one of the most popular forms of entertainment for rural people throughout China. At first glance, opera styles highlight the difference between central and northern Jiangsu: from the nineteenth century on, Huai opera (*Huaiju*) predominated in northern Jiangsu, while Yangzhou opera (*Yangju*) flourished in central Jiangsu. Upon closer examination, however, it appears that the two opera forms actually reflect a division within central Jiangsu—the area of Jiangsu between the Yangzi and the Huai.

Huai opera originated not in the part of Jiangsu north of the Huai, but in the region just south of the river: around Huai'an, Huaiyin, Yancheng, and Funing. It evolved from "incense-burning operas" (*xianghuo xi*) that were performed on holidays such as the Spring Festival or on birthdays, as well as to pray for recovery from illness or to be spared the danger of fire. On such occasions, individuals invited several *tongzi* (male shamans) to sing popular ballads while they burned incense.

These incense-burning operas did not become a full-fledged opera performance until the early nineteenth century, when performers of Hui opera (*Huiju*) came from Anhui to northern Jiangsu. The incense-burning operas thereby incorporated Hui opera styles, and gradually there emerged a corps of professional opera performers who, accompanied by instruments, performed what came to be called Huai opera.[31] Even in the early twentieth century, when Huai opera was first performed in Shanghai, it often either preceded or followed performances of Hui opera, underlining both their similarity and the shared cultural world to which their audiences, natives of northeastern Anhui and northern Jiangsu, believed they belonged.

Yangzhou opera developed from partly similar, yet entirely separate and unrelated traditions. Like Huai opera, Yangzhou opera derived in part from the local custom of incense-burning operas. Yet the incense-burning opera tradition of Yangzhou was not identical to that of the area described above. As in the area around Yancheng and Huaiyin, incense-burning operas were performed for birthdays, to honor the ancestors, and to pray for good health, rain, or fertility. In Yangzhou, however, they were performed on stage from the Tang dynasty onward, often at temples on worship days. They were sung in local Yangzhou dialect and were accompanied by a drum and cymbals. Local incense-burning operas were only one tradition from which Yangzhou opera derived. Equally important were the flower-drum operas (*huaguxi*) that had been popular in the area since the early Qing. When the two forms eventually merged, in the early twentieth century, they were known first as Weiyang opera and later as Yangzhou opera.[32]

That Yangzhou and Huai opera were not simply variations on a single

Subei opera form is attested to by their development in Shanghai. They were performed in different theaters and attracted different audiences (see chapter 5). Cultural criteria, like geographic and linguistic ones, elude a simple "north of the Yangzi" definition of Subei.

Subei: The Idea

If by all these criteria the definition of Subei is problematic, what does it mean then to speak of Subei or of Subei natives? More specifically, what does it mean to those who use the term? Rather than looking at what they believe Subei is, it may be more useful to shift our focus slightly and examine what Subei is *not*. For what permeates writing about Subei, most of which is written by Jiangnan natives, is that it is *not* southern Jiangsu or Jiangnan, which includes northern Zhejiang as well. If there is any regional coherence to Jiangsu north of the Yangzi, it is simply its allegedly stark contrast to the south.

In all the literature, one is struck by accounts of the wealth of the south versus the poverty of the north; the lush scenery of the south versus the drab, dreary north; the soft Wu dialect spoken in the south versus the harsh Yangzhou dialect of north; the industrial economy of the south versus the agricultural economy of north; the fertile soil of the south versus the dry, alkalai soil of the north. As Fan Shuping summarizes in his account of traveling through Jiangsu in the mid-1930s, "'Jiangnan' has fertile soil, beautiful rivers and mountains, convenient transportation, sophisticated culture; 'Jiangbei,' in contrast, has poor soil and poverty-stricken people. Everywhere one looks is wasteland. Transportation is poor. It is backward culturally. Therefore, 'old Jiangbei's' (*Jiangbei lao*) are looked down on by 'Jiangnan' people."[33] "'Although Jiangnan and Jiangbei are divided only by a river," Feng Hefa concluded in 1933 in his study of the rural economy, "a thousand years of history separates them."[34] Some Subei natives challenged this representation of Subei as the "bastion of poverty." For example, in his interviews with Buddhist monks in Jiangnan, a large percentage of whom came from Subei, Holmes Welch found that many "denied that [Subei] was poverty stricken. They said that it had much good land, none of which was saline, since it lay far from the coast."[35]

Subei, then, can partly be understood not as an objective place, but as representative of the other, as that which Jiangnan was not or, more precisely, that which Jiangnan had left behind. In the Shanghai environment, both Jiangnan and Subei were simplified and evoked as symbols. Jiangnan, whatever its internal differences, was the embodiment of wealth and urbane sophistication, and Subei, whatever its variety, became the embodiment of poverty and rural backwardness. What Subei symbolized was more important than what it really was. This almost metaphorical meaning of Subei becomes more comprehensible when placed in a historical context. More specifically, comprehending Subei as an idea—an idea that, to be sure, shaped material reality—requires an examination of the history of that idea, particularly the economic developments in Jiangsu that produced it.

A place called Subei or Jiangbei did not always exist. Only in the mid-Qing do references to it begin to appear with any regularity. Most striking is that prior to that time, when the area north of the Yangzi River was prosperous, it had no generic name Subei. The portrayal of northern Jiangsu as a poverty-stricken, disaster-ridden area from the mid-nineteenth century through the present obscures the fact that it had not always been the economically inferior part of the province. Its prosperity, in fact, had rivaled that of Jiangnan. "The Grand Canal and the Huanghe River along with the waterways branching out from them," observed the anthropologist Fei Xiaotong, "once formed a web of canals resembling those seen south of the Changjiang [Yangzi] today."[36] The northern city of Huaiyin was the center for the tributary grain transport administration during the Qing.[37] Yangzhou, a transshipment point on the Grand Canal, had been considered one of China's most prosperous cities. It was "the jewel of China in the eighth century," according to E. H. Schafer, "a bustling, bourgeois city where money flowed easily . . . a gay city, a city of well-dressed people, a city where the best entertainment was always available, a city of parks and gardens, a very Venice, traversed by waterways, where the boats outnumbered the carriages. It was a city of moonlight and lanterns, a city of song and dance, a city of courtesans."[38] Throughout the Tang dynasty Yangzhou was a flourishing port for foreign trade; it was the object of Marco Polo's marvel during the Yuan dynasty; it later became the paramount symbol of early Qing prosperity and was the home of the salt merchants of Jiangsu, some of the wealthiest men in all of China at that time. Although the economic forces that eventually led to its decline were already at work in the early Qing, Yangzhou remained a city whose wealth and prestige attracted merchants, artists, scholars, tourists, and even the Qianlong emperor himself on six occasions. Described as the "epitome of Southern culture" and "the nerve center of domestic trade," it boasted teahouses, restaurants, literary salons, and some of the most famed artistic talents in China.[39] Yangzhou's prestige and prosperity are reflected in the fact that through the early Qing, the City God of Shanghai was originally from Gaoyou, a district bordering Yangzhou in Subei.[40]

Only in the nineteenth century, at about the same time that Shanghai was developing as a commercial center, did northern Jiangsu decline in prosperity and prestige. Its impoverishment can be attributed to two interrelated events in the mid-nineteenth century. First, the Grand Canal was replaced by sea transport, particularly for the shipment of grain from southern to northern China. Coastal ships, first used in the 1820s when Yellow River silting severely impeded the passage of boats through the canal, became the major means of tribute grain transport in the 1840s.[41] This meant that certain cities and towns in Subei lost their importance as transportation and commercial centers. Yangzhou, formerly the symbol of elegance and prosperity, was, by the mid-nineteenth century, a "skeleton" of its former self. When the scholar-official Ruan Yuan returned to his native Yangzhou in 1839, he described it as "almost unrecognisable from that he knew in his boyhood, with gardens and libraries alike neglected or abandoned and in ruins." The replacement of the Grand Canal by sea transport also meant that the government paid less attention to maintaining and repairing the dikes on waterways connecting with the Grand Canal, thereby leaving parts of northern Jiangsu vulnerable to unprecedented numbers of floods and natural disasters.[42]

The second event contributing to the decline of northern Jiangsu was the shift in 1853 in the course of the Yellow River: rather than flowing into Hongze Lake and then across Subei to the sea, it now ran northeast from Kaifeng, then crossed Shandong. The Huai River subsequently emptied into Hongze Lake with no further outlet, thereby becoming a source of treacherous flooding in Subei.[43] From the mid-1800s on, then, cycles of floods, famine, and poverty characterized large portions of Subei. Whereas during the Ming dynasty northern Jiangsu, including Xuzhou and Hai-zhou, had suffered slightly fewer floods than Jiangnan (eighty-eight in Subei, compared to ninety-one in Jiangnan), during the Qing Subei had become disaster-ridden compared to Jiangnan (eighty-two floods in Subei compared to sixty-one in Jiangnan).[44]

The impoverishment and decline of Subei were made all the more conspicuous by the simultaneously rapid economic development of Jiangnan, which had its origins in the commercial revolution of the Song and culminated during the Ming and Qing dynasties. Jiangnan's development can be attributed to several factors. Its proximity to the Yangzi and Grand Canal as well as access to coastal shipping favored its becoming a center of expanded market networks. A geography and climate hospitable to cotton and silk cultivation further contributed to Jiangnan's commercialization. As handicraft textile industries developed, rice had to be imported, thereby contributing to the growth of a market economy.[45] By the early

Qing, Susan Naquin and Evelyn Rawski observe in their survey of the eighteenth century,

The Yangtze River brought rice from interior areas downstream, while the delta also began to serve as a processing center for consumer goods, importing raw cotton from North China via the Grand Canal and exporting finished cotton cloth as well as local silk. Handicraft textiles, produced in rural areas, passed through merchant hands before being sold back to peasants, who bought cloth with money earned from selling grain. Shanghai—long before its discovery by Westerners—became a thriving entrepot for coastal trade. . . . The commercial profits from serving as a national entrepot and manufacturing center thus gave the Yangtze delta the economic foundations that underlay its political and cultural preeminence."[46]

The increasing gap between economic development of Jiangnan and Subei is reflected in the policies of Qing statecraft officials: they promoted handicraft weaving by women in Jiangnan as a model to be emulated by women in "poorer Subei."[47]

By the early twentieth century, Jiangnan was as famous for its wealth as Subei was for its poverty. The differences between the two parts of the province were more than impressionistic. They were evidenced in levels of commercialization, urbanization, and industrialization.

Describing the poverty and backwardness of Subei relative to Jiangnan, one Republican-period writer declared that the Yangzi truly demarcated wealth and poverty. In Jingjiang, right on the northern bank of the Yangzi, "if you want to buy a pound of cookies it is extremely difficult. Even if you want to buy white rice, you must go across the river to Jiangying," she complained.[48] The relative availability of goods was indicative of the fact that most of Jiangsu's commercial wealth, by the twentieth century, was concentrated in Jiangnan. Native banks provide a quick index to the location of capital: in 1915, though northern Jiangsu boasted a greater number of native banks than Jiangnan (136 compared to 111), those in the north had only about one-fourth of the money (927,715 *yuan*), while those in Jiangnan (including Shanghai) had nearly three-fourths (2,791,500 yuan).[49] Chambers of commerce attest to a similar pattern: in 1911, Jiangnan (excluding Shanghai) had 39 chambers of commerce, including 11,981 members and an income of 68,676 yuan, whereas Subei had only 25 chambers of commerce, with 5,471 members and an income of 35,439 yuan.[50] The disparity between the levels of commercialization of northern and southern Jiangsu was not merely statistical, but visible to the observant traveler as well, as reflected in the following account of northern Peixian in 1930:

> Entering the city of Pei is like walking into a rural village. The people are all farming. If there is someone hawking by the roadside from a cart on which is loaded some coarse material, that constitutes the clothing store. The only shops we could find were on the order of what would be considered tiny stands in the South. . . . In all of Pei County, only some thirty stores had capital investments of more than 1,000 yuan. Adding all this capital together, one would attain the level of only a small firm in Shanghai—despite the fact that in territory Pei is thrice the area of Wuxi County.[51]

The different levels of commercialization of Subei and Jiangnan were paralleled by the vastly different degrees of urbanization, Jiangnan being far more urbanized (see map 5).

Modern industry, as it developed in Jiangsu, was also centered almost entirely in cities of the Jiangnan. In 1931, for example, some 95 percent of Jiangsu's 403,152 industrial workers were employed in Shanghai and in such cities of the Jiangnan as Wuxi, Changzhou, and Hangzhou. In Subei, only the city of Nantong could boast a significant number of factory workers; cities farther north, such as Yangzhou, Yancheng, and Funing, had fewer than 100 industrial workers each.[52] Whereas industry was a growing part of the Jiangnan economy, Subei continued to depend on agricultural production: it was a major producer of raw cotton, salt, and pigs[53] (thereby giving rise to the derogatory expression "Jiangbei swine" in Shanghai dialect). As Wang Nanbi observed in his study of Subei villages, "In this vast area, except for a very few number of capitalists and big landlords and officials concentrated in the towns, the majority of people are farmers."[54]

Even when it came to agricultural production, Subei could not compete with Jiangnan, as reflected in the relative values of land in the two parts of the province. In the mid-1930s, while wet fields in such counties of Jiangnan as Wuxi or Changshou sold for an average of 100 to 140 yuan per *mu,* they cost only 30 to 50 yuan per mu in Subei; a mu of dry land that cost anywhere from 55 to 120 yuan in Jiangnan was worth only 20 to 40 yuan in Subei.[55] Compared to Jiangnan, one of the wealthiest agricultural and commercial regions in all of China, Subei was indeed poor and undeveloped.

These economic data shed light on the meaning of Subei in several ways. First, they suggest another criterion by which Subei was defined. In addition to geography, language, and culture, Subei was defined by

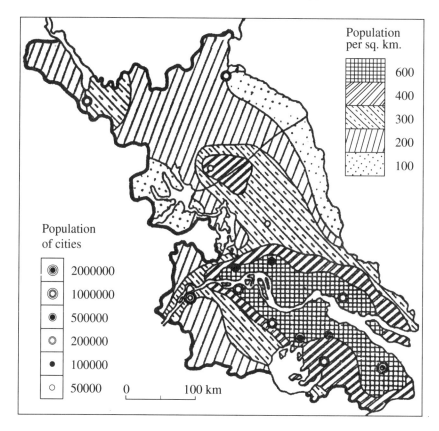

Map 5. Population distribution in Jiangsu Province

economics: that which was poor was Subei. This criterion, like the others, does not neatly correlate to a division at the Yangzi: one finds that poor areas south of the river are considered part of Subei, while wealthy areas north of the river are thought of as being part of the south. Nantong, as Fei Xiaotong points out, illustrates the problem. In his discussion of administrative districts in Jiangsu in the mid-1980s, he observes that Nantong has usually been considered part of southern Jiangsu, "because they have something identical in their economic development." Indeed, Nantong by the 1910s was one of Jiangsu's major industrial centers: its cotton industry was surpassed in size only by Shanghai and Wuxi.[56] Fei therefore proposes refining this correlation of economic development and geographic identity. "If the matter is given more thought," he remarks, "it can be seen that the northern part of the Nantong Municipality that includes Hai'an and Rudong counties is not very much influenced economically by Shanghai." Only the wealthier southern parts of Nantong, by his proposal, should be included in a southern administrative region.[57] Wealthier places north of the river, in other words, are economically Jiangnan.

A second point suggested by the economic developments described above is that the notion of a place called Subei emerged only when northern Jiangsu became poor relative to the south. That the belief in a Jiangnan/ Subei divide emerged only in recent times is underlined by political history. Although in the early Qing separate financial commissions and literary chancellors were appointed to northern and southern Jiangsu, only in the early twentieth century do we begin to find aggressive attempts to treat the two parts of the province differently because of their unequal levels of economic development.[58] In 1905, for instance, the Empress Dowager proposed making the part of Jiangsu north of the Yangzi an entirely separate province called Jianghuai, allegedly to alleviate the official neglect to which northern Jiangsu had been subjected.[59] Implementation of this plan was revoked after only three months. Jiangsu was subsequently divided into two separate administrative regions in 1909: one covering the area south of the Yangzi, the other the area to the north.[60] Through the 1930s, individuals both south and north of the Yangzi continued to petition for the division of the province, though they did not always agree on the boundaries.[61] Finally, as noted above, when the Chinese Communist Party organized in Jiangsu in the 1940s, it set up entirely separate base areas north and south of the Yangzi, though it separated the part of Jiangsu north and south of the Huai as well.[62] After 1949, however, emphasizing the division at the Yangzi, the party established separate North Jiangsu and South Jiangsu administrative regions, not reuniting the province until 1952.[63]

The concern with dividing the province politically paralleled and reflected broader perceptions of the gap between northern and southern Jiangsu. When northern Jiangsu was prosperous, it was never suggested that the Yangzi represented an obvious division. Only in the context of the economic decline of northern Jiangsu did the notion of Subei as a quasi-political unit emerge. Subei, that is, was not an ever-present, consistently defined place, but rather represented a belief that developed in a specific historical context.

Although patterns of economic development help account for the emergence of an emphatic belief in a gap between northern and southern Jiangsu, they do not completely explain the notion of a homogeneous, north-of-the-river area called Subei. Given the terminology and wisdom popular at the time, it seems just as likely that the area north of the Huai, Huaibei, could have been singled out as the backward, undeveloped, poverty-stricken contrast to Jiangnan.

To understand why the notion of Subei emerged and ultimately to make sense of the meaning of Subei, one final factor must be considered: patterns of migration in Jiangsu. As the commercial and industrial economy of Jiangnan expanded in the nineteenth century and as northern Jiangsu became the victim of natural disasters at an increasing rate, large numbers of peasants began to move south, forming an underclass there. Speaking a northern-sounding, as opposed to a Wu, dialect, they were perceived as quasi-foreigners. That some came from Yancheng, some from Yangzhou, and others from Nantong were subtleties that did not matter to the people they encountered in the south. To Jiangnan residents, they were all northerners of a sort. Most likely, it was only because of the influx of such a large immigrant population from north of the Yangzi that people in the south became so concerned with distinguishing Jiangnan and "Subei"—it was an essential part of declaring their separate identities.

Because it derived from migration patterns, the notion of Subei people actually preceded the belief in a place called Subei. *Subei ren* was most likely a label used to describe the immigrant population in Jiangnan and Shanghai. Once Subei people existed as a group, the idea of Subei as a place emerged to define their place of origin. If Subei was defined as a place chiefly for the purpose of describing the immigrant population, it becomes less surprising that the geographic region was only vaguely defined and in some ways defied definition, that a range of often contradictory criteria were used to define Subei, or that Subei might even include parts of Anhui or Shandong. It did not matter that a place that symbolized Qing prosperity, Yangzhou, was lumped together with one that had epitomized despair and lawlessness, Peixian. What mattered was that a name be given to the "northern" immigrants who became an increasingly permanent presence in the south.

3

FROM IMMIGRANTS

TO ETHNICS

The belief in a place called Subei came into being when northern Jiangsu natives began migrating south to Jiangnan and Shanghai. Only as immigrants did they first encounter prejudice and discrimination; only as immigrants were they first labeled Subei people. The designation enabled natives of southern Jiangsu to distinguish themselves from these impoverished northern neighbors with whom they shared a racial (Han) and provincial (Jiangsu) identity. This confrontation of Jiangnan and Subei people led to the articulation of what anthropologists call boundary markers, thereby beginning the process of ethnic formation.[1]

Attempts by Subei people to establish residence in Shanghai generated resistance by both the Jiangnan-based Chinese elite as well as the foreign-dominated municipal government. Subei people constituted a threat to the modern, sophisticated identity aspired to by the Chinese elite; they were regarded by the Shanghai Municipal Council as a blemish on the treaty port's status as a "model settlement." To both Chinese and foreign elites, Subei people were outsiders or guest people (*kemin*).

From Subei to Jiangnan

By the nineteenth century, poverty provided the background to most migration from north to south. From the time of Subei's decline, Jiangnan, including Shanghai, became the destination for refugees from the northern part of the province. Northern Jiangsu, it seemed, was a notorious producer of refugees, as the so-called Jiangbei refugee became a common and despised figure in the Jiangnan landscape. Having fled their homes because of natural disasters or simply because it was the winter slack season, peasants congregated in Jiangsu's cities and towns, hoping to take advantage of the relief services—food, clothing, and medical care— that were often provided. "Before the coming of floods," Fei Xiaotong observed, "peasant families [in Subei] sealed the doors of their houses with mud and then fled their homes. In some localities like the Lixiahe area [near Yangzhou], whole villages were deserted during the flood seasons."[2] Towns within northern Jiangsu were the first destination for many. In 1876, for example, some sixty to seventy thousand refugees were reported in Huaiyin and forty-two thousand in Yangzhou; in 1898 approximately one hundred thousand camped in Huaiyin, arriving allegedly at the rate of two thousand per day, and forty thousand in Yangzhou.[3]

The experiences of one northern Jiangsu family, described in an issue of the missionary journal *Chinese Recorder* in 1912, illustrates the plight of these refugees. The Zhang household included thirteen members: a seventy-year-old grandmother, her son and his wife, their five unmarried sons and daughters as well as a married son, his wife, and their three children. They owned a fourteen-mu plot of land (about two acres), and under ordinary circumstances were able to survive. In 1909, however, they could not make ends meet and sold two mu; the following year, due to famine, they sold six of the remaining mu:

> Last summer and autumn, nearly all the small crop they had was destroyed by floods. About November 1, counting all they had saved and all gleaned from other fields, they found they had enough grain to last the whole family if they should eat "dry" (i.e., bread, as opposed to gruel) for just six weeks. By mixing what they have with turnips, turnip tops, sweet potato vines, and other herbs they have been able to raise or gather, and eating gruel made very thin, they have enough for the whole family to exist on for three months or more. But it is seven months till harvest—what could they do? It is impossible to find work even in a good year, but this is a famine year with revolution too.

So the family had a "council." They decided that Mr. Chang, his oldest daughter (15), and two of the younger children, together with the oldest of the grandchildren, would remain at home. The married son would take his wife and two little children, two brothers and one sister and the old grandmother and go where they can. They leave most of the little store of grain at home as they hope to get down to Chinkiang or Nanking and live on the gruel kitchens there, if they cannot find any work to do. They start out with a wheelbarrow, the man pushing, the woman pulling; there are two of the little ones, a lot of millet stalks for fuel, the kitchen pot and the large reed mat, which is to be their cover at night, on the barrow. The others trudge along behind. Day after day they go on, foot-sore and sick. They beg from the villages as they go.

At Tsingkiangpu they camp awhile and try to beg a living. But they fail. With crowds of others, they pile on to an old rotten boat, and, after a few days, are at Yangchow. From here they are driven back by official orders.[4]

Those who headed for rural Jiangnan may have had better luck than the Zhang family. The desperate need to attract cultivators to the parts of Jiangnan that had been depopulated as a result of the Taiping Rebellion provided resettlement opportunities for many northern Jiangsu migrants during the second half of the nineteenth century. The historian Kathryn Bernhardt, in her study of Jiangnan peasants, observes that refugees fleeing the famine of 1866 in northern Jiangsu were among the first immigrants to settle the devastated parts of Jiangnan. In the 1880s another wave of Subei immigrants relocated to Jiangnan.[5] Even when post-Taiping reconstruction was no longer an issue, cycles of famines and floods (and, in the 1930s, war) continued to cause large numbers of Subei natives to cross the Yangzi to seek their fortune as farmers in the south.[6] In extreme cases, as at Jinta and Piaoyang in 1931, close to two-thirds of the peasant households consisted of northern Jiangsu migrants who had settled wild land.[7]

Throughout the Jiangnan countryside, migrants from northern Jiangsu, certain that even the worst circumstances in Jiangnan were better than those at home, formed an underclass. Fei Xiaotong recalled often having seen, as a child, migrants from Subei cultivating the newly formed land surrounding Lake Tai. Vulnerable to flooding whenever the lake water rose, this land was undesirable to natives of the area.[8] Yuji Muramatsu, in his study of landlordism in Jiangnan, corroborates this portrait of northern Jiangsu immigrants forming an underclass among the Jiangnan peasants: they were "willing to be content with rather poor conditions to get a start in life as tenant farmers."[9]

Not all migrants to Jiangnan settled in rural areas. Particularly as industrialization expanded job opportunities in Jiangnan cities, large numbers headed directly for such urban areas as Suzhou, Wuxi, Changzhou, or Nanjing. There, as in the rural areas, they formed an underclass, living in shack settlements and doing coolie work that southerners considered beneath their dignity.[10] Men commonly pulled rickshaws or hauled freight at the city docks; women, some of whom migrated seasonally, sought jobs as servants: according to one account, every October, when it was slack season, women crossed the river to look for work as maids.[11] (Another report, however, observed that in Jiangnan cities women from northern Jiangsu rarely found work as maids, as their incomprehensible dialect made them undesirable.)[12] So commonly recognized was Subei people's underclass status in Jiangnan cities that almost every Republican-period survey of Jiangsu repeated the observation that "men and women who have grown up in the Jiangnan see people from Jiangbei come to the cities and towns of Jiangnan every year. They become peddlers, factory workers, rickshaw drivers, and do all the lowest class jobs. They live, eat, and raise their children on small, dilapidated boats."[13]

Whether in cities or rural areas of southern Jiangsu, Subei refugees, or Jiangbei vagabonds, as they were commonly called, were considered a source of disorder. As early as 1814, officials from Jiangsu and Zhejiang complained to the emperor about disruption caused by the Jiangbei vagabonds in such Jiangnan areas as Hangzhou, Jiaxing, Huzhou, Suzhou, and Changzhou. "Every year during the autumn and winter slack season," stated the edict,

> there are vagabonds from the Jiangbei places of Huaiyin, Xuzhou, and Haizhou areas. Usually several hundred band together as a group. They come by boat, pushing small carts, or on foot. They are dressed in every which way and almost look like beggars. They call themselves famine victims. Whenever they pass through a village they sit there and beg for free meals, a place to stay, or money. You must give them whatever they want so that they will leave. Otherwise they will rob you, since they have a lot of people. Everyone is afraid of their tough nature; no one dares argue with them. . . . Some wealthy shopkeepers have moved to avoid trouble.[14]

In his study of Jiangsu, the historical sociologist David Faure observes that throughout the second half of the nineteenth century there were constant reports of incidents—from petty thieving to conflicts provoked by "famine-begging"—involving Jiangbei vagabonds. Officials in some northern Jiangsu cities were so determined to dispose of these undesirables that they actually paid for their transport to Jiangnan, where they were presumably headed anyway. And officials in Jiangnan cities, partly resigned to the seasonal influx of the refugees, waited for winter's end and then provided the refugees a "travel fee" so they would return north.[15] These efforts were not always successful, as attested by the complaint of the author of an article in the Shanghai newspaper *Shibao*. "Refugees from the Huaiyang [Huai'an/Yangzhou] area have gathered together and come east," he observed. "Their leaders are hooligans . . . and they create disturbance along the way. Last year we gave them money and sent them to open new land. But now they have returned—some 7,000 to 8,000 of them."[16]

Throughout Jiangnan, then, Subei migrants became a despised, stigmatized group, and it is this characterization that gave rise to the belief that people from "north of the river" formed a coherent, homogenous social category, Jiangbei folk. Yet did the Jiangbei vagabonds of Jiangnan constitute an ethnic group? One would have to know more about the social and economic relations between Jiangnan natives and Subei immigrants to determine whether this regional appellation assumed ethnic dimensions outside of Shanghai. Ethnicity, as myriad anthropological studies have shown, certainly does not require an urban setting. But even if the construction of a Subei ethnicity originated in the countryside, it did not acquire the prominent meanings it did in Shanghai. In southern Jiangsu, the relationship between Subei and Jiangnan people was a straightforward native–immigrant one: Jiangnan people's claim to native status was not subject to dispute. In Shanghai, however, Jiangnan and Subei people alike were immigrants. It was largely in the struggle of Jiangnan people to appropriate the status native, to claim Shanghai as their own, that they magnified distinctions between themselves and Subei people.

Guest People of Shanghai

It is in the context of settlement throughout Jiangnan that a community of Subei people formed in Shanghai, one representing, through most of the Republican period, roughly one-fifth of the city's population.[17] We cannot know the precise number of migrants from northern Jiangsu to Shanghai, but we can outline the major periods of migration. Although natives of northern Jiangsu continually migrated to Shanghai throughout the period from its opening as a treaty port in 1842 to 1949, the largest waves of migration occurred in response to natural disasters and war. The famine of the late 1860s, as noted above, combined with the aftermath of the Taiping Rebellion, prompted large numbers of northern Jiangsu natives to settle in Shanghai. As early as 1907, so many families had fled natural disasters that a Jiangbei Famine Relief Committee was established in Shanghai to attend to the problem of Subei refugees.[18] The population of northern Jiangsu migrants was sufficiently large and conspicuous at that time to at-tract the attention of a Japanese observer, who described a "class of Jiangbei people."[19] Floods in 1911, 1921, and 1931 forced even more people to leave Subei and seek their fortunes in Shanghai. The last flood was the most severe, leaving more than sixty-one million mu of cultivated land under water (in some areas twenty feet deep), and nearly four million families on the verge of starvation.[20] According to government estimates, some 78,045 refugees from Subei came to Shanghai at that time.[21]

In subsequent decades war overshadowed natural disasters as the cause of emigration to Shanghai. Large parts of northern Jiangsu were occupied by the Japanese during the late 1930s and early 1940s, causing many natives to leave their homes. Of the 75,000 refugees who poured into Shanghai in 1937, for example, those from Subei, approximately one-third of the total, represented the largest single contingent.[22] Nearly a decade later, when northern Jiangsu (parts of which had become one of the Communist base areas) was the battleground between Guomindang and Communist armies, still larger numbers of Subei people left their homes for Shanghai. In 1946, close to 59,000 Subei natives, the majority from Yancheng and Funing, registered with the Shanghai office of the Committee for the Sal-vation of Subei Refugees. "The poor Subei people cannot survive in the countryside," observed the reporter for one of Shanghai's daily papers, "and so old and young alike have come to Shanghai to beg for a living. They are all over Shanghai, from the north train station to downtown— along Nanjing Road, the Bund, and East Zhongzheng Road. At night they sleep on the street. Their situation is really tragic."[23]

The migrants who came to Shanghai during the civil war differed from their predecessors in one important respect. Although the ranks of previ-ous migrants had always included individuals of some wealth, most had been relatively poor peasants. The migrants of the late 1940s, however, were more often landlords, petty businessmen, or students. Of the reg-istered refugees who listed an occupation, 21,649 were peasants, 7,059 workers, 13,170 engaged in business, 4,400 were students, and 541 were government officials.[24] The number of students was sufficiently large that the Committee for the Salvation of Subei Refugees established a special committee to deal with their plight.[25] The number of landlords from Subei was sizable enough to constitute an obstacle to Communist organizers in the shack settlements of Zhabei.[26]

The background of this new group of refugees and their reasons for leaving home are highlighted in the petition to the Bureau of Social Affairs for the establishment of the Association for the Relief of Refugees from the Subei District of Haimen (Subei Haimen liuwang nanmin jiuji xiehui). "Because our Haimen district is harassed by communist bandits and forced conscription, reduced rents and land distribution, the destruction of houses, and ruthless killings," the founder of the association argued, "many people have had to flee and are now wandering in Shanghai." He was especially concerned with the five-hundred-odd high school and university students from Haimen who were unemployed in Shanghai. "These people are from excellent families," he declared, "but their families have been ruined by the communist armies."[27] These refugees were clearly not the poverty-stricken peasants of previous decades.

Although northern Jiangsu natives still did not constitute a major presence among the Shanghai elite, the economic status of the migrants in the late 1940s was very different from that of the ones who had arrived earlier. Nevertheless, the arrival of greater numbers of immigrants who were not destitute failed to alter the equation of Subei people with poverty and backwardness. Perhaps initial stereotypes are seldom altered by subsequent developments. More likely, however, was the continuing need of the Jiangnan elite for an other. If anything, the derision of Subei natives may have intensified following the arrival of better-off immigrants, whose presence potentially challenged the Jiangnan community's claim to elite culture in Shanghai.

Almost from the moment large numbers of Subei people began arriving in Shanghai they were regarded as a group that did not belong. They were seen as tarnishing the urban landscape through their ignorance, unsanitary habits ("their children urinate and defecate wherever they want," complained one article), and poverty.[28] Shanghai residents sometimes tried to prevent them from settling in the city, as had their rural counterparts throughout Jiangnan. At the time of the flood of 1911, for instance, residents of the Shanghai suburbs of Kunshan and Jiangwan fought with the several hundred Subei natives seeking refuge there, trying to keep them away.[29] Officials in Jiangwan gave them money to "drive them out of the area." In the Yangshupu district of Shanghai, police were summoned to contend with Subei refugees.[30] About the same time, some two hundred Subei refugees "causing disturbances" in Pudong were put on boats and sent back home by the local militia.[31] The salvation associations for Subei refugees that were formed in response to the influx of migrants after each major natural disaster aimed not simply to provide relief but to assist the refugees to return to their homes. Ideally they would not establish residence in Shanghai. As in Jiangnan, the presence of these undesirable refugees generated the label and belief in the coherent category Subei people.

Sometimes attempts to keep northern Jiangsu migrants from settling in Shanghai involved the foreign-dominated Shanghai Municipal Council. Only rarely did the council identify and denigrate Subei people as such. One such instance involved resistance by some Chinese residents of Shanghai to a vaccination campaign undertaken by the council's health office during World War I. Its report of 1917 complained about the resistance of the so-called Kaung-pok* (Jiangbei) people, who "form the bulk of that innumerable class whose sole occupation appears to be the picking up of unconsidered trifles." The report observed that Subei people "as a class are hard working but unintelligent, living under very primitive conditions in the poorest property, in beggar-boats and beggar villages, grossly overcrowded." These people, the report concluded, were "so ignorant that they reject vaccination even when it is brought to their doors."[32]

Rather than targeting Subei people per se, the Municipal Council more often contributed to the construction of the social category by describing their enterprises and dwellings as emblems of poverty that should be eradicated. Rag picking ("disseminating dust, dirt, and vermin"), cotton waste sorting ("causing dust"), feather cleaning ("causing dust"), and pig raising—all occupations associated with Subei migrants—were considered "nuisances and offensive trades" by the Shanghai Municipal Council.[33] Pig raising was considered especially repugnant, and city officials occasionally attacked groups engaged in the business. A police report from 1925, for instance, observed, "The Shanghai City Magistrate issued an order on December 4, for the dissolution of a club at No. 8 Ping An Li, Si Ka Pang, Nantao, the members of which are all pig dealers from Kompo [Jiangbei]. This step was taken through a fear that these dealers might use the organization furnished by the club to resist the toll which is being imposed by the Authorities for all pigs entering Shanghai."[34] Even more disturbing to the Council was the Subei-dominated occupation of rickshaw pulling. From the late nineteenth century, foreign officials battled with little success to replace rickshaws with more modern trams. In 1894 the author of a guidebook to Shanghai pointed out,

Ragged and filthy coolies would no longer lounge about the streets, blocking up every passage and endangering our lives and property; pedestrians would not be pestered by the constant touting for fares . . . foreigners would not run the risk of being taken into the country and robbed there of their valuables by these wretches, as is only too often the case; and last but not least, by the introduction of tramcars,

* "Kaung-pok," or, more commonly, "Kompo" is the way foreigners spelled the pronunciation of "Jiangbei" in Shanghai dialect.

people would gain an immense advantage by being able to ride in a clean, comfortable and well-appointed vehicle, adapted for all kinds of weather.[35]

These charges profoundly influenced the Jiangnan elite's beliefs about what constituted modernity. What foreigners described in terms of occupation, the Jiangnan elite described in the language of local origins: what to foreigners was a rickshaw problem, was, to the Jiangnan elite, a problem of Subei people.

The most dramatic example of attempts to remove Subei people from the Shanghai landscape that involved both the Shanghai Municipal Council and the Jiangnan elite is the shack settlements, where the overwhelming majority of Subei people lived. Although not all residents of the shack settlements were from Subei, Chinese writers consistently associated these shantytowns with Subei natives. The battle between local authorities (Chinese and foreign) and the shack dwellers became a major arena for the creation of Subei ethnicity.

The Battle of the Shack Settlements

When large numbers of northern Jiangsu natives began to migrate to Shanghai in the mid-nineteenth century, many set up residence in makeshift shack settlements. For some, building or renting a shack was a step up from life on the "little hat boats" (maomao chuan) which they had used to bring them to Shanghai.[36] (Before the shack settlements developed, Suzhou Creek and other waterways that criss-crossed the suburbs of the International and French settlements were crowded with such houseboats.)[37] In many cases, migrants lived on the boats until they began to fall apart, then moved them onto shore and used them to construct a shack. Or they simply used the sail to make a low, tunnel-shaped, windowless gundilong to cover themselves at night.[38] Only after several years' work were most able to buy some bamboo or straw which they could mold with mud to made a more durable straw hut. Others, unable to afford to build a hut, rented them for 0.5 to 1.5 yuan a month.[39]

The huts provided precarious shelter. Holes in the wall functioned as windows; a piece of worn-out cloth was the door.[40] Tar paper, when available, provided a roof, which otherwise was made of less water-resistant straw.[41] Inside, straw spread over bricks served as beds, and old tin cans as stoves.[42] Often a loft was constructed in the hut to accommodate additional families: at least two families lived in most huts, and sometimes as many as four.[43] No running water was available in the huts, and the small quantity of water obtainable from local wells was usually dirty, so many residents depended on water from the neighborhood fire hydrants that the Municipal Council opened for an hour each morning.[44]

Clusters of hut dwellers, found throughout Shanghai from the 1870s on, gradually evolved into neighborhood-like shack settlements. Charles Darwent, in his guidebook to Shanghai (1905), describes one such community:

> On the higher reaches of the creek [Hongkew], from Scott Road northward, the visitor may see genuine beggar villages, if he wishes. These people are from north of the Yangtse, which is a poor region. Their huts are made of anything handy—mud, reeds, brickbats, old planks, coats, sacking, and enamelled iron advertisements of somebody's invaluable soap. There is a large supply of babies, dogs (much fleabitten and mangy), urchins (clothed in winter, naked in summer).[47]

The shack settlements emerged in different parts of Shanghai at different times. In the late nineteenth century, the first such settlements developed along the banks of the Huangpu River, inhabited mostly by Subei migrants who had come to work on the Shanghai docks. By 1900, the Pudong shantytowns of Caonitang, Bailianjing, Yangjinggang, Laobaidu, and Lannidu existed.[47] As factories were built in the early twentieth century in the eastern Shanghai district of Yangshupu and in the western districts of Caojiadu and Xiaoshadu (along Suzhou Creek), northern Jiangsu migrants who came to work as loaders inside the factories and along the nearby docks built shack settlements in these areas. For example, before the construction of factories, what became the shack settlement of Yaoshuilong (Medicine-water Lane) had been empty land along Suzhou Creek where no more than ten-odd peasants lived. By the 1930s, Yaoshuilong was a settlement with more than one thousand hut dwellers.[48] On the northern bank of Suzhou Creek, Piaoziwan became another large settlement. Between the two, the creek itself was home to a large number of "floating shacks" constructed on the small boats that had provided transport from northern Jiangsu to Shanghai.[48] At the same time, settlements sprang up in Yangshupu along Yangshupu Road and Pingliang Road.[49]

Japanese attacks on Shanghai in 1932 and 1937 resulted in a proliferation of shack settlements, particularly in Zhabei, which suffered heavy damage owing to the presence of the train station, a major target of attack. The shack settlements along Xinmin, Datong, and Guangpi roads in Zhabei, including Fangualong (Pumpkin Alley) all emerged at this time on land that had been devastated by the bombings.[50] Finally, as yet a new

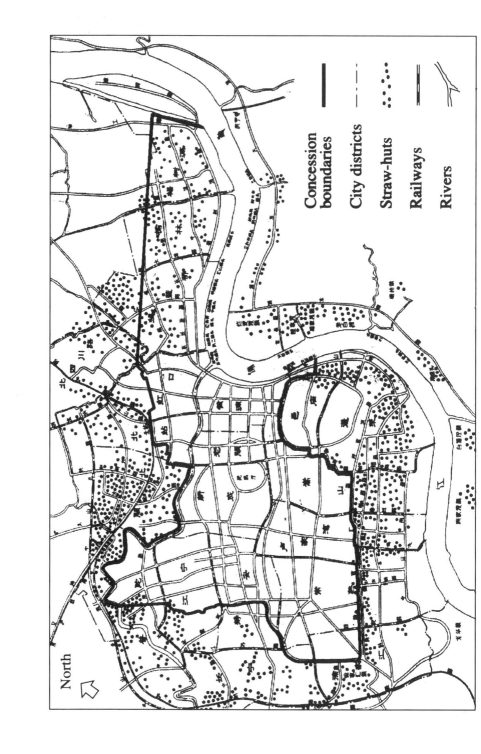

North

Concession
boundaries

City districts

Straw-huts

Railways

Rivers

wave of immigrants from northern Jiangsu came to Shanghai during the civil war, shack settlements began to appear along creeks at the edge of the relatively prosperous district of Xujiahui. Zhaojiabang, for instance, developed during these years.[51] By 1949, when close to one million individuals lived in huts, some 322 settlements with populations of at least two hundred huts each existed in Shanghai.[52] Fangualong itself had some sixteen thousand hut residents.[53] Almost all these shantytowns were outside the foreign concessions where most of the Chinese elite lived, emphasizing the geographic isolation of Subei people. Hut settlements formed an almost perfect circle around the concessions (see map 6).

Almost as soon as the shack settlements emerged, city officials and real estate investors undertook efforts to get rid of these eyesores on the urban landscape. As succinctly phrased by the author of one newspaper account of attempts to remove a hut settlement, "The Concession is a pure and clean place!"[54] Makeshift huts—considered "harmful to public sanitation and safety," "offensive to the eye," and "harboring of criminal elements"[55]—clearly did not belong.

Sometimes natural forces contributed to efforts to destroy the huts. Rain, for example, was a constant threat to their existence. M. T. Tchou, who investigated housing conditions of workers in Shanghai in the 1920s, described what typically happened to the huts during a rainstorm:

Because the place is full of cess-pools, the inmates are finally obliged to fill up the roads with earth in order to secure some sort of passage. But this makes the surroundings higher than the mud floors in the houses. So that when there is a heavy rainfall, the cess-pools overflow and the water saturated with dirt and gas enters the houses, making them into human ponds. After a storm the writer has seen men and women walking in the huts with filth and water up to their knees, while their little ones were placed on islands formed out of beds, chairs and tables. Often the water does not subside for several days.[56]

Not surprisingly, many huts never survived.

Fires, another frequent threat to the huts, occurred regularly, often caused by oil lamps or by the charcoal-burning stoves that were brought inside during winter months both for cooking and for the meager amount of heat they provided.[57] In one typical incident, a woman from Gaoyou was holding her infant while cooking inside her family's hut in Pudong. When the baby began to cry, she stepped outside to hand it to her husband. Meanwhile, the wall near the stove caught fire. Their hut as well as a number of neighboring huts was destroyed, and some five hundred people were injured by the fire.[58] Similar incidents involving fire were commonplace in the hut settlements, sometimes destroying entire communities. For example, a fire in a hut settlement in Zhabei that occurred in January 1949 burned six hundred huts and left more than two thousand people homeless.[59] In the one-year period from June 1948 to May 1949, at least thirty-seven fires in hut settlements were reported in the daily newspaper.[60]

The impact of fires was perhaps unnecessarily severe, as local fire departments were often less than enthusiastic about saving the huts. For instance, when a large fire broke out in a hut settlement in 1940, firefighters at the closest station in the French Concession decided little would be gained by extinguishing the fire and therefore did not respond to the call for help. In another instance, in January 1949, firefighters responded to a call about a fire in the Hongkou district. When they discovered the fire was in a hut settlement, they lost interest in fighting it, claiming that the dirt road was too narrow for the fire truck to enter.[61]

The fires, however, were not always accidental. Arson was often the last resort of landowners desperate to have the huts removed. For example, in 1936 the owner of the land on Yutong Road in Zhabei, where several hundred huts had been built, ordered the residents to move. The residents petitioned the government for a postponement of the deadline by which they had to move. Before the issue was resolved, however, a fire suddenly erupted, burning ten huts before firemen from the concession arrived. Certain that the fire was set by arsonists, some four hundred of the hut residents, carrying banners to publicize their cause, marched to the Public Security Bureau demanding that the truth be exposed.[62]

Elimination of the huts was not usually left to natural or human-made disasters. Instead, from the mid-nineteenth century, city officials relied on legal procedures to remove the huts. At the time the Land Regulations were enacted in 1845, the huts were already considered sufficiently distasteful to foreigners that Article 33 prohibited their construction—a rule which provided the basis for their later destruction in the International Settlement.[63] Newspapers from the 1870s include frequent reports of police efforts to destroy settlements. For example, an article from 1872 entitled "To Destroy the Huts" described the frustrating efforts to expunge the huts constructed by Subei refugees on vacant lots within the International Concession. The police repeatedly tried to disperse the hut residents, arresting those who refused to destroy their huts for violating the laws of the concession. "But these 'guest people' (kemin)—if you drive them to the east they move to the west. It's hard to get rid of them," complained the author.[64] The huts continued to haunt officials in the early twentieth century: continued attempts to eliminate them were chronicled in news articles with titles such as " 'Guest People Occupy Land and Won't

Move" and "The Dispersal of Jiangbei Guest People along the Pujiang."[65] In one highly notorious incident the Shanghai Municipal Council, one night during the winter of 1925, razed more than a thousand huts in a settlement on Pingliang Road in Yangshupu.[66]

As the above accounts imply, hut residents did not passively accept these efforts to eliminate their homes. They resisted, often in highly organized ways, engaging in struggles that have been largely ignored in histories of popular protest in Shanghai. Conflict between the hut dwellers and city authorities became intense in the 1930s, perhaps because the number of huts dwellers had swelled after the floods in Subei in 1931. The annual reports of the Shanghai Municipal Council chronicle, among other municipal problems, quasi-battles between the police and hut dwellers. In 1931, for instance, the annual report proudly declared that some 4,590 huts had been cleared.[67] The next year, however, the authors of the report admitted that "the existence of large numbers of straw huts, usually referred to as 'beggar' huts, has been a cause of anxiety for several years."

In 1931 it was decided to register the existing huts with a view to their gradual elimination, as they are a definite menace to public health and also constitute a serious fire hazard, and 2,041 huts were so registered. In the spring when there was a large movement of refugees and routine supervision was relaxed on account of the state of emergency existing, a large number of additional huts were erected and it was ultimately decided to demolish these huts after giving the occupants one month's notice.[68]

The results of these efforts fell short of the Council's hopes. After complaining that the squatter huts "have given their usual amount of trouble during the year [1932]," the report described its frustrated attempts to remove them:

The demolition of unregistered huts was commenced by the Public Works Department at the beginning of October and then passed over to the Public Health Department at the beginning of November. The pulling down of these huts has resolved itself into a war of attrition between the squatters and this Department, for no sooner is a hut demolished than it is erected again. The occupants were very persistent. For instance, during the month of March a large squatter village was destroyed by fire and despite the vigilance of the Police this village was entirely re-erected within two months.[69]

The battle between city authorities and the hut dwellers came to a head in 1936–37. Conflict had begun in 1935, when the Shanghai Municipal Council decided to order the approximately ten thousand hut residents of the eastern concession area to do away with their huts. Those east of Lan Road were to be removed by July 11, 1936; those west of Lan Road had until August 8. Once the deadlines passed, any remaining huts would be torn down by the police. Meanwhile, policemen were sent to the hut settlements to paint green numbers on the doors of each hut and require the residents to pay rent to the Council (which most never did).

When the first deadline arrived, the hut settlement was still thriving, and at 8:00 P.M. the Municipal Council sent fifty armed Chinese and Western police to order the residents to leave. The hut dwellers showed no inclination to comply; some two thousand of them staged a protest. Women armed with chamber pots, men carrying brooms, and children waving the brushes used to clean chamber pots accused the police of acting "against the hearts of the people." When the women used their chamber pots to construct a wall surrounding the police, they surrendered and agreed to give the residents five more days to move before returning with more troops.[70]

The hut residents intensified their organizing efforts: representatives from the eastern Shanghai hut settlements went to the settlements of northern and western Shanghai and established a Federation of Shanghai Concession Area Hut Residents (Shanghai gonggong zujie gequ penghu lianhehui).[71] Eventually representatives of this association worked out an agreement with the municipal council to postpone removal of the huts until the autumn, while the hut dwellers promised to establish a responsibility system to ensure that no new huts would be erected.[72]

The truce was short-lived, as a new round of conflict was triggered by a seemingly minor incident in early September. A man whose hut was dilapidated and rotting decided to repair his dwelling to prevent rain from pouring in. The Council considered this a violation of the moratorium on building new huts and dispatched police to remove his hut. Neighbors gathered to protest; the police beat them back with sticks, wounding some. This prompted the mobilization of the hut dwellers' so-called women's army (niangzijun), whose members hit the policemen with chamber pot cleaning brushes while throwing the contents of the chamber pots at the police. "The air stunk!" observed the Shenbao reporter. A number of women were arrested and sent to the Yangshupu Prison for "disturbing public order."[73] Ironically, the hut whose refurbishing triggered the incident was destroyed in the course of the riot that ensued.

Conflict between the dwellers and the Municipal Council diminished after this incident, largely because the Council apparently relaxed its determination to eliminate the huts. But no sooner had it announced new deadlines for hut removal in spring 1937 than the dwellers once again organized in defense of their residences. Hut dwellers on each street held meetings, the result of which was a petition signed by some ten thousand individuals pleading for the preservation of their homes. When their request was denied in April, they staged a demonstration. To contend with the four thousand demonstrators, the city dispatched not only the police but a platoon of the Russian Regiment of the Shanghai Volunteer Corps, equipped with machine guns. The demonstrators then withdrew and sent a delegation to meet with T. K. Ho, assistant secretary of the Municipal Council. They reached a compromise whereby the representatives agreed to assume responsibility for the demolition of 476 huts and to clear away the remaining waste straw and bamboo sticks as well. In return, the Council offered what the editors of the left-leaning *China Weekly Review* sarcastically described as a "compassionate grant" of $14 (US$4.05) to the dwellers of each hut. The money would be issued only after all 476 huts were torn down.[74]

The results of this plan are unknown and perhaps irrelevant, as war with Japan began shortly after its implementation. Whatever small number of huts were demolished was surely overshadowed by the massive number of new huts built by wartime refugees.[75] At the war's end the number of huts was so large that their elimination became one of the major projects of the Guomindang-led city government. In late 1945, it enacted a law forbidding the construction of new huts. "To ensure the peace and safety of the majority of citizens, we must sacrifice the interests of a minority group," government officials explained. "Particularly in light of the health problems during summer and the fire danger in winter, these huts are really a danger to all the city's residents. . . . They must be eliminated!" The ineffectiveness of the law is suggested by the fact that only one year later, an almost identical law was passed, this time providing a special police patrol that would be responsible for its implementation. The policemen assigned to this patrol issued a statement to the hut residents that they were not acting on their own but following government orders.[76] These laws—even with the police patrols—seem to have scarcely affected the hut problem. There is no evidence of a decrease in hut dwellers during this period; if anything, their ranks were swelled by refugees from the Communist-occupied areas of northern Jiangsu. When the Chinese Communist Party finally assumed control of Shanghai in 1949, the massive number of hut dwellers was one of the first major social problems it confronted. Although it never succeeded in eliminating the huts, it radically reduced the number of such dwellings by building public housing that was affordable to the hut residents and, at the same time, prohibiting migration from rural areas to Shanghai.[77]

The attempts by previous governments to obliterate the huts, no matter how constant and determined they were, never enjoyed even a modicum of success. So long as rural immigrants continued to flow into Shanghai, the proliferation of these shantytowns was as inevitable as is their existence in cities of third world countries today. From the government's perspective, the battle to eliminate the huts was a losing one. Yet the battle is significant, for even though it was not directed explicitly at Subei people, it was in effect an attack on the niche they occupied in Shanghai's urban landscape. It was an attempt to expunge or at least move to the periphery of the city, the poverty associated with Subei people.

Attempts to eradicate the huts, however, cannot be understood as a straightforward conflict between the Jiangnan elite and Subei immigrants. The foreign-dominated Shanghai Municipal Council, as we have seen, played a major role in attacking the settlements, illustrating the indirect ways in which the foreign presence in Shanghai contributed to the construction and stigmatization of the category Subei people. For foreigners, the fact of paramount importance was the proliferation of shack settlements that blemished their image of a modern city. Precisely who occupied these shacks was largely irrelevant.

But for the Chinese elite observing and participating in this battle local origins were crucial. They went to great lengths to define the shack settlements as a Subei phenomenon. "The slum districts of the south city, Zhabei, Pudong, Xujiahui, and Tushanwan are inhabited by the Jiangbei poor," read one magazine article. "Grass huts are being built by the Jiangbei poor," noted a newspaper report about the slums of Zhabei; another referred to the "Jiangbei guest people" (keren) who occupied the slums."[78] So close was the equation of Subei people with the shantytowns that they were often described as Jiangbei shack settlements. One writer coined the term Jiangbei colony to portray these areas.[79] In daily parlance, they were referred to as Jiangbei villages (Jiangbei cun). Underlining the equation of Subei people with the shack settlements and poverty, one writer observed, "There are some people who say, 'Shanghai is a place that is both heaven and hell.' The areas where Jiangbei people live are truly tantamount to hell."[80] Yet another writer remarked that "'Shanghai has become like a colony for Jiangbei people. The grass huts of Pudong, Zhabei, Nanshi, and West Shanghai are all homes for Little Three's and Little Four's [common names for Subei people]."[81] By ascribing the shack settlements to Subei people and labeling them Jiangbei shack settlements, they could separate themselves from a Chinese phenomenon so offensive to the foreign elite. The shack settlements, then, became a central arena in which the category Subei people was constructed and imbued with symbolic meanings.

The battles over the shack settlements had a different but nonetheless significant meaning for Subei people's construction of their identity in Shanghai. When Subei people organized to protect their dwellings, they did so as shack residents, not as Subei natives. Yet these struggles against the state most likely instilled in the shantytown residents a new sense of community in Shanghai. Even if they did not lead to an explicit articulation of Subei identity, they presumably forged alliances among northern Jiangsu natives who had previously experienced and insisted upon more locally based solidarities.

Contested Terrain: The Battle over Shanghai Culture

The repeated attempts to send Subei refugees back to their villages and to eliminate their dwellings in Shanghai represent a willful effort to marginalize migrants from northern Jiangsu, to keep them from becoming a part of cosmopolitan Shanghai. This effort had a less deliberate dimension as well, one that concerned the cultural aspects of Subei people's presence in Shanghai. Through a process that remains largely intangible, the culture that northern Jiangsu migrants brought to and redefined in Shanghai was denigrated and excluded from the formation of what became known as Shanghai culture. It was as if an unacknowledged battle took place among immigrant communities to define a new urban culture. In Shanghai, it was migrants from Jiangnan who ultimately won, having defined Shanghai culture as one derived in large part from their own traditions, rather than one that integrated influences from Subei. This is evidenced in language, entertainment, aesthetics, and cuisine—all of which reflected the dominance of Jiangnan natives in the Shanghai elite. This does not mean that Subei people abandoned their culture in Shanghai, but rather that they, along with their cultural practices, were kept separate and on the periphery.

The fate of local operas from northern Jiangsu exemplifies the ways in which Subei culture persisted but was marginalized in Shanghai. First, they exerted no influence on the development of the hybrid Shanghai local opera (*huju*), based primarily on Jiangnan styles.[82] Second, performances of northern Jiangsu operas were denigrated. From the early 1910s, Huai and Yangzhou opera troupes performed in Shanghai.[83] But they almost never appeared in the prestigious theaters of the International Settlement or French Concession, where performances of Yueju (Shaoxing opera) and Peking opera predominated. According to a guidebook from 1947, for example, one could hear Peking opera in six theaters and performances of Yueju in twenty-six. But not a single one was listed for Huai or Yangzhou opera.[84] Moreover, advertisements in the daily newspaper *Shenbao,* which regularly included publicity for Shaoxing and Peking opera performances, rarely listed operas from northern Jiangsu. No advertisements for Huai opera appeared, and only occasionally was there an advertisement for Yangzhou opera troupes performing at the Great World. One such occasion, ironically, was when the Yangzhou opera troupe performed "The Beauty of Jiangnan."[85] (Yangzhou flower-drum opera, *huagu xi,* was given an extraordinary chance in Shanghai when Lu Lanchun, the concubine of Green Gang leader and owner of the Great World Huang Jinrong, took a liking to it while worshiping at a temple in Hangzhou. She persuaded Huang to find performers, and Yangzhou flower-drum opera was then granted a ten-day run, during June 1921, at the Great World. However, no subsequent performances appear to have taken place.)[86]

Even the Tianchan Wutai, owned by Gu Zhuxuan, the powerful Green Gang leader from Yancheng called the Subei Emperor by Subei natives in Shanghai, never featured Subei opera. "We couldn't even sing at Gu Zhuxuan's theater," complained Xiao Wenyan, one of the most well known Huai opera performers in Shanghai.[87] Performances of northern Jiangsu operas most commonly took place not in formal theaters, but on makeshift open-air stages or in teahouses in the districts where northern Jiangsu natives lived. If they were held in theaters at all, it was in relatively unknown places located far from the concessions: the Minle Theater in Nanshi, the Fengxiang Stage in Zhabei, the Great Huangshan Theater near Xieqiao, and the Great Western Shanghai Theater and Great Gaosheng Theater, both in western Shanghai, where cotton mill workers were concentrated.[88]

None of these theaters was well known outside the working-class districts of Shanghai, and to the extent that they were known at all, had a somewhat less than glowing reputation. "The theaters where Yangzhou opera are performed," observed a local reporter in 1947, "are usually troublesome places. Hoodlums (*sanguang mazi*) come and go. If the ticket collector does not have experience with the gangsters, he won't be able to do his job. Often there are fights caused by people who try to get in without tickets."[89]

These theaters were enterprises whose origins were enmeshed in and reflected the experience of Subei people in Shanghai. The Minle Theater, for instance, was owned by Liu Muchu and his wife, known as Big Pockmarked Liu (Liu *damazi*). Originally from Huai'an, he first worked as a rickshaw puller in Shanghai; she came to Shanghai to escape an arranged marriage and supported herself by mending clothes for rickshaw pullers and dockworkers. By pledging a powerful gang leader as their master, they eventually managed to open a teahouse. Through her skills as a mediator of disputes, Big Pockmarked Liu attracted a number of pledged goddaughters, becoming a woman of considerable power in the South City (Nanshi) district. In the late 1920s, she and her husband used the money they had saved to open the Minle Theater, more popularly called the Forty-Rooms (*sishi jian*) by the northern Jiangsu natives who went there to hear their local opera performed. (Meanwhile, they owned twenty or thirty rickshaws that they rented to pullers in the neighborhood.)

It was in this theater that Xiao Wenyan, who had been sold to the Lius as a child daughter-in-law, first learned to sing Huai opera and perform.[90] As she established a reputation among the northern Jiangsu community in Shanghai, she earned the nickname the Jiangbei Mei Lanfang, an expression of her comparability to the renowned singer of the elite Beijing opera.

Northern Jiangsu opera, then, was popular among Subei natives, yet it never became part of Shanghai elite culture. To journalists and guidebook writers, it was almost invisible, not even worthy of mention. It was peripheral, irrelevant to the Jiangnan styles that dominated the opera world in Shanghai.

The peripheral status of Subei culture is also evident in language, specifically, the development of Shanghai local dialect. Shanghai dialect is not based primarily on the language spoken by its only genuine natives, the people of Pudong, but rather is a conglomeration of the dialects spoken by immigrants. Given both the early presence of migrants from Subei as well as their relatively large numbers in the Shanghai population one might expect some of the northern Jiangsu dialects to have been a major ingredient in Shanghai dialect. Instead, the Wu-derived dialects of Suzhou and Ningbo provided the major influence. As two scholars pointed out, describing how the Ningbo word for "we"—*ala*—replaced *woni*, "Most of the people who immigrated from Ningbo to Shanghai were merchants. . . . Since the status of Ningbo businessmen was relatively high, people were willing to use their language."[91] Yangzhou dialect is mentioned only as one of at least a dozen other local dialects that influenced Shanghai slang.[92] Furthermore, as is evidenced by the comments of Shanghai residents today (see chapter 7), Subei dialect was considered harsh-sounding and inferior to southern speech. Even Yangzhou storytellers, when performing outside Subei districts of Shanghai, used Suzhou dialect to tell their tales—their native dialect was apparently unacceptable to Shanghai audiences.[93]

The minimal influence of Subei culture on what became known as Shanghai elite culture is also apparent in notions of beauty, although in ways that are not easily identified. Beliefs about female attractiveness are

one measure of popular notions of beauty. Despite the reputation of Yangzhou as home of the most famed prostitutes during the Qing, in Shanghai
it was Suzhou women who were considered most beautiful and desirable.
Not only were northern Jiangsu women considered less physically attrac-
tive, but their language was not as pleasing to the ear as that spoken by
the women of Suzhou. That this scorn for Subei beauty was confined to
Shanghai is suggested by the fact that in Guangzhou and Hankou, Yangzhou prostitutes were highly prestigious.[94]

Clothing styles, too, reflected the dislike of Subei tastes. Jiangbei
women, observed the authors of a major survey of Shanghai's working
class in the late 1930s, "like to wear red and green silk clothes, embroidered
shoes, pink or red stockings, and other brightly colored clothes." Women
from Jiangnan, in contrast, "always wear more tasteful blue, black, or
gray colored garments."[95] The bright red and green colors associated with
Subei natives were shunned by Shanghainese. "Even today," complained
a woman originally from Subei, "if you buy a piece of red cloth people
will say, 'You Jiangbei ren—that's ugly!' "[96] And apparently among the
Shanghai natives who live in Taibei today, bright red and green are still
associated with Subei ren and despised.

Food more clearly illustrates the marginalization of northern Jiangsu
culture. Of the northern Jiangsu areas, only Yangzhou could boast a presence in the Shanghai culinary world, and its status was precarious at
best, even though Yangzhou restaurants were prestigious in other parts
of China.[97] Guides to Shanghai typically listed the several most famous
cuisines in Shanghai. Yangzhou/Zhenjiang cuisine, treated as one type,
usually appeared on the list along with Shanghai local, Cantonese, Bei-
jing/Tianjin, Ningbo, and Sichuan cuisines. But a closer examination of
these lists reveals the relatively low status of Yangzhou food. One guide,
for example, devoted a full page or two to descriptions of Beijing, Tianjin, Sichuan, Guangdong, Huizhou, Ningbo, and Shanghai local cuisines,
replete with lengthy lists of the restaurants serving each. Yangzhou/Zhen-
jiang cuisine was mentioned only in passing, in the final section listing
miscellaneous other cuisines that could be sampled in Shanghai.[98] *Shanghai chunqiu* (The Shanghai annals) was more blunt in its assessment of
Yangzhou/Zhenjiang food: it "once was common in Jiangnan and Jiangbei, but its method is conservative (*moshou*), and has gradually come to
be looked down on by people. In Shanghai, except for Yangzhou snacks
(*dianxin*), there is very little advertisement for Yangzhou/Zhenjiang food.
Lion's head and cured pork are the only dishes it can claim, and they can't
compare to the achievements of the cuisines of other places."[99]

Almost all aspects of culture, then, from dialect to food, evidence the exclusion of Subei influences or styles from that which was considered sophisticated, urbane, and truly Shanghainese. This exclusion should not be construed as the willful machination of the Jiangnan elite; they did not *conspire* to marginalize Subei culture. Instead, it was the inevitable result of their struggle to define Shanghai culture as their own, such that fashion and sophistication in Shanghai reflected the styles of such places as Ningbo, Shaoxing, and Wuxi.

In some instances, as we have seen, Subei culture was not simply marginalized but actively denigrated as well. This may partly be due to the relatively high status that Yangzhou culture, in particular, had formerly enjoyed: if Jiangnan tastes were to claim superiority, it was almost imperative that those of Yangzhou be actively dismissed. The denigration of Subei culture may also have been a necessary component of the definition of Jiangnan styles, establishing the other against which Jiangnan natives could define themselves and claim, eventually, a Shanghai identity. The denigration was therefore a crucial element in the construction of the negatively charged category Subei people.

The marginalization and denigration of Subei culture, along with the attempts to destroy the hut settlements, represent the ways in which Subei people were kept on the periphery of Shanghai. At the same time, *Subei* (or *Jiangbei*) became the adjective predictably attached to all distasteful and despicable elements of Shanghai life ("Jiangbei refugees" or "Jiangbei hut dwellers"), even when they were not solely the purview of Subei people. Little wonder, then, that by the 1920s, *Jiangbei swine* was one of the most common curse words in Shanghai dialect.[100] It both reflected and reinforced the status of Subei people as unwelcome outsiders in Shanghai, as a group that did not rightly belong—as immigrants who had become ethnics.

4

ETHNICITY AT WORK:

SUBEI NATIVES IN THE

SHANGHAI LABOR MARKET

Work, more than any other experience, determined Subei people's social and economic status in Shanghai. The jobs they could secure influenced where they lived, their standard of living, and their relationship to other immigrant communities. Their employment patterns were crucial in shaping popular perceptions of Subei people as low-class. Conversely, popular beliefs about Subei people were a significant factor in defining their job opportunities. The category Subei people not only described Shanghai's subproletarian underclass, but also provided an explanation of its constituents. The Shanghai labor market, in other words, produced ethnicity just as it, in turn, was shaped by it.

The Regional Nature
of the Shanghai Labor Market

Natives of northern Jiangsu who migrated to Shanghai entered a labor market that was vastly different and in some ways far more complex than that of other Chinese cities in the late nineteenth and early twentieth centuries. Shanghai's labor market was shaped by its prominence as a commercial and industrial center. Domestically produced handicraft and manufactured goods, raw materials for industrial production, and goods imported from abroad were all handled by the Shanghai port.[1] Shanghai was the unrivaled center of Chinese industry as well: in 1911, approximately one-fourth of all China's factories were located in Shanghai, by 1933 almost half, and by Liberation in 1949, some 60 percent were concentrated there. Not only was Shanghai China's major industrial center, but it was also the center of the colonial enterprise in China. More than in other Chinese cities, a large proportion of enterprises in Shanghai—from cotton mills to rickshaw companies—were owned by foreigners.[2] It is in this complex and highly differentiated labor market that the niche occupied by Subei people can be described.

Much like the Irish who immigrated to London in the nineteenth century, most Subei natives in Shanghai worked at low-skilled, low-paying jobs.[3] Whether they had migrated from Subei themselves or were the offspring of Subei migrants, whether they were poor peasants fleeing the prospect of starvation or wealthy landowners fleeing land reform in the 1940s, Subei people in Shanghai concentrated in jobs that Shanghainese regarded as inferior. Republican period surveys of the Shanghai work force reveal three general patterns: such unskilled, physically demanding occupations as coolie labor were dominated almost exclusively by people from Subei; occupations attracting people from Jiangnan as well as Subei were stratified, with Subei people performing the lowest-paying, lowest-status jobs; jobs requiring high levels of skill or education were rarely available to Subei people.

Rickshaw pulling, more than any other occupation, was associated with and symbolized the status of Subei people in the Shanghai labor market. From the beginning of Shanghai's rapid development in the mid-nineteenth century, transport vehicles that depended on human labor power were considered the domain of Subei migrants. In the 1860s, well before the appearance of rickshaws, wheelbarrows used to transport both materials and people were called Jiangbei carts, as northern Jiangsu migrants represented the majority of cart pullers.[4] When rickshaws began to be used in 1875, Subei natives immediately took over the work of hauling rickshaws. By 1913, when there were approximately ten thousand rickshaw pullers in Shanghai, an estimated 80–90 percent were from Subei.[5] By the mid-1930s, when the number of rickshaw pullers had soared to eighty thousand, 90 percent were of Subei origins, the majority from Yancheng and Funing.[6] So extreme was the dominance of rickshaw pulling by people from Subei that one Republican-period surveyor complained that the prevalence of Subei dialect among rickshaw pullers was an obstacle to his research work.[7]

In the minds of the Shanghai elite, rickshaw pulling epitomized the lowly status of Subei people. One reporter observed that only Subei people, plagued by natural disasters and economic destruction in their home villages, would condescend to do this "bestial" and "inhuman" work.[8] Rickshaw pulling not only reinforced the association of Subei people with physically demanding, almost animal-like labor, but also confirmed a belief that the people who performed such jobs in Shanghai were ignorant and unsophisticated. "Almost all of Shanghai's rickshaw drivers are brothers from Jiangbei," began one poignant critique. "Those Jiangbei people can tolerate a great deal of hardship, and are part of the struggling race. . . . Almost all of them are illiterate, so their knowledge is very superficial." This semisympathetic tone quickly gave way to sarcasm and disgust:

> Their minds are very simple, so when they are situated in such a sophisticated, complicated, and prosperous city as Shanghai, they lose their original innocence and adopt a kind of greedy, dishonest, barbarian, and despicable nature. So Shanghai residents, whether male or female, feel totally hateful whenever rickshaw pullers are mentioned. They have no positive feelings toward them.

After enumerating the variety of ways in which rickshaw pullers cheated their passengers, most of which indicated sheer stupidity to the author, he continued his denunciation:

> Their knowledge is so superficial that they only know that all foreigners are rich. They can't even tell who are the Jews who are even stingier than they themselves, or the White Russians who are even poorer than they themselves. They treat them all like people from England and America. They are so silly that they just bend down in front of the foreigners like a hen trying to mate! They are full of pidgin English—nonsense like Mai-da-mu [Madame], Mai-si-dan [Mister], li-ke-xi [rickshaw]. It just makes you laugh.

"The manifestations of their evil and disgusting image are too numerous to be listed here," the author concluded.[9] The concentration of Subei people in rickshaw pulling thus not only located them in one of the least skilled, most physically demanding jobs, but also contributed toward popular prejudice against them.

In the eyes of the elite rickshaw pulling may have represented the lowliest livelihood imaginable, yet for some Subei natives getting a job pulling a rickshaw represented upward mobility of a sort. For example, a Yancheng native, Chen Caitu, recalled his progress from the time he was forced by natural disasters to leave his village around 1900. First he went to Yangzhou and supported himself by selling vegetables and fruit, saving enough money to marry at the age of twenty-two. Shortly after that it became difficult for him to make a living in Yangzhou, so he moved to Shanghai. "At first I transported rocks in Pudong," he recalled, "but the work was hard and paid little. A friend introduced me to rickshaw work and my life got better day by day. After two or three years I had enough money to bring my wife to Shanghai."[10]

Many rickshaw pullers never shed their peasant identity, coming to work in Shanghai only seasonally. Numerous pullers from the area around Yancheng and Funing returned home every spring for the busy agricultural season, coming to Shanghai only after the fall harvest was finished. A smaller number of pullers from Chongming and Taizhou, who mostly cultivated crops of peanuts, migrated on an opposite schedule, coming to Shanghai in the spring and returning home in the fall.[11]

While rickshaw pulling may have been the job most immediately associated with Subei people, migrants from northern Jiangsu also dominated the ranks of freight haulers. The approximately fifty thousand dockworkers in the 1930s were dominated by the so-called Subei bang. The predominance of northern Jiangsu people among the loaders at the Shanghai docks was so extreme that, as in rickshaw pulling, Subei dialect was the language of the trade.[12] And like rickshaw pulling, dock work did not offer stable employment. Although many docks employed small permanent crews, these were composed mainly of workers from Ningbo;[13] employees from northern Jiangsu were hired on a temporary basis, usually for fifteen to twenty days a month.[14] Most of the workers who hauled freight at the Shanghai train station were also from northern Jiangsu.[15]

The final category of jobs dominated by northern Jiangsu natives belonged to the service sector. For example, the overwhelming majority of barbers, of which there were some twenty-four thousand in 1920, were from Yangzhou.[16] Some worked in formal barbershops, but the majority plied their trade on the street, carrying a shoulder pole with a stool for the customer on one end and a washbasin containing a towel and instruments on the other. A few barbers set up makeshift shops at the entrance to residential alleys: a cloth tent with a chair and mirror inside.[17] Bathhouse workers, too, came predominantly from Yangzhou. In 1920, the sixty-odd bathhouses in Shanghai employed an estimated two thousand workers to do pedicure, massage the guests' backs while they bathed, and serve them tea as they rested afterward.[18]

Cobblers, night soil collectors, and garbage collectors were also from northern Jiangsu.[19] Particularly the latter two occupations—quite literally shit work—were jobs that only Subei people seemed willing to do, both confirming and reinforcing their lowly status. As one description of Shanghai Municipal Council employees noted, "Country people from Jiangbei, the Chinese who are most able to swallow hardship, are concentrated in the garbage department. Although there are individual Jiangbei people in other departments, the garbage department is really theirs."[20] So demeaning was it to be a garbage collector that a man from Yancheng preferred the hardship of unemployment to working as a garbage collector. When, in order to survive, he finally had no choice but to become a garbage collector, he did not want anyone to know. "Garbage collectors employed by the city had to wear a red shirt," he recalled. "I hated wearing that red shirt because everyone could then see who I was and what I did. So as soon as we finished work each day I would take off that shirt!"[21]

Not all occupations in the service sector were dominated by northern Jiangsu natives. A small number were in fact the purview of Jiangnan natives. The majority of tailors, for example, came from the Jiangnan areas of Ningbo and Changzhou. Yet an enormous gap separated the livelihoods of Jiangnan tailors and northern Jiangsu people engaged in service sector jobs: while tailors earned 3–7 yuan (dollars) a day in 1920, barbers, who earned more than most Subei service sector workers, could count on making only 2–3 *jiao* (dimes).[22]

In addition to the occupations described above—ones completely dominated by Subei natives—a number of enterprises employed workers from both Jiangnan and northern Jiangsu. Almost all such enterprises had a hierarchy of jobs in which Jiangnan natives were at the top and Subei people at the bottom. The most important such case, because of the number of employees, was factory work. As noted above, the majority of Subei people worked outside the ranks of the industrial proletariat. For them, securing factory employment was the highest-status job to which they could aspire. Recalled a man from Yancheng who worked as a garbage collector, "We really wanted to work in a factory, and I was very envious of my relatives who had factory jobs. But we just couldn't get in."[23] Another man who worked for the city's sanitation bureau insisted with absolute certainty that "no people who were themselves born in Subei could get jobs in cotton mills. The only Subei people who were able to work in cotton mills were ones who had been born and raised in Shanghai."[24] In fact, a sizable number of women born and raised in Subei worked in Shanghai's cotton mills.[25] The man's distorted impression underlines the fact that securing a factory job was considered a step up for Subei people.

The elite of Shanghai's industrial working class—those who performed highly skilled jobs, became technicians, and were employed at the highest wage rates—were primarily from Canton and Jiangnan. The scarce information available about the native-place origins of factory workers in the late nineteenth and early twentieth centuries suggests that northern Jiangsu natives were quite possibly latecomers to factory work in Shanghai.[26] The earliest groups of factory workers were from Canton, Ningbo, and Shanghai proper. For example, when the first machine-building factories were established in the 1850s, skilled workers were recruited from Canton, where a foreign-owned shipbuilding factory already operated. Peasants from Ningbo and Shanghai were employed to perform the unskilled jobs. No mention was made of any workers from Subei.[27]

When, in the early 1920s, Subei people began to appear in records of factory workers, they concentrated in industries that generally required the least skill and offered the lowest pay, such as silk reeling and cotton spinning. For example, while workers in the machinery industry earned an average of $.85 a day in 1934 and those in shipbuilding $1.24, workers in silk filatures earned only $.31 and in cotton spinning only $.47. This disparity partly reflects the difference in the earnings of male and female workers, as the machinery and shipbuilding industries were dominated by men while textiles primarily employed women. Yet even within the female-dominated textile industries, those dominated by Subei natives— cotton spinning and silk reeling—offered substantially less pay than industries in which the majority of workers came from Jiangnan. In underwear knitting factories, workers earned an average of $.79 a day in 1934, in silk weaving $.90, in cotton weaving $.61, and in tobacco $.57[28]—all higher than the figures for cotton spinning and silk reeling cited above.

Even within cotton mills and silk filatures, the relatively higher-paying skilled jobs went to people from Jiangnan. In the cotton spinning industry, one of the largest employers of Subei workers, Subei women, considered strong, robust, and accustomed to dirt, were channeled into the workshops where the work was most arduous and dirty. Initially they dominated the undesirable jobs in the reeling workshops; in the 1930s, when mill managers began to hire women instead of men in the roving workshops, they recruited Subei women for the jobs.[29] "This was because natives of Shanghai were not willing to do that work," a mill manager explained. "The wages were not necessarily the lowest, but the work was rough. In roving there was more dust and the air was not very good. Since the work was hard, Subei people were more able to do it."[30] Women from Jiangnan villages concentrated in the weaving department, where the jobs generally required more skill and paid better: in 1934, women weavers earned an average of $.64 a day, while women in the spinning department earned $.46, in roving $.53, and in reeling $.43.[31] Furthermore, a number of Jiangnan women who worked in the mills eventually became factory supervisors, secretaries, and bookkeepers, advancements unimaginable to women from Subei.[32]

A similar division of labor between workers from Jiangnan and Subei was apparent in the silk reeling industry. (The separate, and more prestigious, silk weaving industry was dominated by workers from Zhejiang, Changzhou, and Suzhou.)[33] When the head of the YWCA Labor Bureau, Cora Deng, visited a Shanghai silk filature in the late 1920s, she was especially struck by the concentration of Subei women in the worst jobs, which often involved the painful work of bobbing silk cocoons in boiling water. Women from Jiangnan, on the other hand, having personal connections to the factory management, were hired to work under much better conditions.[34] Likewise, in the tobacco industry, where most of the workers were from Zhejiang, the minority of Subei workers were hired to perform only the unskilled tasks. Women from Subei concentrated in the leaf department, where the work was more onerous and the wages lower than in the packing department, which was staffed by women from Jiangnan.[35] "Probably no part of the factory offered a less pleasant work environment than the Leaf Department," observes Elizabeth Perry in her study of Shanghai labor protest.

> As one former worker recalled, "Life in the Leaf Department was like the life of an adopted daughter-in-law. Only the Number Ones were allowed to talk. We were barely allowed to breathe." Temperatures were kept hot and humid to prevent leaf breakage. In winter time, the contrast between the cold weather outside and indoor temperatures in the high eighties caused chronic bronchitis problems for many of the workers. This was exacerbated by the dust particles that filled the air as tobacco leaves were ripped from their stems and shredded into tiny pieces. Yellow steam permeated the workshop, lending workers' sweat and phlegm a yellowish hue. Handling the hot, wet leaves left more than a few workers with sopping clothes and blistered hands. As a consequence of the cluttered, unsanitary conditions under which they labored, Leaf Department employees . . . commonly referred to theirs as "garbage work" (laxi shenghuo).[36]

Employed on a temporary basis, many of the male workers from Subei were reportedly "maltreated and abused practically all the time, sometimes even being punched and kicked."[37] In the flour industry, dominated by workers from Ningbo, Wuxi, and Changzhou, those from Subei worked primarily as coolies, loading the heavy sacks of flour to be transported for sale.[38] And in the Shanghai Arsenal, where the majority of jobs were far more highly skilled and remunerated than in textiles and tobacco, a small number of Subei natives were employed as riveters.[39]

Shanghai's tramway industry also illustrates the hierarchical division between employees of Jiangnan and Subei origins. All three tramway companies in Shanghai (the French Tramway Company, the British-owned Shanghai Tramway Company, and the Chinese Tramway Company) consisted of a machine department employing a small number of skilled technicians and a traffic department, where the larger corps of drivers and ticket collectors were employed. The majority of technicians in the machine department were from Ningbo and Shanghai, while the less skilled employees in the traffic epartment were mostly from Subei; some were from Hubei, Hebei, and Shandong. In the late 1930s a large number were beholden to Xu Dejing, a "native of Kompo and a high-interest money lender." Not surprisingly, Jiangnan mechanics earned more than the Subei drivers and conductors.[40] Moreover, the tram conductors were a despised lot, "their corrupt practices known to all," according to a *Shenbao* report.[41]

Even among prostitutes, the division between women from Jiangnan and Subei and the further division between Yangzhou and the northern parts of Subei were obvious to observers. The highest class prostitutes (*changsan*), who lived in lavishly furnished brothels, acquired skills as entertainers, and catered only to wealthy businessmen and officials, came from Jiangnan. Second-grade prostitutes (*yao'er*), reputed less for their entertainment and social skills and more for their sexual services, were primarily from Yangzhou. Women (and more commonly girls) from Subei, many of whom had been kidnapped from their home villages, made up the overwhelming majority of "pheasants" (*ye ji*), prostitutes who wandered the streets of Shanghai's red-light district soliciting customers.[42] Some Subei women specialized in providing sexual services to sailors on junks moored in the Huangpu River, rowing small boats out to solicit their business.[43]

The dominance of Subei people in unskilled, low-paying jobs may obscure an equally important aspect of the work experience of Subei people in Shanghai: many never entered the formal labor market at all or worked outside of it for long periods of time. Large numbers of Subei migrants eked out a living by peddling food, collecting and selling paper, hulling rice, making and selling charcoal briquettes, or doing other people's laundry. Garbage collector Zhou Guozhen spent several years supporting himself by peddling vegetables before securing a regular job in the city's sanitation bureau.[44] One man who eventually worked as a rickshaw puller survived by picking and selling garbage when he first came to Shanghai in 1925; another made shoes and repaired umbrellas; a woman helped support her family by making charcoal briquettes and selling vegetables and fish.[45] Chen Dewang, selected as a model worker in the 1950s, recalled that upon arriving in Shanghai from Hai'an in 1944 he lived with a group of rickshaw pullers in Nanshi, all men from Subei who had come to Shanghai alone. "I couldn't pull a rickshaw then because I was too small. People felt sorry for me because I had no parents, so they let me wash their clothes, clean vegetables, and help them cook." When he was finally tall enough to pull a rickshaw he still could not afford the rent, so he spent several years pulling other people's rickshaws when they were between shifts. Only after several years was Chen able to borrow enough money to rent a rickshaw with three other men and begin to work regular shifts.[46]

Subei women, except for those who secured jobs in silk filatures or cotton mills, were particularly likely to work outside the formal sector of the labor market. A large number of women gleaned some cash by working as "poor people's seamstresses" (*feng qiong po*), sewing and mending clothes for shop clerks, factory workers, apprentices, and job-seekers whose wives remained in the countryside. These women would roam the streets carrying a bamboo basket supplied with scissors, needle and thread, as well as a small stool to sit on while working.[47] Other women served the same clientele by doing laundry. Still others—called "pickle devils" (*yancai gui*)—carried baskets of rice and salted vegetables which they sold to coolies.[48] While some of these female peddlers were the wives of Subei natives working in Shanghai, others were peasants who crossed the river only to work for the duration of the agricultural slack season and then returned to their Subei homes.[49]

Children of Subei natives were also likely to work outside the formal labor market. Beginning at the age of seven or eight, unless they could secure jobs as child workers in cotton mills or silk filatures, children in Subei families were expected to contribute to the family income by picking salable pieces of paper, cloth, and glass from garbage heaps, peddling produce, or selling popsicles.[50] Others helped support their families by begging.

In the early 1930s, some twenty thousand individuals begged for a living in Shanghai. Becoming a beggar, however, required joining a native-place-based gang ruled by an elder. Beggars were then required to turn over a certain portion of their daily earnings to the elder, who in return took care of the welfare of their charges, helping them, for example, when they were sick.[51] Begging was not a straightforward activity in Shanghai, as some twenty-five distinct styles were practiced; some beggars, for example, publicized their pitiful circumstances with a statement written in chalk on the ground while others helped rickshaw pullers over the steep part of bridges and then solicited coins of gratitude from the passengers. Subei natives were known to specialize in "playing the green dragon"— holding a large green snake and teasing passersby who refused to give them money.[52]

Working on the fringes of the formal labor market was another, albeit smaller, group of Subei natives, those who made a living by joining the criminal underworld. Many engaged in the lucrative business of recruiting girls from Subei to sell to *yao'er* or pheasant brothels. Subei women in Shanghai were famous for monopolizing the kidnapping business.[53] For example, after the death of her father, who ran a pheasant business just outside the Small East Gate, a woman from Yangzhou known as Old Five Hong (Hong *laowu*) engaged in the business of "issuing tickets" (*kai tiaozi*), or trafficking in young girls. Hoodlums who went to Subei to kidnap the girls brought them to Old Five Hong, who then sold them to brothels. As the demand for prostitutes increased, Hong herself went to Subei to kidnap young girls. For some women, joining the criminal underworld represented upward mobility of a sort. For example, Shen Kouzhu had first worked as a servant and then as a prostitute on arriving in Shanghai from Taixing. After living with the Green Gang leader Feng Zibao, she established connections that enabled her to become a trafficker in kidnapped children from Subei, eventually becoming a well-known female hoodlum in her own right. She sold young girls to brothels and boys to labor bosses. Both Old Five Hong and Shen Kouzhu belonged to the "ten sisters" (*shi jiemi*) of the Green Gang.[54] Like most women kidnappers, these female gang leaders were sworn disciples of the Green Gang boss from Subei, Gu Zhuxuan (see below).[55]

Many people from Subei, in other words, worked for long periods of time outside of or on the fringes of the formal labor market, some never securing regular jobs at all. For them, regular employment as a rickshaw puller, night soil collector, or garbage collector was a step up. The status of Subei people in the Shanghai labor market can perhaps best be described as subproletarian. The jobs they dominated, from rickshaw pulling to garbage collecting and vegetable peddling, were lower in status than factory work. In some cases, such as when they made a living by mending clothes or doing laundry, Subei people were providing services for members of the industrial proletariat, in a pattern similar to the employment of Mexican women as maids by Chicana factory workers in present-day border cities of the American Southwest.[56] Moreover, as we have seen, when Subei people were able to secure factory jobs, they were generally low-paying, physically demanding ones that workers from other areas were not willing to perform. If economic status helps to account for the prejudice against Subei people, the question that must be asked is, How can we explain the concentration of Subei people in the unskilled sector of the labor market? We need to understand why they in particular dominated the ranks of laborers in low-paying, physically demanding jobs.

The Origins of Native Place Hierarchy

An explanation of the concentration of Subei people in the unskilled sector of the Shanghai labor market must begin with an examination of the circumstances under which they arrived in Shanghai seeking work. Most immigrants, as observed in chapter 3, were poverty-stricken refugees of natural disasters or war, and for them almost any work in the city was an improvement over what they had left behind. It mattered little that by Jiangnan or Shanghai standards the conditions under which they lived and labored may have appeared intolerable. A man who left Yancheng in the early 1940s to work on the Wuxi docks explained that "life in Wuxi was *completely different* from life in Subei. My own opinion is that life in Subei was very tough. We ate turnips and sweet potatoes. Actually sweet potatoes were considered really good food in Subei. But when I came to Jiangnan I ate rice. Rice was one of the best things about Jiangnan!" When asked whether having to work as a coolie lessened the desirability of living in Wuxi, he emphatically replied, "Of course Wuxi was still better—I was eating rice there!" Even when he moved to Shanghai, where he worked as a night soil collector and lived in one of the shack settlements, he remained certain that he was better off than in Subei. "At least we could earn some money in the shack settlements," he explained. "In the countryside we couldn't earn a cent."[57]

The picture that emerges, then, is that throughout Jiangnan, Subei refugees, whether they migrated seasonally or moved permanently to the south, accepted a much lower standard of living and hence poorer working conditions than Jiangnan natives. This at least partly explains the concentration of Subei people in the unskilled sector of the Shanghai labor market. They were, as conventional wisdom holds, fleeing poverty and amenable to do jobs that no one else would do, much like the Irish who had fled famine and migrated to the United States in the early nineteenth century. Furthermore, the migration experience of Subei people to Jiangnan suggests that the stereotype of them as willing to do the lowliest jobs may even have preceded Shanghai's modern development; people from Jiangnan who moved to Shanghai most likely brought with them an impression of Subei people as being poor, menial laborers, for that is what they had observed in the countryside.

This alone, however, does not fully account for either the concentration of Subei people in the unskilled sector of the Shanghai labor market or their domination of that sector. Subei was not the sole source of poverty-stricken peasants who migrated to Shanghai. What of those who came from the Jiangnan districts of Wuxi, Changzhou, Ningbo, and Shaoxing? Despite the relative prosperity of these regions, they, too, were the source of many poor peasants who came to Shanghai hungry for both food and work. Yet they secured very different jobs from their Subei counterparts, as suggested by a survey in 1932 of four hundred immigrants from a Wuxi township. Once in Shanghai they worked in textile mills, machine factories, noodle shops, and food stores.[58] Why do we find such little evidence of these Jiangnan immigrants among the ranks of Shanghai's unskilled and coolie laborers?

Scholars attempting to explain the experiences of different immigrant groups in American history have proposed a connection between the types of job experience immigrants might have acquired in their home countries and their employment patterns in the United States. A study of German and Irish immigrants in nineteenth-century Philadelphia, for instance, suggests that the Irish, coming from an underdeveloped, rural economy, arrived in the United States with no industrial experience and therefore were concentrated in the unskilled sector of the labor market. The Germans, in contrast, came from an industrializing country and were able to use their previously acquired skills to obtain better jobs in Philadelphia.[59]

At least one scholar has suggested a similar connection between rural handicraft industries and the kinds of jobs held by people of different local origins in Shanghai.[60] At first glance this seems a compelling explanation. Jiangnan was as well known for its handicrafts as Subei was for its lack of them. That men from Wuxi, known for its production of tin, dominated the tinsmithing jobs in Shanghai is hardly surprising. And it should not be surprising that women from Wuxi and Changzhou, areas known for the production of handicraft cloth, dominated the weaving jobs in Shanghai's textile mills. Likewise, to many observers it seemed obvious why Yangzhou natives dominated the ranks of bathhouse workers, coming from an area famed for its bathhouses. As one writer put it, "Yangzhou bathhouses are famous throughout the world. No matter what port you visit, all the back rubbers and pedicurists are Yangzhou natives. It seems that providing service in bathhouses is the only profession of Yangzhou people."[61]

Under scrutiny, though, this explanation is problematic. First, Subei was not completely lacking in handicrafts, although their development may have been less advanced than in Jiangnan. For example, the Subei districts of Taixing and Taixian were known for the production of handicraft cloth.[62] Why, then, do we not find more women from these areas in the weaving workshops of the mills? Second, there appears to have been little connection between the handicraft traditions of a region and the specific skills brought to Shanghai by peasants migrating from that area. Few women from Wuxi who were employed in weaving departments in the Shanghai mills had themselves engaged in handicraft cloth weaving before leaving the countryside.[63] While Yangzhou's history as a consumption center seems to explain the predominance of Yangzhou men employed in Shanghai barbershops and bathhouses, few had ever worked as barbers or bathhouse attendants before coming to Shanghai. Rather, the majority had been peasants.[64]

An explanation of the correlation between local origins and employment patterns must consider how Shanghai's labor markets operated: how labor was recruited and how individuals sought employment. Previous studies have documented the crucial role of personal and native place connections in obtaining jobs, even in Shanghai's most modern enterprises.[65] People in management and supervisory positions tended to hire relatives, friends, or people from their home district. The important question then becomes the kind of connections available to migrants from Subei, compared to those of people from Jiangnan.

An examination of the local origins of Shanghai's business community —including the owners, directors, and managers of enterprises ranging from factories to banks—indicates that people from Subei indeed had limited personal or native place connections on which to draw in seeking jobs. Of the 2,082 individuals from Jiangsu and Zhejiang (representing nearly 90 percent of the total) listed in a commercial directory published in the 1940s, only 175 (8 percent) were from Subei. Of those from Subei, the majority were from the southernmost areas of Nantong, Haimen, and Rugao, leaving only 88 (4 percent of the total) from Yangzhou north to Funing. A closer look at the individuals from Subei listed in the directory reveals that most were involved in rickshaw companies, barbershops, bathhouses, and construction; only a handful were involved in industry and banking.[66] Typical of the Subei elite were individuals such as Xu Baokun, Wang Bingyan, Yu Lianjin, Ge Jinpiao, and Qiu Jinsheng, all Funing and Yancheng natives who ran rickshaw enterprises in Shanghai; Guan Zhihe, Zhao Degao, and Ju Yongshan, Yangzhou natives who operated barbershops in Shanghai; and Kong Qingcai, Jin Chunhua, and Zhu Guoxun of Jiangdu, who owned bathhouses in Shanghai.[67] Little wonder, then, that Subei migrants concentrated in these enterprises. What is more, this distribution of the Shanghai business elite explains why peasants from Wuxi, who might have at least occasionally been as poverty-stricken as those from Subei, did not end up in the unskilled sector of the Shanghai labor market. They had connections elsewhere. As a woman factory worker from Yuyao observed, "Those of us from Zhejiang could sometimes get jobs in banks because there were a lot of Zhejiang bankers. But if you were from Subei, you could never get a job in a bank!"[68] This may also help explain why poor peasants from Jiangnan areas were not the objects of social prejudice: they came from the districts that were associated with the Shanghai elite.

One can only speculate as to why merchants from Subei failed to join the ranks of the Shanghai business elite. Possibly they lacked sufficient capital to invest in Shanghai as extensively as merchants from Jiangnan and used what little they had to invest in enterprises such as rickshaw companies or bathhouses, which did not require large amounts of capital. One must wonder, however, why the prosperous salt merchants of Yangzhou did not use their funds to claim a stake in the profits to be made from Shanghai's development. Perhaps, as historian Ho Ping-ti suggests, conspicuous consumption and patronage of the arts left them with little capital for potential investments.[69] Nevertheless, these same merchants did succeed in carving out a sphere of influence in the nineteenth-century economy of Hankou.[70] Yet another possibility is simply that individuals from Jiangnan, pushed partly by the Taiping occupation, arrived in Shanghai first and established control over the more lucrative enterprises. If there was competition over Shanghai's wealth during its early development, it was between people from Canton and Ningbo. People from Subei do not appear to have been in the running.[71]

Politics may have contributed to the early economic dominance of people from Canton and Jiangnan. The "rule of avoidance" rendered individuals from Subei ineligible to serve in the *daotai* (the head of local government) office in Shanghai. Individuals from Canton and the Zhejiang areas of Jiangnan—since they were not Jiangsu natives—could, and did, hold political positions.[72] In fact, they battled to control the daotai office, for political power could be used to implement economic policies favorable to merchants from one's native place. For example, Wu Jianzhang, appointed daotai in 1851, was notorious for his pro-Cantonese policies, making "no pretense of concealing his regional prejudices, nor [attempting] to separate politics from commercial interests."[73] Subsequent daotai from Ningbo behaved similarly. This was a realm of power, however, to which Subei people had no access, aggravating, perhaps, their already disadvantaged position.

Shanghai's economic elite was clearly divided according to local origins, with Jiangnan people in positions far superior to those from Subei. Subsequent migrants concentrated in the areas where they had connections; Subei people worked in precisely the enterprises that were owned or managed by individuals with whom they could claim hometown connections (*tongxiang quanxi*).

In addition to connections with individuals based on native place ties, two kinds of institutions played a significant role in securing jobs for people: the Green Gang and native place associations. From the early twentieth century, Green Gang leaders had carved out spheres of influence in Shanghai, subgroups of the gang sometimes controlling entire enterprises.[74] Connections with gang leaders, which often intersected with native place connections, thus assumed importance in the search for jobs. The fragmentary information currently available about the Green Gang suggests that here, too, the resources of Subei migrants were not as plentiful as those of their Jiangnan counterparts. Despite the fact that Subei itself was often described as a center of Green Gang activity, none of the three major Green Gang leaders in Shanghai was from Subei.[75] Du Yuesheng was a native of Pudong, part of Shanghai; Huang Jinrong hailed from Suzhou; Zhang Xiaolin came from Hangzhou. Even among the ranks of powerful women in the Green Gang, those from Subei represented a small minority. Only two of the gang's ten sisters were from Subei; the others were natives of Ningbo, Changshou, Suzhou, and Shanghai.[76] A so-called Jiangbei bang led by Gu Zhuxuan and Jin Jiulin existed within the Green Gang.[77] Neither was ever as influential as the three major leaders, who had "pupils" in almost every enterprise in Shanghai. Gu Zhuxuan, as noted earlier, was called the Subei Emperor by Subei people in Shanghai; he was described as "a great mountain of flesh [who] made his own laws, with gunmen at his beck and call to enforce them." He was powerful in the rickshaw business, where thousands of workers pledged him as their master.[78] In other words, migrants from Jiangnan had a network of people from their hometowns whose position in the gang provided them access to a wide range of jobs; the gang connections available to Subei people, though, offered more limited opportunities and may indeed have contributed to the tracking of Subei migrants into jobs such as rickshaw pulling. Thus, the criminal underworld, often a route through which immigrant underclasses (for example, the Italians and Irish in the United States) get ahead, failed to make a significant difference for northern Jiangsu immigrants in Shanghai. Moreover, although Subei people were among the ranks of Shanghai's racketeers, they never made it to the top, perhaps themselves stigmatized by their native origins.

In addition to the Green Gang, Jiangnan migrants could draw on the influence and services provided by native place associations. The Ningbo Guild, which existed from the 1860s, actively helped nonelite people from Ningbo find jobs in Shanghai. In the early stages of Shanghai's development, the guild had recruited workers and apprentices from Ningbo for employment in Shanghai's foreign shipyards.[79] Previous scholars have assumed that no native place associations from Subei existed in Shanghai.[80] If this was the case, Subei migrants clearly lacked a resource that benefited people from Jiangnan areas. Preliminary research suggests, however, that several Subei districts had native place associations. In the 1910s an association of Yangzhou sojourners existed in Shanghai, and by the 1930s and 1940s most Subei districts had associations in Shanghai.[81] Unfortunately little is known about their activities. Many of the associations appear to have been created at the time of the flood in 1931, which devastated large portions of Subei. They raised money to assist refugees in relocating their homes.[82] Aside from relief work, none of the Subei migrants I interviewed could recall an instance in which they had had any contact with the native place associations from their area. They assumed they were organizations that catered primarily to men of wealth. This suggests that the Subei native place associations did not serve as a quasi-employment agency in the way that the larger, more prestigious Jiangnan guilds did.

All these factors, then, contribute to an explanation of the concentration of Subei people in the unskilled sector of the Shanghai labor market. Often migrants or refugees from poverty-stricken areas, Subei people seemed willing to perform the most menial, low-status jobs in Shanghai. To them, even the worst job in Shanghai was preferable to life in Subei. Most had no training when they arrived in Shanghai, making it difficult for them to secure jobs requiring skill. More important, however, they lacked the personal and institutional connections based on native place ties that might have given them access to those jobs, enabling them to move out of the unskilled sector as migrants from Jiangnan were able to do.

One question remains concerning the jobs dominated by Subei people. A number of Subei people, especially women, worked in factories, and several industries relied heavily on Subei workers, as I have pointed out. Yet factory work was the highest Subei people progressed in Shanghai's job hierarchy; moreover, they never seemed to represent the majority of factory workers. How are we to explain the fact that Subei people never dominated the ranks of Shanghai's industrial proletariat? That most factory owners and managers were from Jiangnan is only part of the answer. Given the cheapness of their labor, one might expect Subei people to have been scooped up as workers. Why did this not happen? Supply was not at issue, particularly after the major floods of 1911, 1921, and 1931 brought massive numbers of Subei people to Shanghai, many of whom were constantly unemployed.

The failure of Subei people to dominate factory jobs requires a consideration of some of the factors that have been used to explain the scarcity of Chinese workers in California factories during the mid- and late-nineteenth century, the initial absence of Irish immigrants in factories of the American Northeast, and the prolonged absence of black workers in factories throughout the United States.[83] In all of these situations, factory owners chose not to draw on the cheapest sources of labor. The most important explanations that have been offered concern popular prejudices among both factory managers and workers.

If popular attitudes toward and beliefs about Subei people are an indication, then they were quite possibly regarded as undesirable workers. People from Subei, as noted above, were commonly perceived as poor, dirty, backward, and lacking in culture. "In general, Jiangnan people are civilized while Jiangbei people are coarse," read a typical description.[84] "People dislike [Subei people] because they are dirty and rude," stated another.[85] Yet another, slightly more specific, observed that "in terms of personality, Jiangnan people are soft and flexible, while Jiangbei people are firm and tough. . . . In terms of customs, religion, and superstition, Jiangnan people tend to be more civilized and open-minded."[86] These perceptions are sometimes evident in observations about the respective work ability of Jiangnan and Subei natives. Assessing sedan chair carriers, for instance, one person noted that the majority, who came from Suzhou and Wuxi, carried the chair very comfortably. Of the minority of carriers from Yangzhou, however, he complained, "Their steps are slower and when they carry the sedan chair it is bouncy. It makes the rider feel drunk!"[87]

Although it is difficult to determine how much these views affected hiring decisions, they most likely contributed to a prejudice against Subei workers among factory managers from Jiangnan, who were willing to pay a higher price for workers more familiar to them. One cotton mill engineer, recalling hiring practices in the 1920s and 1930s, stated this explicitly. "In cotton spinning," he said, "we tried to use as many natives as possible. It's hard to say why. It is not good to say that Subei people are not good workers. It's just that there are certain social attitudes. It's easier to talk to natives. Subei people are harder to handle. We did not like Subei people very much."[88] Subei women who tried to get jobs in the mills often had to dress in a way that would disguise their origins and allow them to pass as Jiangnan natives.[89] Cotton was one of the few industries that employed a large number of Subei people, but this was most likely because by the

1920s roughly half of Shanghai's cotton mills were owned by Japanese capitalists, who did not share the prejudice against Subei workers.[90]

It is possible that the prejudice of factory owners and managers against Subei people was shared by ordinary workers. While they did not necessarily play a major role in hiring decisions (except through the introduction of friends and acquaintances for new jobs), groups of workers could make it difficult for others to maintain jobs, particularly if they felt that the newcomers threatened their job security. Given that Subei people entered the factory work force after people from Jiangnan, it is possible that the latter actively resisted the recruitment of these northerners. In the Jiangnan arsenal, for example, Cantonese and Jiangnan workers made it impossible for people from Subei to become apprentices for skilled jobs.[91] A similar phenomenon is suggested by an incident that occurred in a cotton mill in 1920. A man from the Subei district of Rugao had wangled a job as an apprentice mechanic in a Shanghai cotton mill. Enraged that he worked too hard and fearful that he would eventually get their jobs, the other workers subjected him to physical and verbal harassment until he finally quit his job and returned to the countryside.[92] Incidents like these indicate that territoriality, prejudice, and ethnic conflict among workers contributed to the failure of Subei people to dominate the ranks of the industrial proletariat, much as they did in the bitter protests against the use of immigrant workers by native artisans in nineteenth-century American cities.[93] Moreover, they suggest the possibility that competition over scarce economic resources (in this case, factory jobs) contributed to the definition of *Subei people* as a distinct ethnic group, in a manner similar to that described by Mark Granovetter and Charles Tilly. Evaluating the proposition that racial hostility in the United States becomes most intense when blacks or other racial groups pose an economic threat to the dominant white population, they surmise that

> if the offending groups had been absolutely identical racially, but only different in point of origin . . . these differences would have been magnified to the point where they became quasi-ethnic, and the focus of hostility. If, for example, the First World War had seen a large influx not of blacks but of southern whites, who are quite similar to white northern Protestants in their ethnic background, Northerners would almost surely have constructed derisive categories, or used existing ones—"crackers" or "white trash"—to help preserve their own economic position. Similarly constructed "ethnic" animus can be observed, on a smaller scale, against white "hillbillies" in Chicago or "Okies" in Los Angeles.[94]

This is precisely the type of "ethnic animus" that was created in Shanghai: to protect their status, Jiangnan workers may well have contributed to or at least reinforced the belief that a marked difference existed between themselves and Subei natives.

Discrimination, then, combined with other factors to account for the tracking of Subei people into the unskilled sector of the Shanghai labor market. We have seen that Subei people initially came to Shanghai because of poverty and natural disasters in their home villages and therefore performed the most menial tasks to eke out a living. Because hometown connections played such a major role in the securing of jobs in Shanghai, subsequent waves of immigrants from Subei continued to be tracked into these jobs, for that is where they had connections. Eventually, as Shanghai industrialized and more complex and highly differentiated labor markets developed, the jobs performed by Subei people assumed an even lower status. As the attitudes toward rickshaw pullers indicate, the association of Subei people with unskilled, physically demanding labor created and continually reinforced the belief that they were poor, ignorant, dirty, and uncivilized.

It would be misleading to imply that a simple relationship existed between bias and the status of Subei people in the labor market, that there was first prejudice and subsequently an inferior economic status. Popular beliefs about Subei people may well have prevented their entrance into preferable labor markets, but the divisions in the labor market themselves contributed to the creation of these beliefs. The propagation of negative stereotypes about Subei and Subei people was partly a product of the development of segmented labor markets in Shanghai, and it served to justify the unequal access of different groups of people to job opportunities. Defining Subei people as ethnically distinct, in spite of their shared Han identity, provided Jiangnan natives with an explanation of why these immigrants from the north were suited for coolie labor. The labor market both demanded the construction of Subei ethnicity and was shaped by it.

5

ETHNICITY CONTESTED:

THE SELF-IDENTITY

OF SUBEI PEOPLE

Did Subei people themselves believe that they constituted a coherent, homogeneous group with a shared identity? Under what circumstances, if any, did natives of such places as Nantong, Yangzhou, and Yancheng believe they shared a common geographic origin, heritage, culture, and experience in Shanghai that could be described by the label *Subei ren*? Did Subei people think of themselves as Subei ren or was it simply a social category used by others to describe them? Did they, in short, perceive of themselves as a distinct ethnic group?

Since the idea of Subei as a place and Subei people as a category emerged only in conjunction with the development of Jiangnan and Shanghai, any sense of Subei ethnic identity would naturally be forged only through the experience of migration and living in the south. The majority of Subei people had most likely not even heard the term *Subei* before coming to Shanghai. Furthermore, when they arrived, they appear to have identified not as Subei ren, but as natives of the district from which they came, much as Italian migrants to the United States saw themselves as Genoese, Venetians, Neapolitans, Sicilians, and Calabrians rather than as Italians.[1] "Ethnicities rarely coincided with the initial self-identification of the industrial recruits," observes Eric Wolf about migrants to the United States, "who first thought of themselves as Hanoverians or Bavarians rather than as Germans, as members of their village or parish (okolica) rather than as Poles, as Tonga or Yao rather than as 'Nyasalanders.'"[2] So Subei people, too, initially thought of themselves not as Subeinese, but as Yangzhouese, Yanchengese, or Nantongese. Did their sense of identity change over time?

At first glance, it appears that Subei migrants to Shanghai gradually accepted the belief that they formed a coherent group, that by the late 1910s local identities had gradually given way to a growing sense of Subei identity. This is the picture that emerges if we use the organizations they formed, specifically, native place associations, as an index of their self-identification.

Native Place Associations

The Subei native place associations, as noted, were never as large or powerful as those—among them the commanding Ningbo Guild—organized by migrants from Jiangnan areas, but most Subei districts did have associations in Shanghai. More notable here are the number of associations that represented Subei as a whole. A Jiangbei Natives' Preservation Association (Jiangbei tongxiang weichi hui) and a Subei Friendly Confederation (Subei lianshanhui) existed in the early 1920s; in 1936 an Office for the Confederation of Shanghai Sojourners from Each District in Jiangbei (Jiangbei gexian lühu tongxianghui lianhe banshichu) was formed.[3] During the late 1940s, the number of Subei-wide organizations in Shanghai multiplied. These included a Service Society for Subei Sojourners in Shanghai (Subei lühu tongxiang fuwushe) and a Relief Committee for Shanghai Sojourners from Each Subei County (Subei geshu lühu tongxiang jiuji weiyuanhui) as well as a Subei Refugee Center (Subei nanmin shourongsuo), a Subei Nursing Home (Subei yanglao yuan), and a Subei Compulsory Primary School (Subei yewu xiao xuexiao).[4] Aside from the sheer fact of their existence, little is known about any of these organizations, their members, or their activities. Their formation, though, suggests that a Subei identity was replacing or supplementing the more local Yangzhou or Yancheng identities. The charter of the Service Society for Subei Sojourners in Shanghai, for example, declared the society's goal of helping Subei natives win the respect they deserved for their contribution to Shanghai's development.[5]

Scrutiny of the native place associations, however, calls into question the Subei identity that their existence might seem to represent. First, these organizations were not always established by Subei people. For example, the Organization to Save Subei Refugees (Subei nanmin jiuji xiehui), formed in 1946, was initiated and directed by Du Yuesheng, a Pudong native, and several individuals from Zhejiang and Anhui as well as influential people from Subei such as the Green Gang leader Gu Zhuxuan.[6] Likewise, the Subei Flood Relief Organization formed in August 1947, when a severe flood destroyed large parts of Xuzhou and Haizhou, was organized by "Shanghai citizens."[7] Some organizations bearing the name Subei therefore represented the benevolence of non-Subei people concerned with the plight of this destitute community. Although the rosters of some organizations indicate that the founders and members were all of Subei origins, the above examples caution us not to assume that organizations with the name Subei inherently represent the efforts or identities of Subei natives.

Second, most of the Subei-wide organizations appear to have been short-lived. After 1925, for instance, no references to the Jiangbei Natives' Preservation Society exist, suggesting that it may have disbanded. Likewise, the Confederation of Shanghai Sojourners from Each District in Jiangbei, initially formed in response to a major strike of rickshaw pullers (most of whom hailed from Subei) in 1936, seems to have dissolved once the strike ended.

In addition to the fact that the organizations were short-lived, the basis of the bond represented by their formation seems to have been precarious. This is suggested by the comments of the chairman of the first meeting, in 1936, of the Office for the Confederation of Shanghai Sojourners from Each District in Jiangbei. "The groups from each district have no spirit of unity," he complained. "Every day the number of migrants from Subei districts increases, but it is impossible to unify them."[8] Zhu Hua, a native of Dongtai and the founder of the Service Society for Jiangbei Sojourners in Shanghai, bemoaned the isolation of Subei people: "The majority of people [in Shanghai] are countrymen from Jiangbei, [yet] they have very little contact among themselves, and this is a pity."[9] Little wonder, then, that many of these organizations and confederations were established in response to specific issues such as famine relief or a strike and then disbanded once the issue was resolved.

A final qualification of the Subei-wide identity represented by these organizations is that they were often overshadowed by the existence—if not proliferation—of associations representing natives of specific Subei districts in Shanghai. From at least the 1910s, for example, Yangzhou migrants had their own association, the Yangzhou Guild, and later an Association of Sojourners in Shanghai from the Eight Counties of Yangzhou.[10] By the early 1930s, separate associations for sojourners from Dongtai, Xinghua, Huaiyin, and Haimen also existed.[11] And by the late 1940s, these were joined by associations for Funing, Yancheng, Huai'an, Nantong, Baoying, Qidong, Taixing, Taixian, Gaoyou, and Rugao.[12] Almost every Subei district could boast its own native place association in Shanghai.

Not only were the majority of associations locally based, but the issues that concerned them tended to be locally defined as well. Only rarely did associations become involved in an issue of concern to migrants from another Subei district. This is perhaps most dramatically exemplified by an incident that absorbed and enraged Shanghai's Yangzhou community in 1934: the publication of Yi Junzuo's *Xianhua Yangzhou*—a book that primarily describes the history, people, and places of interest to tourists in Yangzhou. In part, Yi's book reads like an advertisement for Yangzhou and its famed culture, praising Yangzhou people for being refined and more sophisticated than their cruder Subei brethren.[13] These compliments notwithstanding, Yangzhou natives felt that the book maligned them. Specifically, they objected to the author's statements that prostitutes were the pride of Yangzhou, that Yangzhou was cluttered with chamberpots and the sight of natives relieving themselves in public, and that Yangzhou people were notorious collaborators, first with the Manchus and more recently with the Japanese.[14]

No sooner did the book appear than the Association of Sojourners from the Eight Counties of Yangzhou in Shanghai called an emergency meeting to plan a protest. The heads of the association held a press conference and denounced the book as "an insult to all the people of Yangzhou." They demanded that Yi resign from his position as director of the Editing and Censorship Office of the Jiangsu Provincial Bureau of Education and later filed suit against him. Meanwhile, they asked that stores refuse to sell (and preferably burn) the book.

The results of their efforts are not clear. More significant here, however, is that this was a strictly Yangzhou-defined issue in Shanghai. It was the Yangzhou community that was offended and the Yangzhou community that responded. The attempts to rectify the book's insults were organized entirely by the Yangzhou native place association in Shanghai. No other Subei native place association came to their assistance or defense. Conversely, the Yangzhou association did not involve itself in issues concerning natives of other Subei districts. So, for example, when the cotton mill worker Gu Zhenghong, from Yancheng, was killed by a Japanese guard in 1925, the Yangzhou associations did not join the Association of Jianghuai Sojourners in sponsoring a memorial. This, then, underscores the local identities represented by the district-based native place associations.

No discussion of the Subei native place associations would be complete without reference to the Association of Jianghuai Sojourners in Shanghai (Jianghuai lühu tongxianghui). Of all the associations—Subei-wide or district-based—this was the single most enduring and powerful association of Subei natives in Shanghai. Established at the time of the May Fourth Movement in 1919, it continued to exist through the late 1940s, by which time it had branch offices in most of the districts where Subei people lived in Shanghai and operated a school as well.[15] This association represents an identity that *did* extend beyond specific localities: according to its charter of 1947, it encompassed the districts of Huai'an, Huaiyin, Lianshui, Siyang, Yancheng, and Funing, the majority of its members coming from those areas.[16] It did not, however, serve natives of all of Subei: those from the southern part of Subei, such as Yangzhou, Taixing, or Nantong, were not affiliated with the Jianghuai association. In other words, while the Jianghuai association may represent a belief in the commonality of experience of migrants from Jianghuai, it indicates a profound sense of difference between natives of northern and southern Subei.

This split is corroborated by other associations that represented several Subei districts, for almost all were federations of districts either in the south or in the north. For example, in the 1940s, an Association for Sojourners in Shanghai from Nantong, Rugao, Chongming, Haimen, and Qidong (Tong-ru-chong-hai-qi lühu tongxianghui) served natives of the southernmost part of Subei, while an Association for Sojourners in Shanghai from Yancheng and Funing (Yan-fu lühu tongxianghui) represented those from the north.[17]

The existence of several Subei-wide organizations, then, cannot be immediately equated with the emergence of a Subei identity among migrants from northern Jiangsu. If organizations are at all indicative of identity, they suggest the persistence of localism and perhaps a growing sense of commonality among natives of specific parts of Subei, such as Jianghuai. It does not appear that the conviction held by the Shanghai elite that Subei people represented a coherent group with a common heritage and experience was shared by Subei people themselves. This becomes overwhelmingly evident when it comes to the beliefs and experiences of Subei migrants to Shanghai.

Self-Identities

We cannot know how most Subei people identified themselves, how the self-identity of individuals changed over time, or how the self-identity of migrants from a Subei district in the 1870s differed from that of their counterparts in the 1940s. Nevertheless, the fragmentary evidence provided by interviews with individuals who migrated in the 1930s and 1940s as well as data about their cultural practices, work, and residential patterns outlines their persisting localism and the northern/southern Subei rift suggested above.

The more local identities of migrants from Subei are expressed, first, in attitudes toward one another, as migrants from different Subei districts often went to great lengths to distinguish themselves. For example, a cook at the Yangzhou Restaurant in Shanghai insisted, "Our customs were completely different from those of Yancheng natives. Our language was different and our food was different, too. Yancheng people ate yams while we ate rice. We don't consider Yancheng people as belonging to our same native place."[18] That natives of one Subei district did not consider those from another to be *tongxiang ren* (people of the same native place) is confirmed by the admission of Xia Keyun, himself from Huai'an, that "if someone came to Shanghai from Huai'an we would help him, but if he came from Yangzhou we'd ignore him."[19] They did not, that is, share a common Subei identity.

The sense of separateness expressed by people of different Subei origins sometimes extended to attitudes of hostility or condescension. For example, a woman from Huaiyin described the contempt of Huaiyin natives for residents of the neighboring city of Huai'an. When asked why Huai'an natives were despised, she replied, "First of all, their language is extremely ugly-sounding. Second, people from Huai'an have no sense of shame. For example, during the Spring Festival it's a custom that we never refuse to give food or money to beggars. Huai'an people take advantage of this: every year, during the Spring Festival, they all come to Huaiyin to beg. All over Huaiyin you can see the Huai'an beggars. They're really awful!" More frequently, it was natives of the more prosperous southern parts of Subei who expressed contempt for their neighbors to the north. People from Yangzhou, for instance, frequently expressed precisely the same attitudes of scorn and disgust toward Yancheng people that Jiangnan natives more commonly expressed toward Subei people as a group. Their sense of superiority was occasionally so extreme that they insisted Yangzhou was not part of Subei at all. For example, in explaining why the bathhouse bosses hired only people from Yangzhou, one man, himself a pedicurist from Yangzhou, said,

It was because we people from Yangzhou know how to speak well; we speak in a rather cultivated way. It was important for the service people to speak well or the customers would not come. Our speech is very careful and soft, while theirs [people from Yancheng] is

very crude—*wawawawawa*. We were much more refined, while Subei people were very coarse; we were very sophisticated, while they were very poor.
Even though we were from Yangzhou, people still used to call us "Jiangbei folk." It was derogatory and it upset us. We knew we were from Yangzhou and were not really Jiangbei folk, but they did not know the difference.[20]

A similar desire to exclude one's native place from the definition of Subei and thereby deny one's Subei identity was expressed by the late-nineteenth-century reformer Zhang Jian. Himself a native of Nantong, he declared that Subei consisted only of areas immediately south of the Huai, such as Yancheng, Funing, and Huai'an. By implication, neither Yangzhou nor the more southern districts of Haimen or Nantong were part of Subei.[21] Natives of the two areas, as far as he was concerned, did not share a common Subei identity.

The more local identities of Subei migrants were not simply attitudinal, but were also expressed in their separate cultural activities. This is particularly evident in local opera, one of the favorite forms of entertainment for Subei natives. While most Subei districts could boast their own distinctive opera, Yangzhou and Huai opera were the two most frequently performed in Shanghai (see chapter 2). Natives of these two parts of Subei favored performances of opera from their respective region. The Yangzhou barber Zhou Dianyuan recalled that before 1949 "we went to hear Yangzhou opera at the Taiyuan *fang*. The audience was all Yangzhou people, especially barbers. But we never went to Huai opera!"[22] Subei dockworkers, on the other hand, few of whom were from Yangzhou, preferred Huai opera performed at teahouses in their neighborhoods, such as the Kaitian teahouse in Pudong or the so-called Forty Room (*sishi jian*) in Nanshi.[23] Huai opera drew its audience not only from the ranks of dockworkers, but from almost all migrants from the northern Subei areas of Yancheng, Funing, and Huai'an. "Before [1949], we used to all like to go to Huai opera," recalled rickshaw puller Zhang Ronghua. "We liked Xiao Wenyan. There was also Yangzhou opera, but we liked to see Jianghuai opera."[24]

Residential patterns are yet another indicator of the predominantly local identities of Subei people in Shanghai. Although most Shanghai people associated all Subei people with shack settlements, Subei people themselves recognized much more subtle patterns within the so-called Subei villages, as natives of different districts congregated in particular alleys. "Before 1949," recalled Xia Keyun, "we'd say, 'That's the Hubei alley. That's the Yangzhou alley. And that's the Huai'an alley.'"[25] Dockworker

Cheng Jinfan believed that the Pudong area of Yangjiadu was inhabited mostly by Taizhou people; Zhang Ronghua, a former rickshaw puller, recalled that almost everyone who lived in the shack settlement bordering North Zhongshan Road in Zhabei was, like him, from Yancheng; and the Zhabei district of Shenjiatuo was, according to a shoemaker from Yangzhou, the purview of fellow Yangzhou natives.[26]

Household registration records, which would make possible a more systematic study of the relationship between local origins and residential patterns in Shanghai, are not available. However, membership lists of native place associations, which often include addresses of their members, can provide some corroboration to the impressions of Subei natives described above. Although the majority of lower-class Subei natives did not join the associations, the residence patterns of those who did join suggest the ways in which people from particular localities clustered together in Shanghai. For instance, a sizable community of Jiangdu natives resided in lanes number 68 and 82 on Jiaozhou Road; lanes 42, 51, and 162 of Yuyao Road as well as lanes 793–95 on Pingliang Road were dominated by people from Yancheng and Funing; a large number of Huai'an natives lived in lane 68, Changshou Road.[27] It would be misleading to suggest that these patterns were absolute and that all Subei migrants lived in lanes or shack settlements surrounded by people from their precise locality. These patterns most likely varied by class, the wealthier members of the Subei community being scattered throughout Shanghai, for they could afford more desirable housing. Indeed, the native place association records indicate that directors of the various associations, all men of considerable wealth, lived in the International Settlement and French Concession, alongside natives of Jiangnan districts. (They were still seen as Subei natives, in spite of their financial means.) The overwhelming majority of poor, working-class Subei migrants, though, were dependent on personal and native place connections (*tongxiang guanxi*) to find a place to live and therefore tended to cluster together. It is impossible to determine what percentage lived with natives of the same locality compared to those who mingled with natives of different Subei districts. However, compared to the perception of Jiangnan natives that all Subei people lived together in shack settlements that could be described as Jiangbei villages, there was a significant amount of segregation according to specific local origins. This residential segregation both reflected and reinforced the more local identities of Subei people in Shanghai.

Residential patterns suggest that certain aspects of their experience in Shanghai perpetuated the distinctions and divisions among Subei migrants, militating against the formation of a broader Subei identity. This is even more evident in patterns of employment, which suggest that no common Subei work experience existed. Instead, employment patterns often reinforced and reproduced the more local identities of Subei migrants.

Although non-Subei people associated all Subei people with coolie labor, Subei people themselves were aware of a much more complex division of labor in which migrants from each Subei district concentrated in distinct jobs. The most important division was between people from Yangzhou and those from the more northern areas of Yancheng, Funing, and Huai'an. In general, Yangzhou natives had jobs requiring slightly more skill and offering better working conditions than those dominated by people from farther north, reflecting perhaps the prosperity of Yangzhou compared with Yancheng, Funing, and Huai'an. Although some Yangzhou natives could be found among almost all the jobs dominated by Subei people—rickshaw pulling, dock loading, night soil hauling, and garbage collecting—they were especially known for their domination of the so-called three knives: barbers, bathhouse pedicurists, and cooks.[28] Yangzhou was famous as an exporter of barbers, particularly to Shanghai, and the head of the barbers' guild in 1920, Chen Sihai, was a Yangzhou native.[29] People from Yancheng and Funing, in contrast, could claim dominance of the rickshaw pulling profession. A survey of the native place of rickshaw pullers in 1934–35 showed some 53 percent coming from Yancheng and Funing, while only 17 percent hailed from the area near Yangzhou.[30]

The hierarchy of jobs dominated by Yangzhou and Yancheng-Funing people was confirmed by the pride and resentment expressed by people from each of those areas. People from Yancheng knew they could not aspire to enter the occupations controlled by the Yangzhou bang. "The jobs done by people from Yangzhou were much better than ours," a man from Jianhu (near Yancheng) observed bitterly. "Their work was easier and lighter. Being a barber was much better than pulling rickshaws! The worst work was hauling night soil carts, collecting garbage, and sweeping the streets. Not many Yangzhou people did those kinds of jobs. They were mostly in barber shops and bathhouses."[31]

More important than the precision or consistency of these divisions is the consciousness of Subei natives that they existed, for almost all Subei people I interviewed could identify the native place origins of workers in various occupations. Former dockworker Xia Keyun, for instance, explained that "Yangzhou people did service jobs; Yancheng people pulled rickshaws, and Nantong natives pulled *tache* (wheelbarrows) and *laohu che* (tiger carts). People from Taizhou liked to sell things, so they sold peanuts and snacks to us dockworkers from Huai'an."[32] Another Subei native, originally from Yangzhou, described a division of labor as follows: wok repairers were from Gaoyou county; cobblers and sanitation workers from Jiangdu county; barbers, pedicurists, and cooks from Yangzhou city.[33] These descriptions may or may not accurately reflect social reality. As no surveys of workers in these occupations exist, one can only draw on people's memories and beliefs. Yet these beliefs are crucial, for they suggest the ways in which people experienced work as perpetuating the distinctions and boundaries among natives of different Subei districts.

These distinctions, like residential patterns, were not absolute, and certainly many Subei people worked in occupations employing natives of several Subei districts. Cotton mills and silk filatures, for example, employed women from almost every part of Subei. While this did not always contribute to the creation of a broader Subei identity, it did occasionally bring together natives of several districts. A report of a strike at a silk filature in the early 1920s both highlights the local identities and illustrates an instance when they were at least temporarily overcome. "In the past, people referred to Yancheng and Taixing as 'small feet' and 'big feet' [referring to the presence or absence of footbinding]," remarked the author. " 'But in this case the two groups (bang) were able to cooperate. Women workers belonging to the Yancheng bang went to the women's office of the Taixing native place group (tongxiang Taixing bang nügong chu) to ask for strike support." [34] Apparently, under more ordinary circumstances women from the two districts did not get along, much less see themselves as sharing a common Subei identity. The usual separateness between the Yancheng and Taixing women, emphasized by the special office for women of the Taixing bang, was broken down in this case only by the exigencies of a strike.

Dockworkers, too, came from a variety of Subei districts: Taixing and Nantong as well as Yancheng, Funing, and Huai'an. Although workers from each district tended to concentrate in particular jobs, some interaction took place, as attested to by their work chants. On the one hand, workers from each Subei district brought with them chants of their own native place. The chants of Nantong, Yangzhou, and Huai'an were completely different from one another. On the other hand, though, workers on the Shanghai docks adopted chants from districts other than their own, depending on which was most rhythmically appropriate to the job they were performing. Those who hauled sacks of cargo on their back (gang), for example, sang chants from Nantong, as they had a strong beat, while workers who teamed up to carry cargo on shoulder poles preferred the rhythm of Yangzhou chants, even though few were from Yangzhou.[35] This blending of customs had its limits, however. Despite their contact with workers from Hubei, for instance, Subei natives were unwilling to

adopt their chants. "The Hubei chants," exclaimed Xia Keyun, after imi-
tating one, "sound like the songs of minority people to me!"[36] Conflicts
over chants reflected a broader disdain of Subei migrants toward their fellow workers from Hubei, and often fights broke out between the two
groups. In 1926 a brawl between Subei and Hubei workers over unloading
at the Pudong docks resulted in the drowning of two Hubei natives.[37]

Though working together led Subei natives to adapt the chants of
workers from Subei districts other than their own, a knowledge of which
chant came from which district persisted. This was not equivalent, then,
to the formation of a broader Subei identity among dockworkers.

What appears to be continued insistence on distinctions among Subei
migrants of different local origins was sometimes an expression of class
difference. In other words, the line separating class and native place identities was often blurred, and as in the attitude of the Jiangnan elite toward
Subei people as a group, native place sometimes functioned as a metaphor for class. The class dimension of the local identities maintained by
many Subei people in Shanghai is evident in a theme underlying many
of the attitudes and practices described above: the disdain of those from
southern Subei for those from farther north. Most often, it was people
from the southern areas of Nantong, Haimen, and Yangzhou who wanted
to disassociate themselves from natives of the more northern districts of
Yancheng, Funing, and Huai'an.

Because southern Subei tended to be more prosperous than the northern districts, it was often the first destination for migrants from further
north. Refugees from Yancheng and Huai'an eking out a living by collecting garbage were a familiar sight to those who grew up in Yangzhou in
the 1930s. We have also seen that migrants from southern Subei generally
obtained better jobs in Shanghai than their compatriots from the north.
Profiles of members of native place associations from the two areas further
attest to the economic differences between these migrant communities in
Shanghai. We can look, first, at the educational experience of members of
the northern Huai'an and southern Nantong native place associations.

Education	Huai'an	Nantong
University	3 (0.9%)	10 (3.0%)
Law school	1 (0.6%)	7 (2.1%)
Specialized school	2 (0.6%)	18 (5.4%)
Teachers college	2 (0.6%)	5 (1.5%)
Upper middle school (*gaozhong*)	2 (0.6%)	65 (19.8%)
Middle school (*zhongxue*)	12 (3.6%)	68 (20.6%)
Lower middle school (*chuzhong*)	16 (4.8%)	109 (33.0%)

Education	Huai'an	Nantong
Upper primary school (*gaoxiao*)	8 (2.4%)	0
Primary school (*xiaoxue*)	17 (5.2%)	0
Private academy (*sixu*)	91 (27.6%)	18 (5.4%)
Literate	21 (6.3%)	0
Roughly literate	27 (8.2%)	0
Illiterate	53 (16.1%)	3 (0.9%)
No education listed	65	0
Total	320	303

The most notable differences are that more members of the Nantong association had advanced degrees (a total of 13 percent compared to 2.4 percent of the Huai'an association members); a far greater percentage of the Nantong association had middle school education (79.8 percent for Nantong, compared to 9.3 percent for Huai'an); while the number of illiterate or semiliterate members of the Huai'an association far surpassed those from Nantong (24.9 percent for Huai'an, 1.0 percent for Nantong).[38]

Differences in the social and economic status of the migrant communities from northern and southern Subei districts are also evident in occupational patterns. Data are available for occupations of members of native place associations from the northern area of Huai'an and and southern areas of Yangzhou and Haimen in the late 1940s:

Occupation	Huai'an	Yangzhou	Haimen
Government	2 (0.6%)	4 (1.0%)	18 (8.4%)
Lawyer	1 (0.3%)	20 (5.0%)	5 (2.3%)
Teacher	2 (0.6%)	2 (0.5%)	26 (12.0%)
Accountant	0	0	0
Doctor	1 (0.3%)	1 (0.3%)	21 (9.8%)
Business	18 (5.1%)	355 (89.2%)	80 (37.2%)
Journalist	0	13 (3.3%)	0
Engineer	0	0	2 (0.9%)
Factory supervisor	9 (2.6%)	0	0
Company employee	3 (0.9%)	0	0
Store clerk	6 (1.7%)	0	0
Factory worker	93 (26.6%)	3 (0.8%)	8 (3.7%)
Dock worker	18 (5.1%)	0	0
Rickshaw puller	8 (2.3%)	0	0
Sanitation	4 (1.1%)	0	0
Service	6 (1.7%)	0	0
Warehouse worker	31 (8.9%)	0	0

Occupation	Huai'an	Yangzhou	Haimen
Moneylending	20 (5.7%)	0	0
Artisan	1 (0.3%)	0	1 (0.4%)
Peddlar	5 (1.4%)	0	0
Unlisted/unclear	123	0	53
Total	351	398	214

Here, too, we see that members of the Yangzhou and Haimen associations were employed in more lucrative and prestigious jobs than were those in the Huai'an association. Whereas businessmen and professionals represented 95 percent of the Yangzhou and 63 percent of the Haimen associations' members, they comprised only 6 percent of the members of the Huai'an association. And while 52 percent of members of the Huai'an association were workers, only 1 percent of the Yangzhou and 5 percent of the Haimen association were employed as workers.[39]

The membership of these native place associations does not necessarily represent a cross section of migrants from the districts they represent. The vast majority of migrants never joined the associations, and little is known about what qualified certain individuals for membership. Nevertheless, as a rough index of the economic and social status of the various Subei communities, these data illuminate the prosperity of the communities of migrants from southern Subei relative to those from the north. Thus, when natives of the southern districts distinguished themselves from natives of the north (such as the pedicurist who insisted people like him from Yangzhou were not Subei ren), they were not expressing native place identities per se but insisting upon class differences as well, even among the Subei folk perceived as uniformly poor by the Jiangnan-based elite.

Although Subei people represented something akin to an ethnic group in the eyes of Jiangnan natives, for people who had actually migrated from districts north of the Yangzi, a Subei-wide identity was most often muted or nonexistent. Certainly they never bonded together in some form of Subei rights movement to protest their discriminatory treatment. And they did not seem to share the elite's belief that they had a common heritage or experience in Shanghai. For them, *tongxiang* referred to people from the same specific district (such as Yangzhou or Yancheng), not Subei as a whole. Local affiliations, then, remained paramount in their self-identities. This corroborates the findings of anthropological studies of ethnicity, which have frequently observed the difference between the definition of a group imposed by outsiders, on the one hand, and insiders' definition of themselves on the other. For example, in a classic study of ethnicity in Bornu, the anthropologist Ronald Cohen contrasts the Kanuri people's belief that groups of non-Muslim people in the southeast represent a coherent group called Kirdi, while the Kirdi see themselves as belonging to a number of distinctive ethnic groups. "The problem becomes more complex," observes Cohen, "when it is realized that in Kanuri-dominated towns such people often accept the dominant group's term and claim they are Kirdi. Only much closer questioning elicits their home-based subjective identifications."[40] Likewise, while all migrant guestworkers in West Berlin are labeled Turks by the native German population, not all are from Turkey, and even those from Turkey do not consider themselves as sharing a common Turkish identity. As Ruth Mandel observes, "Urban Turks from Western Turkey often feel little if any kinship with their poorer rural compatriots. . . . The self-designated 'westernized' urban Turks sense no end of shame and resentment towards their 'backwards, embarrassing' compatriots, who, they say, give *all* Turks, 'even the well integrated, modern ones,' a bad name."[41]

That the persistence of more local identities is commonly found in studies of ethnicity and immigrant cultures, however, does not mean it should be taken for granted. And Subei people should not be seen as passive participants in the construction of ethnic identities in Shanghai. Despite the prominence of very local identities and the absence of a Subei-wide affiliation, Subei natives did construct some new forms of identity. The belief in a distinct Jianghuai region—as attested to by the powerful Jianghuai Native Place Association as well as the emergence and popularity of Huai opera—did represent the creation of a new social category. Put otherwise, while the Jiangnan elite established the category Subei, some northern Jiangsu natives in Shanghai articulated a category Jianghuai. The two were not synonymous.

Whether adapting a Jianghuai identity or insisting upon more local places of origins, Subei natives were responding to the complex relationship between class and native place identities in Shanghai. Just as the articulation of a Subei identity was, for the Jiangnan elite, part of a discourse about class, so, too, was the articulation of separate Yancheng, Yangzhou, or Nantong identities by Subei natives a way of describing class difference.

But the continued articulation of local identities was not only about class difference among Subei natives. Quite possibly, the insistence upon more local origins was itself a means of resisting the negatively charged category Subei people imposed by the Shanghai elite. Few individuals could have wanted to admit to, let alone assert, a Subei identity. Like migrants from the American Southwest to California, who avoided the label

Okie by insisting upon their more "local" Texan or Missourian origins,[42] natives of northern Jiangsu articulated local identities to avoid the stigmatized label Subei. In other words, this was not simply the persistence of localism, but its recreation and elaboration as an act of defiance.

6

THE POLITICS

OF PREJUDICE

During the entire period from Shanghai's opening as a treaty port in 1842 to Liberation in 1949, only once did the status of Subei people become an explicit political issue, and that was during the Japanese attack on Shanghai in 1932. This otherwise seemingly minor event, dwarfed in history by the far more extended Japanese attack on Shanghai in 1937 and occupation from 1941 to 1945, represents a critical turning point in the construction of Subei ethnicity. It was a moment when all the issues explored in the preceding chapters—Subei people's concentration in shack settlements, their status in the labor market, and the construction of their own identity in Shanghai—converged.

For several months during the spring of 1932, Subei people became visible as a subject of public debate in an unprecedented way. Public response to events surrounding the Japanese attack both reflected the conviction that Subei ren represented a homogeneous group and hardened a prejudice against them, as Subei people were identified as collaborators: all Subei people were presumed to be collaborators with the Japanese; all collaborators were called Subei people.

At the same time, Subei people themselves contested and resisted the category Subei more explicitly and vehemently than ever before.

The "Jiangbei Collaborators"

The January 28th Incident, as Chinese refer to the attack of 1932, must be understood in the context of a rapidly growing Japanese presence in Shanghai since the end of World War I. By the early 1930s, Japanese had in many ways become the city's dominant foreign population. They had replaced the British as the largest community of foreigners in the International Settlement. From a mere eight hundred in 1890, their ranks swelled to ten thousand in 1920 and to thirty thousand in 1930—triple the British population at that time. Hongkou, originally the American Settlement, had become an almost entirely Japanese district, commonly called Little Tokyo.[1] Moreover, Japanese companies controlled much of the Shanghai economy. Cotton spinning, the largest industry in Shanghai, was dominated by Japanese capital.[2] Japanese also owned a number of docks and banks.[3]

It was against this background that the January 28th Incident of 1932 occurred. In response to the Japanese seizure of Manchuria in 1931, a boycott of Japanese goods had been organized throughout China. The refusal of Chinese firms to handle Japanese goods, of Chinese banks to honor Japanese bills of lading, and of dock authorities to allow the unloading of Japanese cargo severely strained relations between Chinese and Japanese officials in Shanghai. In early 1932, the Japanese consul general demanded that the anti-Japanese boycott and propaganda campaign be halted. Shanghai's mayor, Wu Tiezhen, responded too late, for the Japanese navy had already launched an attack. When the Chinese Nineteenth Route Army refused to evacuate Zhabei, the district surrounding the North Railway Station, the Japanese began the "undeclared war" on January 28. "Machine guns rattled day and night," observed Ernest Hauser:

> From behind barricades and window shades, rifles spat death. Horror stalked the streets of Chapei. . . . Bombing planes were roaring overhead. . . . From a height of three hundred feet, they dropped their bombs. Flames shot up where they had hit. Large sections of densely populated Chapei were laid waste. Fighting raged in the streets. . . . Tenement houses burned down or collapsed under incessant shell fire. Industrial plants were blasted to pieces. . . . Refugees came streaming into the Settlement. They scurried across the bridges, through the wrought-iron gates, driven by fear. They carried their

belongings in their hands. Some had managed to fling their miserable "households" into a rickshaw or into a pushcart. Some balanced their bundles on bamboo poles. Women carried screaming babies roped to their backs. . . . They came, six hundred thousand strong.[4]

By the time a peace agreement was signed in early May, the Japanese had, according to Frederic Wakeman, "entrenched themselves throughout the Chinese sector—their 60–70,000 soldiers occupying 47 public and private buildings, all of the municipal and administrative buildings still standing, and 110 elementary and secondary schools." Meanwhile, their claims to the contrary notwithstanding, the Japanese had established a puppet city government, the Zhabei Citizens' Maintenance Association (Zhabei shimin weichi hui), and police force to administer the Zhabei district.[5]

During the spring of 1932, as the Japanese attacked Shanghai and planned to assume its administration, Subei people were blamed for a range of problems. First, they were scapegoated for the criminal activity that plagued many Shanghai districts during the Japanese attack. Almost every day articles in the local papers bore titles such as "Jiangbei hoodlums rob and loot people in Zhabei."[6] As many Chinese evacuated Zhabei, according to one report, "a large number of Komponese were seen busy along the Chapei areas digging into doors of the evacuated civilian houses to commit theft."[7] In the neighboring Jiangwan area, Subei people were allegedly "extremely active, wantonly entering people's homes and stealing their valuables. They take all their jewelry and now they are taking their furniture, too."[8] In other words, a perhaps already existing perception of Subei people as criminals and hoodlums was intensified.

More serious than the association of Subei people with crime was the belief that they were collaborating with the Japanese. As one writer observed, "After the war [the January 28th incident] a new term appeared: Jiangbei traitor [*Jiangbei hanjian*]."[9] The alleged collaboration was manifested in several ways. First, the puppet government established by the Japanese in the Zhabei district of Shanghai in April 1932 was described as the Jiangbei Command (*Jiangbei silingbu*). Common gossip, though not completely accurate, held that the leaders of the puppet government were all Subei ren. The associate director, Wang Du, was from Funing. He had previously worked as a clerk at the Yokohama Specie Bank in Shanghai and reportedly spoke Japanese.[10] The chief of police, Chang Yuqing, was a well-known gang leader from Subei, commonly called the Jiangbei Du Yuesheng. Also known as Two-ton Chang, as he weighed more than three hundred pounds, Chang had worked as a butcher before becoming the owner of a bathhouse on Nanjing Road. His Subei affiliation was consolidated by his chairmanship of the North Jiangsu Residents Guild of Shanghai. His affiliation with the puppet government led newspapers to describe him as "the burly ex-butcher and pro-Japanese gangster."[11] The chief detective, Yao Zhitu, was also a Subei native. "Accompanied by four Japanese soldiers for protection," he was known to visit daily the opium and gambling dens that flourished in Zhabei during the Japanese administration.[12]

In addition to those who held formal positions in the puppet government, a number of prominent Subei natives were affiliated with the government. Gu Zhuxuan, the most well known Green Gang leader of Subei origins and also very active in the Subei native place association in Shanghai, did not hold public office but was powerful in the administration of the puppet government.[13] His brother, Gu San (also known as Gu Songmao), a foreman in the Star Ricsha Company and owner of a so-called Jiangbei theater in Zhabei, was also involved in the puppet regime. Some reports accused him of being its major financer. So, too, was Wei Zhongxiu, a Subei native who had been chief detective of the Public Safety Bureau.[14]

Despite the high-ranking positions held by Subei people in the puppet government, not all its members were from Subei. The traffic superintendent, Chen Ajing, was a native of Ningbo, while Li Fei, the chief police inspector, came from Tianjin.[15] Moreover, the head of the administration, Hu Lifu, was from Anhui. Yet even articles that focused on him propagated the conviction that these so-called traitors were all Jiangbei ren.[16] In fact, some observers seemed utterly unable to determine if he was from Subei or not: detectives for the French police sometimes identified him as being from Anhui and sometimes from Jiangbei. The confusion about Hu Lifu may be due to the inconsistent definitions of Subei, as described in chapter 2. To many Shanghai residents anyone from north of the river who spoke in words resembling Subei dialect was a Subei ren. Hu Lifu, who spoke with an Anhui accent, might therefore have qualified. The fact that he operated a bathhouse in Shanghai, an enterprise associated with Subei ren, may also help account for the conviction that this most notorious traitor was from Subei.

Whether the majority of leaders of the puppet government were actually from Subei is impossible to determine. What mattered was that a corps of Subei natives, or alleged Subei natives, such as Hu Lifu, were visibly involved. This was sufficient evidence to fuel a perhaps popular predisposition to describe the puppet regime as the machination of Shanghai's most despised social group.

In addition to associating prominent Subei people with leadership of the puppet regime, many Shanghai citizens believed that large numbers of ordinary Subei natives in Shanghai were actively assisting the Japanese. Newspaper articles with titles such as "Uneducated Jiangbei people in Zhabei are willingly being used by the Japanese" described how they wore armbands symbolizing the Japanese flag. "The way they look is so stupid and disgusting," the writer of one article exclaimed, "but under the wing of the Japanese they have become really arrogant. . . . It should be noticed that the Chinese who have a friendly attitude toward the Japanese are all those with the armbands, i.e., Jiangbei people."[17] Other articles accused "ignorant and illiterate" Subei people of being "bought" by the Japanese to work as spies.[18] In Jiangwan, Subei people armed with hatchets were observed being led by Japanese plainclothesmen.[19]

In a number of cases, individuals from Subei were accused of being employed as "bosses" by the Japanese, to recruit gangs of workers. For example, one report described a "small foreman" (*xiao gongtou*) from Jiangbei who, paid by the Japanese, recruited more than one thousand workers to take to Zhabei, Jiangwan, and Wusong to do jobs for the Japanese.[20] Another account revealed that Japanese employees of cotton mills were bribing unemployed workers from Subei to go to their home districts and under the pretext of recruiting friends and relatives for factory jobs find people to bring to Shanghai to work for the Japanese.[21]

Reports of Subei collaboration were not confined to the newspapers. Pictorial broadsheets sold on the streets of the International Settlement included illustrations with such subtitles as "Execution of Kompo men who were employed as Snipers by the Japanese," "The arrest of Chinese (Kompo men) who were paid $30 per day for carrying land mines for the Japanese," and "Twenty or thirty sampans plied near the O.S.K. Japanese Wharf by Kompo men engaged in smuggling motors for military purposes."[22]

Public rage at collaboration erupted into incidents of public harassment of Subei natives. For example, in late March unemployed workers at a Japanese cotton mill met and resolved that "Pao Wen Tseng [Bao Wenzeng], alias Pao Lao-sz [Bao Laosi], native of Kiangpeh and owner of the Pao Yong Shing [Bao Yongxing] Coffin Shop, Ferry Road, be severely dealt with for being a running dog of the Japanese and a traitor to the Chinese." The following day workers organized pickets in front of his coffin shop, "with a view of assaulting its proprietor Pao Lau-sz and his Kiangpeh followers who are running dogs of the Japanese."[23]

The accusation of Subei collaboration was not confined to Subei residents of Shanghai but extended to the population of Subei itself, which was allegedly transporting food and supplies for the Japanese. Here, too, writers stressed the relative ignorance of Subei natives. A report from

Nantong in the Shanghai daily *Shibao,* for example, observed that "at each of the docks along the river in Jiangbei there are ignorant, stupid people . . . using large junks to cross the river secretly and assist the enemy."[24]

Given the overwhelming association of Subei people with collaboration in 1932, it is not surprising that prejudice against them turned virulent and blatant. Discrimination against Subei natives became explicit in a way it had never been before. According to some reports, people who wanted to hire maids or rickshaw drivers refused to hire people from Subei; a number of factories and shops refused Subei job applications; even some refugee centers denied admission to people of Subei origins. Moreover, some districts in both Zhejiang and Jiangsu forbade Subei people residential rights.[25] The head of one Subei native place association complained that "anyone who does not speak Shanghai dialect is accused of being a 'Jiangbei traitor.' "[26]

It is difficult to know whether the majority of collaborators were actually from Subei or whether Subei people were simply being used as scapegoats. Certainly Subei people were not the only collaborators in Shanghai. Moreover, many of the Subei people who did work for the Japanese may have been forced into doing so. For example, the Chinese press reported that "refugees who had fled into the Settlement area from Chapei stated yesterday that they witnessed Japanese soldiers in groups of threes and fives forcing the Komponese to direct them to conduct a search of every house in the various districts of Chapei."[27] Also, if accounts of the Japanese attack in 1937 and occupation of 1941 are at all indicative of what happened in 1932, it is likely that a number of Subei people observed working for the Japanese were not doing so of their own free will. The following account typifies reports from that period:

My name is Kyung Yue Chi, age 43 years, M/P.W.D. Highway Coolie No. 524, native of Kaoyue [Gaoyou], Kompo, residing at No. 58 Loong Yi Li, Pingliang Road. I have been working as a Highway Coolie more than 10 years. At 6 A.M. 14/2/41 I left my home and went to report for work at the Sawgin Road Depot. At 7 A.M. . . . I was detailed together with 11 others to work at the corner of Yangtszepoo and Kueiyang Roads. We proceeded to the above place via Yalu Road, Point Road, Muirhead Road and Yangtszepoo Road. 10 of these coolies went away to take their breakfast whilst I together with Tso Ng Zeh Te (P.W.D. Highway Coolie No. 514) continued our journey to the aforementioned place, and on approaching the Sungpan Road market we encountered six Japanese soldiers, two standing on one side of the road and the rest on the opposite side, who stopped and took us together with eight others to the Wing On Cotton Mill godown on Yangtszepoo Road, where on the 1st floor we met about 3 or 4 hundred male Chinese who had also been forcibly taken there by Japanese soldiers. Each of us was issued with a length of yellow cloth which the Japanese soldier ordered to be tied around the right arm.[28]

If occurrences such as this—which were recounted by Subei and non-Subei people alike during the Japanese occupation in 1941—took place during the attack in 1932, then the Subei people observed wearing arm bands and working for the Japanese were hardly enthusiastic, or even willing, collaborators.

A final question must be considered in evaluating the extent of Subei collaboration: how could press reporters (or ordinary observers, for that matter) be so sure that the people they saw assisting the Japanese were in fact from Subei? They may well have looked poor and dressed like rural immigrants, but short of actually hearing their dialect, which was not likely under these circumstances, it is unclear how they determined who was from Subei and who was not. It is even less likely that the Japanese invaders were able to distinguish Subei people from other Han Chinese, single them out, and make a concerted effort to recruit them. At best, then, it could only have been a presumption that most of the collaborators were Subei natives—a presumption that reflected preexisting disdain for Subei people as well as a need to blame someone for collaboration.

Nevertheless, for a number of reasons it would not be surprising if some Subei people in Shanghai did voluntarily work for the Japanese. The first is geographic: Zhabei, the district occupied by the Japanese, was a working-class district where large numbers of Subei natives lived in shack settlements. If poor people who resided in the area occupied by the Japanese were the most likely collaborators, the odds were that they would be Subei natives. A second imaginable reason for collaboration is economic: most Subei people were extremely poor and perhaps not averse to taking jobs that would give them money, regardless of their origins. Moreover, the puppet administration of Zhabei offered them avenues of economic mobility that were otherwise inconceivable. For example, the puppet police charged extremely low license fees for opium dens and gambling dens. In fact, the proliferation of these establishments in the area under Japanese administration earned it the nickname the Badlands. Combined with their *tongxiang* connections with members of the puppet police, a number of Subei natives were quick to take advantage of these new opportunities.[29]

Finally, it is possible that many Subei people did not identify with the sense of nationalism that inspired Han Chinese to resist Japan. History is replete with cases of outcast groups analogous to Subei people refusing to share the elite's version of nationalism. Belgium during World War II, for example, presents a situation remarkably similar to Shanghai in 1932. There, regional identity marked by linguistic difference and overlaid with class affiliation divided the population into two often antagonistic groups: the French-speaking Walloons, associated with the modern industrial sector, and the Dutch-speaking peasant Flemish. The German occupation provided the Flemish an opportunity to challenge Walloon domination and discrimination, and large numbers of Flemish became collaborators. "Quite naturally," a Belgian writer observed, "the Walloons feel a strong kinship with the French and the Flemings with the Germans." Many Flemish greeted the arrival of German soldiers "with undisguised joy; their Germanic brothers had come to 'liberate' them from the Walloon yoke."[30] Unlike the situation in Shanghai, however, Germans actively sought to draw on Flemish discontent, recruiting Flemish to their cause by explicitly presenting themselves as spokespersons for Flemish nationalism.[31] Likewise, the Japanese, in attempting to establish control of Inner Mongolia during World War II, presented themselves as the proponents of Mongolian nationalism, thereby winning a number of Mongolian collaborators to their cause.[32] And in Nicaragua, Miskito Indians of the Atlantic coast, rather than supporting an independent Nicaraguan state, have since the late nineteenth century " 'actively and intentionally espouse[d] Anglo affinity as a resource in their resistance to the state." [33] One of the major dilemmas that the Sandinista government had to confront in the 1980s was that the Miskito population aligned not with the revolutionary government, but with the U.S.-backed Contra forces, who presented themselves as advocates of Miskito rights.[34] The point of these examples is not to argue that outcast groups inevitably become collaborators, but rather to highlight the frequency with which such groups may perceive invaders and occupying forces as representing their interests as well as offering them an opportunity to express their resentment of the native elite groups that had discriminated against them.

The possibility that nationalist sentiments were similarly complex in Shanghai in 1932 is suggested by a fictitious dialogue between a Jiangbei and a Ningbo native published in *Shenbao* in April 1932:

NINGBO MAN: You Jiangbei people are all a bunch of low-class things. Just look: the people who empty toilets and pull rickshaws in Shanghai are all you Jiangbei people. And most kidnappers and criminals are you Jiangbei people too.

JIANGBEI MAN: Shit! It is you Ningbo people who are really low-class. We may empty toilets and pull rickshaws, but at least we rely on our own strength to eat, and we work for Chinese people. But what about you Ningbo people? Hah! You are compradores, slaves for foreigners. Now that is really low-class!

NINGBO MAN: You mean to say that you don't kiss ass to foreigners?! You've been running dogs for the Japanese. Wasn't it you Jiangbei people who have been traitors, killed people, and set fires?

JIANGBEI MAN: Not bad! We might be traitors, but at least the Japanese give us money. But you slaves for foreigners—you're always dressed up in Western suits, and when you ride in rickshaws you're not willing to pay even a copper more. You're always doing your best to think of ways to exploit us. . . . It is because you live so well that some Jiangbei people became traitors.

NINGBO MAN: Who taught you not to know how to earn money? Who taught you to be poor? Poor people deserve it if they starve to death.

JIANGBEI MAN: Ah, right! You have money, so you are even less willing to fight the Japanese. Instead you are determined to think of a way to sell the country. From the head of some committee at the top, to owners of banks at the bottom, there is no one who does not advocate compromising with the Japanese. Is it possible that the defeat in battle this time was not the fault of your honorable *tongxiang* people?

NINGBO MAN: Okay. But our *tongxiang* people have ability. They are capable of selling the country. But you people—can you do that?

JIANGBEI MAN: Ha-ha-ha! So it's like this: if people have a country they sell it. Then what's so odd about poor Jiangbei people becoming traitors?[35]

If the statements of the Jiangbei man reflect popular sentiments, they suggest that Subei people may well not have identified with Han nationalism and that events of 1932 provided Subei people an opportunity to express a perhaps long-brewing resentment toward the elite for its condescending attitude.

Other incidents confirm that many Subei people may have felt a closer affinity with Japanese than with the Jiangnan-based Shanghai elite. For example, Deng Yuzhi, head of the YWCA Labor Bureau who was assisting unemployed women workers find jobs during spring 1932, was initially stunned to find that a number of Subei natives were unwilling to work in Chinese-owned cotton mills, but in fact preferred the Japanese mills. "Most people do not understand the situation very well, and think that these are Jiangbei people who have no conscience at all and are traitors to China," she wrote. She then related a conversation she had with a woman from Subei. When asked why she preferred the Japanese-owned mills, the woman replied, "Japanese people are just as polite to us Jiangbei people as they are to Shanghainese. They treat us like people. Every day when we go to work they nod their heads to greet us, and smile. But in Chinese mills they treat us like trash. They swear about how terrible us Jiangbei people are." "Those two sentences: 'Japanese people are just as polite to us as they are to locals; they treat us like human beings,'" concluded Deng, "'can typify the oppression faced by Jiangbei people in the hands of people from Jiangnan."[36] These experiences prompted Deng Yuzhi to write a most impassioned critique of the treatment of Subei people in Shanghai. "Workers, foremen, managers, as well as lettered people all hold Jiangbei people in contempt, treat them as inferior, and are mean to them," she began.

> Truthfully speaking, our cruel behaviour towards Jiangbei people is no different from the way in which imperialists treat our coolies, and it is no different from the way in which American people treat black slaves. We oppose imperialist exploitation of our people; we oppose Americans making slaves of black people. But what about our treatment of Jiangbei people—who are our own countrymen?
>
> Furthermore, we are always accusing Jiangbei people of not being patriotic, and cursing them for being traitors. But we might do a little more research about what it means to be patriotic: On behalf of the Japanese, Jiangbei people kill people, set fires, and help Japanese invade China. We can say that is not patriotic. But is it patriotic to always discriminate against Jiangbei people, to curse them and beat them? If we are going to talk about loving our country, we had better begin by loving our fellow countrypeople.[37]

In the context of resentment toward the contemptuous treatment they received from the Jiangnan elite, it would not be surprising if Subei natives felt a closer affinity for the Japanese than for their fellow–Han Chinese. Under these circumstances, they may well have—like their Flemish and Mongolian counterparts—worked for the enemy during the invasion. Doing so offered a fleeting chance to dominate those who had for so long dominated them.

Ultimately it cannot be known whether Subei people really were the majority of collaborators or not; more significant is the popular perception that they were and the discrimination against them that ensued, a discrimination that both reflected and intensified the belief that they constituted a coherent, despised social category.

Moreover, events of 1932 had a legacy that extended far beyond that spring. For years to come, many Shanghai residents clung to the conviction that Subei people had been collaborators, and on that basis discriminated against them. Even after two years, according to one social commentator, "Whenever the name 'Jiangbei' is mentioned in Shanghai, no matter who one is talking to, their expression immediately changes to contempt and disgust. It is clear that, like the Indochinese in the eyes of Europeans, Jiangbei people are considered a sub-civilized people in the eyes of Shanghainese."[38] That same year, the author of an article in a popular magazine, obviously attempting to defend the reputation of Subei people, admitted that their image was tarnished by a record of collaboration. " 'It is only a pity," he lamented, "that [Jiangbei ren] are somewhat lacking in knowledge and guidance. Because of this they could not help becoming 'Jiangbei traitors' during the January 28th affair."[39] The writer Lu Xun, living in Shanghai at the time, was also a critical observer of the enduring prejudice. In an essay he wrote in 1934 entitled " 'Toys," he complained that "ever since the year before last, men from north of the river have been generally abused, as if this were the only way to prove the speaker's own integrity."[40]

Even the book *Xianhua Yangzhou* propagated the conviction of Subei collaboration with the Japanese and argued that Subei people were collaborators by nature. "If you read the historical account *A Record of Ten Days in Yangzhou (Yangzhou shiri ji)*," advised Yi Junzuo,

> you will see that when the Qing army massacred Yangzhou the people who really caused this massacre were the Yangzhou local residents. From just this one example, we can see how bad-hearted Yangzhou people are. I would have hoped that after these few hundred years, the tormented Yangzhou people would try to improve. But how could you guarantee that the Jiangbei people who are traitors do not include Yangzhou natives?[41]

Yi Junzuo's claims notwithstanding, *A Record of Ten Days in Yangzhou* is not, in fact, replete with evidence of Yangzhou natives' collaboration in the notorious sacking of their city.

Sometimes the legacy of prejudice against Subei people for collaboration jeopardized individuals' careers. For example, in 1936, a Subei native who was the Chinese chief detective of the French police, Chen Ziqing, was accused of spying for the Japanese when in fact he was collecting information about troop movements throughout China for the French police. "This gave rise to a misunderstanding," the report concluded, "particularly so as the officer is a native of Kiangpeh, and it is common belief among Chinese people that mostly natives of Kiangpeh are working for Japanese as spies."[42] Charges against Chen were subsequently dropped.

Given the legacy of 1932, one would expect that the subsequent Japanese attack on and occupation of Shanghai would have deepened the perception of Jiangbei collaborators. However, there is little evidence that this was the case. A number of Subei natives were in fact associated with the puppet regime of that time. Chang Yuqing, widely thought to be a collaborator in 1932, became even more renowned in the late 1930s for his association with the Japanese. In addition, Wu Shibao, a Gaoyou native whose allegedly hideous, deformed features generated the nickname Rotten Wintermelon (*lan donggua*), was a major figure in the Japanese-run police force.[43] Nevertheless, Subei people as a group do not seem to have been singled out or scapegoated; almost no articles in the press identified Subei people as collaborators.[44] One can only speculate as to why this was the case. Perhaps the fact that the most notorious collaborator, Wang Jingwei, was Cantonese made it difficult to construe Subei people as the source of the problem. It is also plausible, given the greater power and geographical reach of the later attack, that there were many more collaborators of Jiangnan origins during this period. If more Jiangnan natives joined the Japanese, it would be harder to single out Subei people as villains, even if just as many collaborated as in the earlier period.

Despite the brevity of the Japanese attack of 1932 compared to the war of 1937–45, its legacy in terms of the construction and stigmatization of the category Subei people was far more profound. That Subei people were not perceived as being more inclined to be collaborators during the latter period failed to negate the perceptions formed earlier. Even in the 1980s, when I raised the subject of Subei people with retired factory workers, many voiced the complaint that they had collaborated with the Japanese.[45]

Subei Solidarity

Did the Japanese attack of 1932 contribute to Subei people's acceptance of the category Subei? Did it create a sense of solidarity among them, even if only to defend their reputation? At first glance, the Japanese attack seems to be one of the few instances in which there is an explicit record of what might be considered a Subei consciousness, of Subei people publicly declaring a Subei identity. In response to the accusations that Subei people were collaborators, the native place associations of the three Subei districts Huai'an, Yangzhou, and Nantong formed a joint office. The announcement of its founding deplored popular propaganda that unfairly blamed natives of those districts:

> How dare those people, acting according to the "Shanghai custom," accuse all those who do not speak Shanghai dialect of being "Jiangbei traitors." For instance, a local newspaper published an article charging that all Jiangbei people are traitors. This has a negative impact on all of us; everyone feels threatened and blacklisted. . . . The word

"traitor" [*hanjian*] has nothing to do with Jiangbei people. It originally referred to those Chinese loyal to the Manchus. Now we are all one family. Using the word to attack Jiangbei people only divides the Chinese people and helps the Japanese.[46]

Whether or not Subei (or Jiangbei) people represented a coherent category was not questioned; rather the announcement was simply defending their reputation.

In addition to institutional response, a number of individuals from Subei districts spoke out in their own defense. When they did so, they invariably invoked a Subei (rather than a more local Yangzhou, Yancheng, or other) identity. "For someone who is from Jiangbei," complained one man in a letter to the editor of a local magazine, "walking on the street and hearing people make fun of us feels worse than being a Chinese in a foreign country." He criticized the public for blaming all Subei people for the activities of what he believed constituted only a small minority of Subei natives working as collaborators.[47]

Some reports suggest that not only in the press, but in daily encounters as well individuals from Subei defended themselves. One writer described the following incident: while chatting with friends in a teahouse, a fruit vendor, identified by them as a Subei native, offered to sell them fresh water chestnuts. Outraged by the seemingly high price, one of the writer's friends declared, "You guys are so greedy—why don't you just go work for the Japanese? Then you can make more money!" Infuriated, the peddlar delivered an impassioned defense of his people. "You gentlemen are intellectuals and have manners," he began. "So why do you say these disgusting words to me?"

> Those people who are traitors are not all from Jiangbei. There are traitors from other places as well. It is only because Jiangbei people are the majority of traitors that this reputation of disloyalty has been extended to all Jiangbei people.
>
> Although I am ignorant and low-class, I still learned to be patriotic ever since I was young. So, during this incident, although some people asked to go to work as a collaborator, I refused. Of course I know that if I worked as a traitor I could earn much more money, but ultimately it would not be good for me if the Japanese took over China. So I would rather take this low-class job. Although it is difficult, I feel good about myself.[48]

Other Subei natives, rather than denying the accusations, rallied their compatriots to behave more patriotically. The Office of the Association of Sojourners in Shanghai from Huai'an, Yangzhou, and Nantong issued a statement that, while deploring the accusation that Subei people were traitors, admitted that "some of our people have totally lost their hearts and minds and are helping the enemy." It resolved to investigate cases of Subei people being used by the enemy and threatened those found guilty of collaboration with severe punishment: "Anyone found to be engaged in such heartless activity will face confiscation of all home property in the village and capital punishment in the city. No lenience will be granted to those traitors who damage our Jiangbei people's reputation. . . . To get rid of the traitors among us is everyone's responsibility."[49] The Jianghuai Native Place Association likewise delegated members to investigate cases of Subei people working for the Japanese.[50]

The native place associations were not the only ones to express concern about Subei compatriots working for the Japanese. According to one report, a group of Subei natives who were intellectuals printed and posted leaflets calling on their fellow Subei ren to stop working for the Japanese. "Dear pitiful Jiangbei compatriots," began the leaflet. "We have long been aware of the nature of your daily life, but there is nothing we can do [now]. . . . You must please tolerate it for the time being and we will find a way to help you in the future. You cannot only think of your own narrow interests. Please do not help the Japanese kill people and start fires. . . . Wake up! Wake up!" The poster was signed by "a tearful Jiangbei ren."[51]

These statements by the native place associations and the intellectuals may be interpreted as signifying a consciousness among Subei natives that they belonged to a coherent group or at least a recognition and acceptance of the label Subei ren imposed on them by the Jiangnan elite. In all these instances, they refer to themselves as Subei-nese and assume responsibility for others presumed to share that identity.

These statements do not, however, show that all, or even most, Subei natives subscribed to this belief. Instead, the pleas are issued by members of the Subei elite and as such express a kind of ethnic anxiety: concern among the literati that the activities of their less-wealthy, less-educated compatriots will tarnish their own reputation. How the majority of poorer Subei natives responded to the accusations of collaboration and to the pleas of their compatriots remains unclear.

That Subei solidarity, even if only among the elite, emerged in the context of the Japanese attack is not surprising, for as studies of ethnic identity elsewhere have shown, "ethnic unity, ascribed by outsiders, was accepted as part of the defense against prejudice and hostility." Adversity, argues Jonathan Sarna in an essay describing the transition "from immigrants to ethnics," is what caused immigrants to the United States to transcend their village identities and accept a national identity ascribed them by outsiders.[52] And if there were ever a time when Subei people in Shanghai experienced adversity, the early 1930s was it. However, the adversity experienced during 1932 does not appear to have resulted in a lasting acceptance of the category Subei by Subei people themselves. Instead, it was a short-lived, class-based sense of identity that dissipated once the intense hostility toward Subei people subsided. Its impact on the Shanghai elite's belief in the category Jiangbei ren was far more profound and long-lasting than its effect on Subei people's own sense of identity.

The Japanese attack of 1932 represents a singularly discrete episode in the construction of Subei ethnicity. It illustrates dramatically how politics intersected with economic status and geography, not only to harden prejudice against Subei people, but to deepen the belief that this despised group indeed represented a meaningful social category.[53] The need for such a category intensified at this time, as Shanghainese required a scapegoat, a means of assuaging their own potential guilt: there were no collaborators, only Jiangbei collaborators. The meaning of *Subei people* therefore expanded during the events of 1932. The category not only described poverty and backwardness, but encompassed traitors and troublemakers as well.

The Japanese attack is also the most visible instance of politics shaping Subei ethnicity. Its development, however, was undoubtedly punctuated by other, less dramatic events that did not generate extensive media attention and remain largely invisible. For example, when women silk filature workers began to organize a union in 1924, Subei women were singled out as the culprits. One factory owner dealt with the labor unrest by firing all the women from Subei, whether they were involved or not. Workers from Jiangnan who may have been involved in organizing were not fired. According to at least one newspaper account, the labor activities of women silk workers at this time generated popular antagonism toward Subei people, who were perceived as the source of the problems.[54] It is impossible to determine how frequently Subei people were scapegoated during strikes and other events, but this account suggests that they were seen as the cause of political problems more often than the historical record documents.[55]

In these events, as in the Japanese attack of 1932, the line between popular beliefs and social reality is even more indistinguishable than in analyses of Subei people's housing and employment. It is impossible to determine whether Subei people really are the culprits they are made out to be or whether they are being used as scapegoats. Is the already pejorative expression *Jiangbei ren* simply being extended to encompass a newly problematic group of people? Or does the perception of Subei people as politically problematic account for their stigmatization as a poor underclass? The two dynamics were most likely inseparable, but they constituted equally essential ingredients in the transformation of immigrants from northern Jiangsu into despised Jiangbei swines.

7

INVISIBLE INEQUALITIES:

SUBEI PEOPLE IN

POST-1949 SHANGHAI

When the Chinese Communist Party took power in 1949 one of its major concerns was how to analyze and eliminate the vast inequalities that structured Chinese society. During the 1950s and 1960s, a number of political campaigns aimed to reduce class differences as well as to eradicate the discriminatory practices of the Han Chinese toward peoples identified as national minorities, such as the Miao or Zhuang. At the same time, many of the bases of native place identity were eradicated: native place associations were abolished, and from 1958 migration from rural areas to cities such as Shanghai was prohibited. Subei people being the victims of ethnic discrimination and the epitome of the disenfranchised working class heralded by the party, one might have expected the Subei problem to have diminished.

Yet four decades after Liberation, many of the phenomena described in previous chapters continue to exist. Subei ren is still a metaphor for low-class, and Subei people continue to be regarded as the scum of Shanghai. In spite of official emphasis on classification by class, cleavages by native place, particularly Subei/non-Subei, have remained central to popular categorizations of the Shanghai social landscape. Though scarcely evident in documentary sources, popular prejudice against Subei people thrives; its constant expression in casual conversation can be confirmed through more formal interviews as well as social surveys. In short, Subei people continue to be regarded and to function as a distinct ethnic group.

The Subei population of contemporary Shanghai is somewhat different from that of the pre-1949 past. First, the majority of so-called Subei people in Shanghai today were not born in Subei; they are the children, grandchildren, and in some cases great-grandchildren of migrants. Indistinguishable from the rest of the Shanghai population by physical appearance, only language betrays their identity. Although most contemporary Subei people speak Mandarin or Shanghai dialect, they grew up in homes in which Subei dialect was spoken and speak Mandarin with an allegedly Subei accent. (At least one linguist argues that Subei people who learn Shanghai dialect speak it with a distinguishable accent.)[1] Since language is the only recognizable marker of a Subei person, those with no accent can effectively disguise their native place origins—at least until friends visit their home and hear their relatives speaking Subei dialect. At the same time, however, those whose pronunciation bears any resemblance to Subei dialect, even if they are not from Subei, are likely to be called Subei ren, as often happens to people from Nanjing or Anhui.

Another feature distinguishes the Subei population of contemporary Shanghai from that of the pre-1949 past. Historically, the overwhelming majority of migrants from Subei were peasants fleeing natural disaster and poverty; notably few Subei people were to be found among the ranks of Shanghai's political and economic elites. This changed in 1949: the Communist soldiers who crossed the Yangzi River and liberated Shanghai, members of the New Fourth Army, came mostly from Subei. After Liberation many were appointed officials and cadres in the city government. So well recognized is the political prestige of Subei people (several of the post–Cultural Revolution mayors and Communist party secretaries of Shanghai and an even larger number of municipal bureau heads hailed from Subei) that when citizens are dissatisfied they commonly say, "No wonder we have so many problems—our leaders are all from Subei!" In the decades since 1949, then, the Subei community in Shanghai has consisted not only of manual laborers, but of members of the political elite as well.

The political context for the articulation and recreation of Subei ethnicity after 1949 was also radically different from that of the past. Shanghai was no longer the semicolonial treaty port it had been since the mid-nineteenth century; no longer did a foreign-controlled administration or occupying force shape the contruction and meaning of social categories. Instead, class and ethnicity in post-1949 Shanghai were constituted in the context of a state, one dominated by the Chinese Communist Party, that was far more intrusive and active in establishing acceptable categories than any previous government had been. Native place identity, including Subei ren, was not a category sanctioned by the state, yet for reasons explored below, it continued to be profoundly meaningful.

Pride and Prejudice in Contemporary Shanghai

How have Subei people been regarded in Shanghai since Liberation? Do they still function as a distinct ethnic group? The most immediately visible evidence that the category Subei ren remains profoundly meaningful is linguistic: derogatory references to Subei people permeate the language of Shanghainese. Moreover, whereas before 1949 the term *Jiangbei* was used in a variety of ways, only some of which were derogatory, since 1949 it has become clearly and strictly pejorative. The expressions *Jiangbei ren* and the more insulting *Jiangbei lao* (old Jiangbei), *Jiangbei danzi* (Jiangbei egg), and *Jiangbei zhuluo* (Jiangbei swine) continue to rank among the most common curses in Shanghai dialect.[2] These terms are used not only in reference to someone who is literally from Subei, but also to accuse someone of being low-class or unreasonable. *Subei* remains a synonym for almost anything distasteful. People who speak crudely, for example, are criticized for "speaking Jiangbei dialect"; individuals who fail to conform to standards of cleanliness are scolded for "being dirty and unsanitary, like Jiangbei folk"; sexually promiscuous men are accused of "having a rotten cock (literally, *lan diao*), like a Jiangbei person"; and those who push and shove on the ever-jammed Shanghai busses are chastised for being "rough like Jiangbei people." (Some Shanghai residents are convinced that *all* the people who push and shove on busses are of Subei origins.)

Even Subei dialect itself bears the brunt of prejudice. Shanghainese, notorious for belittling anything that is not Shanghai dialect, single out Subei dialect as being particularly noxious. As one historian (of Jiangnan origins), himself sensitive to the problems faced by Subei people in Shanghai, unashamedly declared, "Subei dialect really is ugly-sounding (*nanting*). For example, in Mandarin, people say *nali* when they want to ask where something is. In Shanghai dialect we say *sa difang*. That sounds pretty nice, doesn't it? But Subei people say *la kui*. Now you have to admit, that really is ugly, right?" In the early 1970s, the belief that Subei dialect was markedly foreign and distasteful led some primary and middle school teachers (mostly non-Subei natives) to refuse their assignment of teaching Mandarin. "It is little use," they declared, "since they [the Subei residents] could not learn to speak the standard spoken language."[3] If it was so difficult to teach Mandarin to speakers of Subei dialect, which is closer to Mandarin than Shanghai dialect is, one wonders why more teachers did not express a similar sense of futility in trying to convert speakers of Shanghai dialect to the national language.

Aesthetics, too, reflect the belief in a distinctive Subei style, as anything smacking of Subei tastes is ridiculed or condemned. Purchasing a piece of bright red cloth or donning a red garment is likely to provoke friends or onlookers to comment, "That's so ugly—it's like what Jiangbei people wear." A young woman recalled that whenever a primary school classmate wore a red ribbon in her hair, friends would inevitably mimic Subei dialect and call her Xiao Sanzi (Little Three)—since Subei people allegedly gave their children numbers for names: Xiao Sanzi, Xiao Sizi (Little Four), and so on.

Prejudice against Subei people extends to popular culture as well. Save for a brief moment of glory in the 1950s when Zhou Enlai, himself from the Subei county Huai'an, dedicated a Huai opera theater in Shanghai, local opera from Subei continues to have a poor reputation. My efforts to convince some Chinese friends to accompany me to a performance of Huai opera were fruitless; members of the foreign affairs office who were responsible for my research arrangements, certain that Huai opera would disappoint me, offered me tickets to the more prestigious Shaoxing opera instead. Residents of Subei districts complain about the infrequency of performances of Huai opera. Members of the Huai Opera Troupe in Shanghai speak bitterly about the low-class status accorded their art. "We only get to perform in theaters in Shanghai when they do not have good business," the well-known Huai opera singer Xiao Wenyan complained. "We are required to report all our new operas to the Cultural Affairs Bureau, but they always pick the Shaoxing operas for performances. They are the decision-makers, so there is nothing we can do about it." "Whenever it is opening night for one of our operas," a director for the troupe added, "we invite the city leaders to attend. If it were a Shaoxing opera, they'd be glad for the invitation. But to get them to accept the invitation to our Huai opera we have to phone several times. And even if we send cars to pick them up, they still usually say that they are busy and cannot come." The officials in charge of local radio and television stations share the scorn for Subei opera, granting priority to Shanghai, Shaoxing, and Peking opera instead. Some Subei residents complain that the radio broadcasts only two Huai opera programs a day, one in the middle of the night.[4] As mentioned earlier, when I accompanied the troupe for part of a two-month tour of Subei, the performers were ecstatic, for the presence of a foreigner conferred on them an almost unprecedented prestige.

The attitude of Shanghainese toward Subei opera is not simply lack of interest in an unfamiliar art form, but rather represents hostility toward something considered base and unsophisticated. This was made most clear to me when I naively asked an old woman worker from Subei whether she ever went to see performances of *yueju* (Shaoxing opera). An older male factory official present at the interview—himself from Shaoxing—indignantly interrupted to explain to me that "they [people from Subei] did not go to see yueju. Most people in this mill are Jiangbei people, and so they would not go to see *our* Shaoxing opera. Yueju—that's something for us Shaoxing, Ningbo, and Yuyao people to see. Subei people would go to see *their* Jianghuai operas."[5] A similar attitude was expressed by one of the directors of the Shanghai Huai Opera Troupe. A native of Shanghai, he recalled his anger and shame when assigned to the Huai Opera Troupe after graduating from a drama institute.[6] This prejudice against Huai opera is confirmed by a survey of cultural life in Shanghai, conducted in 1984: the declining size of audiences for Huai opera, surveyors found, could be largely attributed to social prejudice against Subei people.[7]

Popular culture not only reflects the prejudice toward Subei people, but in some cases actively perpetuates it. This is most conspicuous in performances by comedy troupes in Shanghai. Evil characters are played by someone from Subei or someone who speaks with a Subei accent; Subei dialect is often the brunt of jokes; whenever the characters include a rickshaw puller or cobbler, they are called Xiao Sanzi or Xiao Bazi (see above), pronounced by the other characters in imitation Subei dialect.[8] The category Subei folk, in other words, functions as an indispensable embodiment of backwardness, much like hillbillies in American popular culture (to wit, the television series "The Beverly Hillbillies").

Literature, too, both reflects and perpetuates prejudice toward Subei people. In short stories and novels characters described as country bumpkins are inevitably from Subei. For example, in Zhou Erfu's fictional account of workers and capitalists in Shanghai during the early 1950s, *Morning in Shanghai,* a cadre from Subei, Mr. Zhang, is described as wearing a "grey cotton cadre's suit with the bottom of his white shirt showing beneath the bottom of the jacket." His country-style black cotton shoes were "covered in dust." "Everything around him and all that was going on seemed to him strange and new." Little wonder, then, that he was duped and cheated in a business deal with a pharmaceutical company.[9]

The insistence on defining Subei people as a coherent and despised social category finds its most concrete expression in the search for marital partners. No self-respecting Shanghainese would consider marrying a Subei native, and most are unabashedly explicit in stating this preference. Individuals seeking introductions to prospective mates commonly remind their friends of their requirement that the person not be from Subei. Even the marriage introduction bureaus established in the mid-1980s report that when young people in Shanghai register their preferences for a mate, many specify that they will not consider an introduction to someone from Subei. "Anyone but a Subei person," "a southerner," "will refuse a Subei person," are commonly written on the registration forms.[10] That the forms include the question "What are your preferences for a spouse's native place?" itself underscores the continued importance of native place identity.

Many an otherwise satisfactory match has dissolved at the revelation of a person's Subei origins. The young woman writer Wang Xiaoying recalled the plight of a cousin whose girlfriend of two years was from Subei. When his mother heard her Subei accent she opposed the marriage, and the young couple separated. "You probably don't realize that Subei people are the most poor, vulgar, and low-class people," his mother proclaimed.[11] A young Subei man angrily lamented his rejection:

> My mother had introduced me to a prospective mate. Before I met the girl we had exchanged photographs, and based on our requirements, it seemed that this match would succeed. My mother took me to the Anhui restaurant at the corner of Shaanxi Road to have a meal with her family. After the meal, based on arrangements made by both our parents, I took the girl for a walk to the Bund. Several days later my mother heard that the girl did not want to continue with me. When I heard this I couldn't figure it out. I wondered whether my actual appearance was that different from my photograph. Several days later I found out by coincidence that the girl broke it off because she heard my mother speaking Jiangbei dialect.[12]

Still another young man, whose father was from Shandong and mother from Yangzhou, recalled that his fiancée's parents forced their daughter to break off the engagement. "My father being from Shandong was acceptable, but they just couldn't tolerate the fact that my mother was from Yangzhou and I was therefore a half-Subei ren." One university graduate was so discouraged and angry at the number of girlfriends who rejected him upon learning about his Subei origins that he took the unusual step of requesting a job outside Shanghai. "When I'm in other places, northerners all respect me, thinking I am a 'southerner' and therefore smart. But the moment I return to Shanghai everyone scorns me for being a 'Subei ren'. . . . I'd rather live somewhere else."[13]

Statistics confirm these attitudes. A survey conducted in 1984 found that approximately 70 percent of the younger generation of Subei people in Shanghai married other Subei natives.[14] The marriage registration records of 1986 for Shanghai's Zhabei district are even more extreme: some 80 percent of the individuals who listed Subei as their native place chose spouses of Subei origins. Moreover, in 75 percent of the cases of mixed marriages, it was the bride who was from Subei, suggesting that marrying a southerner represented a form of upward mobility for Subei women. As an official originally from Subei explained, "I have seven daughters, and not a single one is willing to marry a Subei person; they all hope for something else."

When asked to explain their strong objection to marrying people from Subei, Shanghainese offer several explanations. First is the association of Subei people with poverty. The issue of economic status involves more than a disdain felt by intellectuals or members of the middle class at the idea of marrying workers. Among workers, at least, Subei people are perceived as a substratum of the working class, as evidenced by the comments of a young woman interviewed by the writer Zhang Xinxin for her oral history collection *Chinese Lives*. The father of this woman's fiancé had opposed their marriage because her family came from the "lower quarters" (*xia zhi jiao*), the working-class districts of Shanghai, while his was from the "upper quarters" (*shang zhi jiao*). She was a skilled factory worker, her fiancé a teacher in a key middle school. Yet to her, a crucial distinction exists between ordinary residents of the lower quarters like herself and people from Subei. "Jiangbei people all belong to low-class occupations," she explained. "They are coolies in bathhouses, barbershops, and sanitation stations. If their children don't do these kinds of jobs then their parents do. Therefore, you cannot marry a Jiangbei person. Let those Jiangbei people find other Jiangbei people to marry!"[15] In many cases, then, the rejection of Subei mates is a class issue: marrying someone from Subei is perceived as downward mobility, whether from the middle class to the working class or from the working class to a disadvantaged substratum.

Yet more than class is at stake, as suggested by the difficulty encountered by the sons and daughters of officials of Subei origins when they seek mates.[16] "The problem of Subei ren is not an economic one," explained a young historian, "but rather one of customs. Subei people are coarse and dirty." The undesirability of Subei people as mates involves beliefs about differences in habits and customs between them and Shanghainese. One Shanghai native, the head of the cultural affairs station in a predominantly Subei district of Shanghai, offered the following explanation of why intermarriage between Subei and Ningbo people was problematic:

> The habits of Subei and Ningbo people are very different. Ningbo people are much more picky. For example, when they make *tangtao* [sweet soup dumplings]: Ningbo people make very small, delicate ones, while Subei people make large, coarse ones. Or *kaufu* [balls of wheat gluten]: Ningbo people deep fry it and use sugar and a lot of oil, while Subei people don't care about the flavor. The same with *suji* [mock chicken, made of bean curd skin]: Subei people just fry it and eat it, while Ningbo people add soy sauce.

These differences, he concluded, would make a couple incompatible.[17] A young woman concurred: she called off her engagement to a man from Subei after visiting his home and being served a platter laden with eight *pidan* (preserved eggs). "A Shanghai person would consider *pidan* a delicacy, and delicacies should be served in small quantities. I realized that if I married this man I would have to contend with things like this." Perceived character differences exacerbate the problem: Subei people are allegedly "frank and coarse," "talk very loudly," "like to argue a lot," "have a different sense of logic," and "are stingy with money." Several individuals who had siblings married to someone from Subei complained that these "coarse" Subei customs had replaced their formerly refined manners as a result of living in Subei districts. One man whose Subei wife lived with him in the "upper quarters" of Shanghai, refused to let their child visit the wife's parents in the "lower quarters," for fear that the child would be exposed to the noxious habits of Subei natives.[18]

These beliefs about cultural and personality differences between Shanghainese and Subei natives are also expressed in housing assignments. Many Shanghai residents will do anything to avoid living near Subei natives, regardless of their economic or political status. "No one wants to live near Subei people because they are just too different from us," declared a young man whose downstairs neighbors are from Subei. "They play disgusting popular music all day and they slam the doors shut," he complained. The desire to maintain a distance from Subei people is also expressed in the employment of maids (*baomu*). "Everyone would rather have a Zhejiang baomu than one from Anhui, and they'd rather have one from Anhui than one from Subei," observed the director of a baomu introduction service center in the Jing'an district of Shanghai. The problem, he concluded when asked to account for these preferences, is beliefs about cultural differences between Shanghainese and Subei natives, making it undesirable for Shanghainese to have Subei natives in their homes.

From the vantage point of Shanghainese, then, Subei people continue to represent a different ethnic order: not only do they come from a different region and speak a different dialect, not only are they relatively poor and uneducated, but in addition they have different cultural practices and personality traits. Some Shanghainese, perhaps to confirm that Subei people truly belong to a different ethnic group, insist that physical distinctions exist: Shanghai people are allegedly tall and slender, Subei people stocky and robust. Whether differences actually exist or have instead been distorted and exaggerated by Shanghainese (as they were by the British vis-à-vis the Irish in the mid-nineteenth century) is less important than the fact that Shanghai residents believe in them. They continue to evoke and manipulate geographic origins, language, and cultural practices to establish boundary markers, thereby maintaining a we/them dichotomy.

What of Subei people themselves? Has their acknowledgment or acceptance of a Subei identity changed since 1949? At first glance it seems that Subei people have internalized their inferior status. This sense of shame is most obvious in a reluctance to admit their native place. For example, only after reading an article I had written about Subei people in Shanghai did a scholar I had known for some time finally reveal his Subei origins. First praising me for dealing with a "very important subject," he then whispered, as if revealing some deeply guarded secret, "My father was from Subei, and so I am really a Subei person."

When asked about their family's local origins, people from Subei typically reply, "Jiangsu Province." On official documents, too, Subei people commonly write "Jiangsu" as their native place.[19] For example, a large number of couples who registered their marriages in Zhabei in 1986 entered "Jiangsu" instead of their specific native place. "You can be certain that all the people who wrote 'Jiangsu' are actually from Subei," the official responsible for the registration records advised me. "They just don't want anyone to know where they are really from." More recently, some people of Subei origins have asked officials at their local police station to allow them to change their native place in order to protect their children from discrimination.[20]

Even in formal interviews, when I asked which part of Jiangsu Province an individual was from, Subei people were reluctant to answer. Only when asked to show me their native place on a map would it become clear they were from Subei. In contrast, people from Jiangnan never hesitated to declare that they were from Wuxi, Changzhou, or Ningbo. One of the few students from Subei in the history department at Fudan University in 1980 informed her classmates that her family was from Nanjing, although their native place was actually Nantong. Perhaps the most flagrant denial of Subei identity I encountered emerged through the attempt of my research assistant to arrange an interview for me with then-mayor Jiang Zemin, known by almost all Shanghai residents to be a Subei native. When my research assistant explained that I was an American scholar studying the history of Subei people, the mayor's secretary, obviously determined to protect the mayor's reputation, retorted, "What makes you so sure the mayor is from Subei?!" The requested interview was denied. (It is of course possible that Jiang Zemin himself would not have denied his origins).

The denial of native place is depicted in the novel *Xiaoyou waizhuan* (The unauthorized history of Lucky Little Rich). Little Rich, who has just been hired as a cook at a Shanghai children's publishing company, repeatedly insists that he is from Yangzhong, an island in the middle of the Yangzi, not Subei. "Little Rich, are you from Jiangbei," He Donghai, a Ningbo native who is his superior asks at one point.

"Me? . . . No, not me. . ."

"Don't be scared to admit it!" He Donghai said, beating up some eggs. "Since Liberation Jiangbei people are just as glorious as anyone else. It's not like before Liberation when people looked down on Jiangbei people."

"I'm not a Jiangbei person. I'm a Taiping Zhou person!" Rich argued. . . .

"I'm telling you you're from Jiangbei. You're up to your ass in it (*qiangdiao ge pi*)!"

"Your granny's! Up your ass!" Rich fired up and started cursing a blue streak.[21]

Subei people in Shanghai often go to great lengths to disguise their identity. Most commonly they do not speak Subei dialect outside their home or neighborhood, partly to avoid harassment, but also to ensure that no one will discover their identity as a Subei person. Members of the youngest generation do not want to speak Subei dialect even at home. "Our children don't want to speak Subei dialect," a director of the Shanghai Huai Opera Troupe complained. "Even at home they just want to speak Shanghai dialect."[22] A woman who worked as a street sweeper had a slightly different attitude: she was proud of her son's ability to disguise his background. "At home we spoke Subei dialect when the kids were growing up," she said, "but when we'd go out, we would speak Shanghai dialect. It was easy for our kids to learn Shanghai dialect because they grew up and went to school here. When my oldest son goes out, no one knows that he is a Subei person. He seems exactly like a Shanghainese."[23]

Language is the most conspicuous and common way in which Subei people attempt to disguise their shameful identity. Less frequently, they disassociate themselves from other aspects of Subei culture. For instance, members of the Shanghai Huai Opera Troupe complained that young people of Subei families in Shanghai refuse to see performances of Huai opera. While this can be partly explained by the increasing availability of television and film, it is also an expression of their fear of being identified as a Subei person. "They feel they've lost face if they go see Huai opera," observed Xiao Wenyan. A director added that fights about Subei opera often erupt in the homes of Subei people: members of the younger generation violently oppose their parents' desire to watch opera performances on television, not only because it bores them but also because they fear the expression of Subei culture in their homes that might be seen by others.[24]

In some cases, the shame of being from Subei is so extreme that young people raised in Shanghai disassociate themselves from their parents altogether. One young man, married to a woman of Subei heritage who had grown up in a Subei district of Shanghai, described his wife's determination to break away from her past. She refused to permit their children to visit her parents' home in Yangshupu, fearing that they would receive the undesirable influences of that environment.[25] Another young man recalled that although his mother was actually from Anhui, everyone called her a Jiangbei ren. By implication, he, too, was a Jiangbei person. "When I was a child I knew that in Shanghai this name was derogatory, so I was afraid to go out with my mother," he later confessed. "I did my best to avoid speaking with her because I feared that people would hear me and call me Little Jiangbei." His predicament was alleviated when he went to boarding school, where no one knew his family's background, and he was able to rid himself of the label Jiangbei ren. Occasionally, however, his determination to disguise his background forced him into painful predicaments. He recalled, for instance, a weekend that he had returned from a visit home, forgetting to bring the money for his boarding fees at school.

> I had no choice but to phone home and ask my mother to bring the money to school. That day when I went to class I watched carefully for my mother. I didn't want her to end up going all over the school using Jiangbei dialect to ask for me. During the third period I suddenly saw her. As soon as the bell rang I dashed out to where she was, grabbed the money, and quickly told her to return home immediately. I am sure my mother originally intended to say something to me, but she saw my panicked look and turned to leave.

He concluded the account with a description of the guilt he felt for having treated his mother so cruelly.[26]

These elaborate attempts to disguise a Subei background—reluctance to reveal one's native place, dissociation from Subei culture and language, and distancing from parents and relatives—all attest to the tenacious hold that the category Subei people maintains. Masquerading one's own individual Subei identity may ironically betray an acknowledgment of membership in the social category.

Acknowledgment of a Subei identity is more directly expressed by individuals who, rather than attempting to refute the label Subei, indignantly denounce its negative connotations. Former rickshaw puller Chen Dewang, a well-known model worker, described his fury when well-meaning acquaintances would say, "Hey, Lao Chen, how can a Subei person be good like you? You don't really seem like a Subei person at all!" "I'd get angry when people said that, and I would tell them why it made me mad," he indignantly recalled.[27] The writer Wang Xiaoying's anger took a slightly different form. So outraged was she at the prejudice against Subei people that she publicly claimed Subei, her birthplace, as her native place even though her family was actually of the more prestigious Ningbo origins. "My grandmother says that I am a typical Ningbo person because my great-grandfather was from Ningbo," she explained in an essay entitled, "The Girl from Subei." "But even my father had forgotten what Ningbo looked like, and I had only seen it on a map." She described her fond memories of a childhood spent in the Subei county of Binhai, where her parents had been stationed as Communist cadres during the civil war of the 1940s. Nevertheless, her grandmother repeatedly warned her that if she identified herself as being from Subei she would never find a husband. Proud of her birthplace and furious at her grandmother's shame, she proclaimed her determination to say "Subei" whenever asked about her native place.[28] A similarly defiant young man, who no longer lived in Shanghai, expressed his anger at the prejudice against Subei people by deliberately speaking Subei dialect whenever he visited Shanghai.[29]

Angry denunciations of the prejudice are accompanied by a burgeoning sense of pride among Subei people in their ethnic identity, not unlike that expressed by various ethnic groups in the United States beginning in the 1960s. The conviction that "Subei is beautiful" is expressed both directly and indirectly. That middle-aged and older people, despite the preferences of their children, persist in using Subei dialect at home and in Subei neighborhoods attests, among other things, to a quiet determination to preserve a cultural identity rather than assimilate. After complaining about the derogatory use of Subei dialect in comic acts, a sanitation bureau worker declared, "But we like to speak our language!"[30]

The pride is more evident in the refusal of some individuals to passively accept the popular notion of Subei as a poor, backward, and culturally impoverished region, but instead to search for and assert the richness of its history. A barber originally from Yangzhou spoke at great length about the famous writers and officials from his hometown. "And the Qianlong Emperor himself visited Yangzhou three times!" he proudly declared.[31] "Anyone with even a slight knowledge of history knows that Subei has always been wealthier than Jiangnan," a professor of literature at Fudan University told sociologists investigating the status of Subei people in Shanghai in 1984. Challenging the pride of southerners, he pointed out that Subei had once been so prosperous that people from Jiangnan migrated to the northern half of the province. "There was no problem of discrimination against northerners by southerners at that time," he observed.[32] Others turned to the more recent past to find evidence of the glory of Subei. That Zhou Enlai hailed from the Subei county of Huai'an is one of the most frequently cited facts. (His Subei heritage, however, is brushed aside by Jiangnan people, who focus on his youth and school years in Shaoxing. Some quite angrily deny Zhou Enlai's association with Subei, insisting that he is a trueblood Shaoxing native.) Shanghai was liberated by the New Fourth Army, composed of soldiers primarily from Subei, a cadre in the research office of the Shanghai Municipal Committee pointed out. "At present there are many Subei people among the leaders at the district, county, and bureau level. Subei people are scattered among the trades and professions of Shanghai, playing an important role in the construction of the Four Modernizations."[33] Yet another took his assertion of Subei pride to the press, challenging the inferior status often accorded Subei dialect. "Actually there is no such thing as a 'good' or 'bad' language," he wrote. "Subei and Shanghai dialect are six of one, half a dozen of another. . . . From the perspective of closeness to standard Mandarin, Shanghai dialect is actually inferior to Subei dialect." He concluded by demonstrating the influence exerted by Subei dialect on Shanghainese.[34]

Structures of Inequality

The pride, anger, and shame expressed by Subei people, like the popular prejudice, attest to the persisting centrality of Subei identity in contemporary Shanghai. Yet given the changes that occurred after 1949—the abolition of native place associations, the prohibition of migration, and the promotion of Mandarin as the "common language"—how is this persistence of native place identity, and more particularly the prejudice against Subei people, to be explained?

The explanation most commonly offered in Shanghai is that the prejudice is simply a historical legacy, a remnant of the prerevolutionary past that will surely disappear with time. Subei people continue to function as a distinct ethnic group, in other words, largely because they always have. Many people, for instance, explain their contempt for Subei people by saying that "*before* 1949, they were the poorest people." Social reality, they imply, has changed since 1949 such that Subei people are no longer actually poor; the association of Subei natives with poverty has simply not yet faded.

There is some merit to this explanation, especially because social structures based on native place identity no longer exist, physical distinctions (such as dress) between Subei natives and other Shanghainese are no longer so clear, and some people from Subei have become members of the political elite. Closer examination, however, reveals that this explanation is inadequate, that the prejudice is not simply a deep-seated value that has failed to disappear. More important than the legacy of old values is the persistence of the very social and economic structures that gave rise to Subei ethnicity, structures that keep Subei people both physically and economically marginal.

Although no systematic data exist that correlate native place identity and job status, preliminary surveys conducted by Chinese sociologists indicate that the Shanghai labor market after 1949, despite its radically changed nature, continues to be segmented along regional lines, at least to the extent that Subei people are still tracked into, indeed dominate, the unskilled sector. For example, a survey of pedicab drivers in 1958 showed that 77 percent were of Subei origins. A survey conducted in the early 1980s indicated that the overwhelming majority of bathhouse attendants and barbers were from Subei. So close is the association of Subei people with haircutting that Subei dialect remains the language of the trade, even among barbers of non-Subei origins.[35] And the majority of the city's sanitation department workers, even in districts where few Subei people live, continue to be Subei natives.[36] Surveys of the jobs held by various generations of members of Subei families suggest little upward mobility. According to one such survey, over two-thirds of the members of the younger generation worked at unskilled jobs.[37] Likewise, in 1984, the records of job assignments for graduating secondary school students in a Subei district of Shanghai bore a remarkable similarity to pre-1949 patterns: the overwhelming majority joined the ranks of Shanghai's unemployed youth; those fortunate enough to secure employment were, with very few exceptions, assigned factory or construction jobs or work in the city's sanitation bureau as street cleaners, garbage collectors, and night soil collectors.[38]

Explaining the continued concentration of Subei people in the unskilled

sector of the labor market requires one to analyze labor allocation processes in China after 1949, and that is beyond the scope of this book.[39]
Only occasionally are Subei people explicitly disqualified from jobs by
dint of their local origins.[40] More commonly, the problem derives from
the educational system, as it appears that Subei people do not have the
same opportunities for higher education enjoyed by other sectors of the
Shanghai population. Unlike their parents, most of whom were illiterate,
the majority of children of Subei families do attain an elementary school
education. But less than half attend upper middle school, and only a scarce
few are admitted to schools that require examinations, including univer-
sities.[41] Older residents of Subei districts in Shanghai boastfully cite the
examples of individuals who have passed the university exams, implying that Subei natives are equally represented among the ranks of college
students. Younger residents of those neighborhoods point out, however,
that the numbers who make it to college are so few that those individuals
become neighborhood celebrities for their achievement.

The most commonly offered explanation of the relatively poor performance of Subei children in school is environmental: they grow up in
homes lacking an intellectual tradition and in neighborhoods not con-
ducive to study. A young man raised in a predominantly Subei district of
Shanghai describes the problem in somewhat melodramatic terms:

> Some children grow up hearing the sound of their mother's violin;
> listening to Andersen's fairy tales; lying on a heap of toys and chil-
> dren's books. But other children [grow up in places where] they are
> awakened from their dreams by the noise of cleaning chamber pots;
> where they eat rice porridge (*paofan*) and dried turnip in the midst of
> smoke that burns one's eyes and nose; at school they listen to teachers
> recruited from the ranks of housewives; then they do their homework
> listening to the noise of adults playing cards, arguing, and cursing
> each other.[42]

Other differences between childhood in the wealthier and poorer districts
of Shanghai may be even more significant. Children in such wealthy districts as Jing'an and Xuhui, for example, are more likely to grow up in
homes where a baomu helps with household chores. Few families in the
working-class districts, such as Zhabei and Yangshupu, can afford to hire
baomu and therefore depend on children to help with household chores
when they are not in school. Sometimes, particularly since the implementation of economic reforms that permit private businesses, school-age
children are expected to work as well, thereby contributing to the family

income.[43] Under these circumstances, it is not surprising that they perform less well in school.

It is difficult to determine whether structural discrimination, too, prevents young people of Subei origins from faring better in the educational system. It is highly unlikely that actual quotas, such as those limiting the number of women admitted to certain schools, are used. Quite possibly, however, fewer educational resources are allocated to the Subei districts, where schools are reputedly inferior to those in the more prestigious parts of the city.[44] College graduates dread the possibility of being assigned to teach in a school in a Subei district, where the students are reputedly "rough and not motivated to learn." Moreover, only those with the lowest grades are assigned to schools in Subei districts, while their more successful classmates can anticipate an assignment in the more desirable parts of Shanghai.[45]

In a semi-autobiographical short story, *Qiong jie* (Poor street), the contemporary writer Cheng Naishan describes the hardships she faced teaching in a Subei district school, where few students were on time for class and many never attended at all. The contrast between the Jieguang Middle School, where she taught, and the Number Three Middle School in the neighborhood where she grew up overwhelmed her. "Graduates from there [the Number Three Middle School] either went on to become graduate students or overseas students; at minimum they'd become doctors or engineers. How could it possibly compare with this Jieguang Middle School, where open chamber pots were drying by the school gate?!"[46] She recalls another teacher explaining to her, "These students in 'the lower quarters' are not cut out for studying, so it's a waste of time to prepare your classes. Ours is a school to prepare the army of laborers. Most of the students will take their parents' jobs—they'll empty night soil buckets or sell *dabing* [flat bread]. How much do they need to learn?"[47] Under these circumstances, it is not surprising that disproportionately few Subei people are found in higher-level educational institutions, where admission is based on examination scores.

Residential patterns, too, contribute to the continued association of Subei people with poverty. Most Subei people live not in the downtown or central districts of Shanghai (comprising the former International Settlement and French Concession), but rather in the old working-class districts of Zhabei, Yangshupu, Nanshi, and Putuo. These are the areas where Subei migrants concentrated before 1949, and little mobility seems to have occurred among subsequent generations. Although no statistics are available to confirm the infrequency with which residents of Subei districts are able to move to more desirable neighborhoods, the children of almost every Subei person I interviewed lived in the same districts as their parents.

Since the 1950s, housing projects have eliminated the worst of the pre-1949 shack settlements, yet these districts continue to be regarded as slums or, in contemporary parlance, the lower quarters of Shanghai. My research assistant, horrified by the conditions in one such district, asked me, "Are slums in the United States *this* bad?" "The Subei districts in Shanghai *are* worse than the black ghettos in the U.S.," declared a Chinese scholar from Shanghai visiting the United States. In "Poor Street," Cheng Nai-shan describes the district where she taught, Aiguo Cun, where some 80 percent of the population was Subei natives.[48] She recounts her first impressions: "The school was only a one-hour bus-ride from my home, but in that one hour it was as if I had gone from the first world to the third world. . . . [I] never would have believed that in Shanghai, the Number One city of the Far East, there existed such a corner, completely neglected by prosperity."[49]

The equation of Subei districts with poverty is not just impressionistic. In Nanshi, for example, 75 percent of the residents have no cooking gas and must still cook on charcoal-burning stoves outside their homes; 89 percent, having no toilets in their homes, still use chamber pots.[50] All the Subei districts, according to one writer, have "the fewest cultural and welfare facilities, the worst housing conditions, and the highest population density in the entire city."[51] Shanghainese who live in other districts perceive the Subei areas as being rough and crime-ridden and warn their children against going to these so-called Jiangbei villages.[52] The name persists even though not all residents of these districts are of Subei origins, suggesting perhaps the extent to which the term *Jiangbei ren* continues to function as a metaphor for anything poor, backward, or low-class.

These problems were magnified, in the late 1980s, by the renewed government tolerance of migration, one result of which was the arrival of new groups of peasants from Subei in Shanghai. According to a local news broadcast, migrants from Subei began to erect shack settlements, eking out a living by performing such menial tasks as collecting and selling garbage scraps, which local residents consider beneath their dignity. (My informal survey of people collecting garbage suggested that most were indeed recent immigrants from Subei.) Local residents complain that these immigrants are dirty, disrupt public order, and are responsible for such petty theft in their neighborhoods as stealing clothing hung to dry on laundry poles. Recalling the response of local government in the early twentieth century, the Public Security Bureau has engaged in what the news commentator described as futile attempts to send the migrants back to their homes in Subei.

The continued concentration of Subei people in the unskilled sectors of the labor market, their inferior levels of education, and their residence in slumlike districts helps account for the continued prejudice toward Subei people as well as for the belief that they represent a distinct social category. Subei ethnicity is therefore not simply a remnant of the past, but rather is actively perpetuated and reproduced by contemporary social conditions.

Political events, too, may contribute to the persistence of prejudice based on native place and the recreation of Subei ethnicity. For example, the arrival of the New Fourth Army to liberate Shanghai in 1949, though welcomed by many, intensified the perception of Subei people as country bumpkins. One former soldier recalled being made fun of by Shanghai residents: "They accused us of trying to light our cigarettes with an electric light bulb. As if we had never seen light bulbs before! And they would say that the Liberation Army soldiers didn't know how to use toilets!"[53] In her memoir of growing up in Shanghai, Margaret Gaan, the daughter of a Chinese father and American mother, describes her encounter with the Liberation Army soldier who came to her home in 1949. Accustomed to speaking with her family's servant, a man from Subei, she was able to understand the soldier's speech. "You're from Kang-poh [Jiangbei], aren't you?" she exclaimed. "Not Kang-poh," he replied. "Now it's called Poh-kang [Beijiang]—'north river'. The People's Liberation Army changed the name so people won't laugh at us any more."[54] It is doubtful that the simple reversal of syllables altered people's perception of the soldiers from Subei as naive and sorely lacking in urban sophistication, though they were probably admired for their honesty and sincerity.

The Cultural Revolution, too, may have exacerbated prejudicial attitudes toward people from Subei. Preliminary interviews suggest that Cultural Revolution factions in Shanghai correlated partly to native place. In her study of the Shanghai labor movement, Elizabeth Perry observes that the "conservative" Scarlet Guards were predominantly skilled workers from Jiangnan, while the leaders of the "radical" Revolutionary Rebels hailed from Subei.[55] Moreover, many people believed that the most violent factions, such as the activist dockworkers, were composed of Subei natives.[56] As was the case in the 1930s, when the belief that Subei people collaborated with the Japanese fueled popular contempt for Subei natives, the popular perception of Subei people as being the most violent in the Cultural Revolution is more important than whether they actually were or not. For it is such perceptions that contributed to and perhaps even consolidated prejudice. Ironically, in the years following the Cultural Revolution, many Shanghai residents identified the despised members of the Gang of Four as Subei natives. Wang Hongwen, for instance, was originally from the northeast, yet people described his career—he worked at the No. 17 Cotton Mill—as a quintessentially Subei one. That his wife was from Subei consolidated the identity.[57]

The continued prejudice against Subei people and persistence of Subei ethnicity cannot be simply construed as remnants of China's feudal past. The curse "Jiangbei swine" remains popular today not merely as a traditional expression, but rather because social, economic, and political conditions have created new bases for the prejudicial attitudes that the term *Jiangbei swine* reflects.

The persisting belief in the social category Subei people can also be attributed to a state that is far more powerful and intrusive than was any government before 1949. After 1949, the state, not just the Shanghai elite, sanctioned and imposed, even if unwittingly, the category Subei in an unprecedented way. In the years immediately following Liberation, for example, it published newspapers whose names—for example, the *Subei ribao* (Subei daily) and the *Subei zhoukan* (Subei weekly)—propagated Subei as a meaningful place-name. In Shanghai, as the state organized cultural affairs, it eliminated the more locally derived forms of entertainment, such as Yangzhou opera. Instead, it homogenized the myriad Subei operas into a single, almost generic Huai opera, thereby contributing to a belief in Subei as a uniform, coherent region. Finally, in post-1949 China, the state has continued to require that on such official documents as household and marriage registration forms individuals declare both their place of birth and native place, thereby contributing to the persisting significance of native place as a meaningful social marker. The state has therefore reinforced the persisting significance of a Subei identity.

The continued stigmatization of Subei people does not mean that its content remains unchanged. *Jiangbei swine,* for example, does not mean what it did before 1949, but has expanded to encompass new circumstances. The number of officials who are Subei natives, for example, has made *Jiangbei swine* a means of voicing antigovernment sentiments that could not be more directly expressed. Perhaps even more important is that since 1949, cursing Subei people has become one of the only acceptable ways of expressing contempt for the working class. In the context of a state that ostensibly represents the proletariat and has such organized campaigns as the class education movement of the 1950s to generate respect for workers, it is politically incorrect to express something less than admiration for laboring people. Cursing Subei people, however, was never considered problematic. It is even possible that the loathing of Subei people became more flagrant after 1949 precisely because the state rendered other scapegoats taboo. In doing so, the state may well have created a script (about class) that does not accord with popular beliefs (such as native place prejudices), which have then intensified.

It would be misleading to assume that the prejudice so clearly evident in contemporary Shanghai has been similarly intense throughout the post-1949 decades. While it is difficult to measure the extent of prejudice in the years immediately following the revolution of 1949, it has become perhaps particularly virulent in the decade since the Cultural Revolution. Resentment of the activities of working-class people during the Cultural Revolution, the post–Cultural Revolution contempt for cadres, and the increased attention to economic status that has resulted from the post-Mao reforms could all account for an intensification of prejudice against Subei people. The revival of migration from rural to urban areas in recent years might also contribute to a heightened sense of Subei ethnicity. The arrival of immigrants from Subei most likely reaffirms the association of Subei people with poverty and consequently intensifies the derogation of Subei people. Once again, they represent the despised Jiangbei refugee, a figure so familiar in the prerevolutionary urban landscape.

If the meaning of the category Subei people ascribed by Shanghainese in the decades following 1949 differs from that of the past, so too does Subei people's own identity. No longer does one find northern Jiangsu natives stressing their specific local origins, such as Yangzhou or Yancheng; when pressed to identify their native place, they declare, "Subei." This is not simply because they have accepted popular beliefs in Subei as a coherent category. Equally important is the cessation (until the late 1980s) of rural migration, so that few young and middle-aged individuals were themselves born or raised in Subei.

One question about Subei people themselves remains: the Communist revolution brought Subei people to political power in Shanghai, yet they have never used that power to challenge their continued concentration in the least desirable jobs and in the old, working-class neighborhoods. At most, Jiang Zemin, a Yangzhou native who before being appointed general secretary of the Chinese Communist Party in 1989 served as mayor of Shanghai, made occasional pleas in his public statements for fairer treatment of Subei people. The reluctance of Subei officials to implement pro-Subei policies may be attributed to the absence of a broad, popularly based Subei rights movement. It may also be that most Subei members of the political elite have devoted considerable energy to "passing," or disguising, their Subei origins, which would be revealed were they to use their political power to advocate an end to discrimination. A final explanation is that Subei people represent a kind of ethnicity—one based on native place—that remains invisible to the state and therefore unacceptable as a basis of policy-making. So long as groups defined by and discriminated against on the basis of native place do not qualify for anything equivalent to national minority status, it might well be inconceivable to Subei members of the political elite to use their clout for the promotion of their cause.

8

THE ETHNIC DIMENSIONS

OF NATIVE PLACE IDENTITY

In Shanghai, native place identity assumed ethnic meanings. It was the basis on which the we/them dichotomies
most central to the structuring of social and economic hierarchies were based; the boundary marker most frequently
invoked and manipulated in claiming and constructing a
native identity. Subei people cannot be described simply
as an immigrant community or underclass, even though
they represented both. Only by understanding Subei natives
as constituting an ethnic group, analogous to African-
Americans or Chicanos in the United States, do the structures of inequality and processes of social construction
bound to native place emerge. Only then does it become
clear that the declaration or ascription of a native place
identity connotes meanings that extend far beyond a literal
place-name, and that, indeed, a place-name may itself be
socially and historically constructed. Thus, Subei is not a
native place per se, for it does not actually exist.

If the concept of ethnicity required a people's belief in a
common language, descent, and heritage—if ethnicity were
still understood as a function of primordial ties—then it

would be a serious distortion to describe Subei people as ethnic. But, as anthropologists from Abner Cohen to James Clifford have argued, notions of common language and culture are themselves historically constructed and derive meaning only in relation to other languages, cultures, and heritages. So, for example, natives of northern and southern Mexico most likely never thought of themselves as speaking a common language or sharing identical customs any more than did natives of the various parts of northern Jiangsu. But once they immigrated to the United States, they were lumped together as Spanish-speaking Mexicans. A belief in their common heritage, in other words, emerged only when they were pitted against North Americans and defined by them as a coherent social category. Only when they migrated did they assume an ethnic identity. Likewise, as Pamela Crossley's study of the Manchus in China demonstrates, the people who during the Qing came to be thought of as Manchus and who called themselves Manchus were actually of extremely diverse geographical, linguistic, and cultural origins. The category Manchu was hardly immutable, but rather acquired and changed meaning in the context of specific historical processes that brought them into contact and conflict with Han Chinese.[1]

Subei people, too, had no sense of peoplehood, shared heritage, common language, or customs or even shared geographic origins before migrating to Jiangnan and Shanghai. The place-name Subei and social category Subei people did not exist. They were created not by Subei natives, but by natives of Jiangnan. For Jiangnan natives it mattered little that no objectively definable place called Subei existed. They created and defined it, not always self-consciously or deliberately and not always consistently. For them, *Subei* was first a term to categorize the poverty-stricken refugees from the north, thereby underscoring the distinction between themselves and this underclass. Indeed, Jiangnan natives may have exaggerated linguistic, personality, cultural, and even geographic distinctions in order to defend their sense of superiority.

The belief in a place called Subei and in Subei people may well have been brought by Jiangnan natives who settled in Shanghai. Nevertheless, in Shanghai the process of constructing the category Subei people intensified, assuming entirely new dimensions. From the mid-nineteenth century until 1949, people from northern Jiangsu continually flocked to Shanghai, fleeing poverty, floods and droughts, and war. Despite efforts to prevent them from establishing residence in Shanghai, many stayed, constructing makeshift homes on their boats or from reeds and whatever other scrap materials they could find; to some degree they accepted the definition of themselves as Subei people. By the 1930s, shack settlements of Subei people formed an almost complete circle around the foreign concessions. Desperate for work, lacking the skills and education required to qualify them for higher-status jobs, and barred from making the personal and institutional connections that would have given them access to those jobs, Subei people concentrated in occupations such as rickshaw pulling, dock loading, vegetable peddling, and occasionally factory work. Discrimination by employers as well as antagonism by workers of Jiangnan origins further contributed to their tracking into jobs that paid low wages and required physical strength. Desperation for work, perhaps combined with resentment at their discriminatory treatment by the Shanghai elite, led some Subei people to work for the Japanese when they invaded Shanghai in 1932—making them more despised then ever before.

Subei people certainly were immigrant refugees, shack settlement dwellers, coolie laborers, and collaborators in Shanghai. They may even have represented the majority of these groups. But Subei identity took on a life of its own, one that derived from but was not confined to the reality of Subei people's own experience. Thus, the name Subei was attached to almost all despised groups: Subei refugees, Subei hut dwellers, Subei collaborators, and Subei swines. An individual did not have to actually be from northern Jiangsu to be called a Subei person. Moreover, the establishing of a non-Subei identity was often the basis upon which people maneuvered for status, good work, and a sense of self-respect.

For Jiangnan natives, the creation and ascription of Subei identity established, in part, the other against which they could define themselves and claim, eventually, a Shanghai identity. Jiangnan tastes defined Shanghai: what came to be known as Shanghai dialect derived from the Wu dialect of Jiangnan and differed from and excluded the Yangzhou-based dialects of Subei; what came to be defined as Shanghai local opera was based on Jiangnan traditions, as opposed to the Yangzhou and Huai operas of the north; Shanghai cuisine, too, derived from Jiangnan tastes. To be a *Shanghai ren* was to be urbane and sophisticated like the Jiangnan elite, in contradistinction to the crude, backward natives of Subei. Subei became the yardstick against which modernity in Shanghai was defined.

The need for Jiangnan natives to distinguish themselves from Subei people may have been especially acute because of Shanghai's status as a treaty port. From the mid-nineteenth century until the dissolution of the International and French concessions in 1945, foreign power in Shanghai could not be ignored. Although it is impossible to know whether Subei people would have functioned as an ethnic group had Shanghai not been a treaty port, the fact of the matter is that foreigners shaped the city's political and social life in profound ways. Among the Chinese population Jiangnan natives may have been the undisputed elite, but they were always subordinate to foreigners. To the extent that foreigners portrayed all Chinese as uncivilized and backward, the antidote to their modernity, Jiangnan natives may have more desperately than otherwise needed to create an other.

The Subei identity, however, was more than a mirror for Jiangnan people's self-definition in Shanghai. It was also a metaphor for class, as the discourse about Subei people was often one about wealth versus poverty. To be poor in Shanghai, to live in the hut settlements, to perform coolie labor was to be a Subei person. Even among natives of northern Jiangsu themselves, the term *Subei* connoted class, as evidenced by the condescending attitudes of Yangzhou natives toward their poorer northern neighbors of Yancheng, Funing, and Huai'an.

The experience of Subei people in Shanghai demonstrates the potential class dimensions of native place identity. However, just as ethnicity is not synonymous with class, so too native place identity cannot be understood as simply a metaphor for class. The two are inextricably bound, but neither can be reduced to the other. "The origins of ethnic groups and consciousness may lie in the structuring of inequality," observes the anthropologist John Comaroff:

> But, once objectified as a "principle" by which the division of labor is organized, ethnicity assumes the autonomous character of a prime mover in the unequal destinies of persons and populations. To wit, just as working class black Americans do not view their blackness as a function of their class position, but their class position as a function of their blackness, so underclass Hutu in Rwanda or Kgalagadi in Botswana see their status as being ascribed by virtue of their ethnic affiliation and not vice versa.

So too in Shanghai did Subei ethnicity take on a life of its own, such that Subei people viewed their inferior class status as a function of their ethnic identity, not vice versa.[2]

That northern Jiangsu natives themselves rarely shed their more local identities to evidence a Subei consciousness was almost irrelevant to the belief in the social category Subei people. In the immigrant city of Shanghai, Jiangnan natives constituted the elite and as such had more power to establish the terms of discourse, both about social categories constructed according to native place identities as well as who qualified as a truly native Shanghainese. Subei people sometimes challenged the categories, but they were not equally positioned in the contest. As the anthropologist Brackette Williams points out in a critical review of theories of ethnicity,

Anthropological analysis of identity formation processes within a population that shares a political unit requires the recognition that not all individuals have equal power to fix the coordinates of self-other identity formation. Nor are individuals equally empowered to opt out of the labeling process, to become the invisible against which others' visibility is measured. The illusion that self and other ascriptions among groups are made on equal terms fades when we ask whether those who identify themselves with a particular ethnic identity could also successfully claim *no* ethnic identification. If their group became the dominant power group in the political unit such a claim might be possible.[3]

In Shanghai, Jiangnan natives were the dominant group; it was they who had the power to formulate *self* and *other*. Subei people, in contrast, could not "opt out of the labeling process." This does not mean, however, that Subei people were passive actors in the process of ethnic formation. They may not have been positioned equally, but they did, as we have seen, articulate somewhat different categories from those imposed by the elite. For many northern Jiangsu natives, Jianghuai was far more meaningful an identity than Subei (or Jiangbei). Moreover, by insisting on their more local origins and identities, they resisted the construction of the negatively charged category Subei. Occasionally, too, they explicitly challenged the negative traits ascribed them.

On the surface it may appear that throughout Shanghai's development in modern times, the belief in the category Subei people as well as the prejudice against them has been an unchanging element of popular thought. However, difficult though it may be to document, the intensity of these beliefs and prejudices most likely varied over time. More important, their content changed. At some times the prejudice against Subei natives reflected a disdain for a people perceived as poor and backward; at other times it also represented a contempt for people believed to be collaborators with the Japanese or troublemakers; in the aftermath of the Cultural Revolution it may have involved anger toward members of the working class; during the post-Mao era it may have coincided with hostility toward officials. Contempt for the poor may be the most constant element in the prejudice, yet even that cannot be understood as something static, for the structure of Subei people's poverty has changed radically over time. What it meant to be poor in early twentieth-century treaty-port Shanghai was very different from the meaning of poverty in the post-1949 socialist state. Indeed, even the structure of poverty in the post-Liberation decade of the 1950s (when poverty was a banner of pride) differed from that accompanying the post-Mao economic reforms of the 1980s (when "to be rich was glorious").

For students of Chinese history, the study of Subei people raises several inevitable questions. The first concerns the broader historical context in which the creation of native place ethnicity in Shanghai took place. From China's defeat by the British in the Opium Wars of the mid-nineteenth century, nationalism was a major theme of Chinese political, intellectual, and social movements: the Self-Strengthening Movement of the 1870s, the May Fourth Movement of 1919, the May Thirtieth Movement of 1925, the Nationalist Revolution of 1927, the anti-Japanese patriotic movements of the 1930s, and the Communist revolution of 1949. It might seem curious, at first glance, that ethnic identities were forged during a period of such intense nationalist sentiment. If anything, one might expect greater Han unity, not inter-Han divisions. Yet nationalism and parochialism are not mutually exclusive, and in fact rarely does nationalism transcend provincial identities and loyalties. Even the casual observer of events in eastern Europe in the late 1980s and early 1990s—events dominated by the resurgence of violent ethnic strife—cannot help being struck by how thin the veneer of nationalist sentiment is, how quickly it has crumbled. Perhaps more pertinent to the case of Subei people in Shanghai is the observation made by David Strand in his study of Beijing workers: rather than transcending ethnic identities, nationalist movements of twentieth-century China may have provided occasions for their public exhibition.[4] Moreover, the formation of ethnic identities quite possibly helped give structure and meaning to the unsettling, traumatic events of twentieth-century Chinese history.

A second question raised by the experience of Subei people concerns the uniqueness of native place ethnicity to Shanghai. Is it only in Shanghai that native place identities have assumed ethnic meanings? There are at least four possible answers to this question: that only in Shanghai did native place identity become ethnic, that it became ethnic in urban contexts throughout China, that it became ethnic only in cities that were treaty ports, and that everywhere in China—in rural and urban areas—native place identity has been socially constructed and embedded in a system of power relationships.

One might speculate that in Shanghai the extremely high percentage of the population composed of immigrants made the formation of social categories different from that of other Chinese cities. Because almost everyone in Shanghai, no matter what their local origin, was an upstart, there was a degree of urgency to the struggle of immigrant communities to rank themselves. Shanghai's status as a treaty port, we have seen, placed an additional edge on the way in which Subei identity was constructed.

Only in the context of Hong Kong, also a treaty port and also a largely immigrant city, has the question of native place ethnicity been addressed. Anthropological investigations almost all assume or conclude that local origins did indeed function as ethnicity in Hong Kong, forming the basis of prejudice and discrimination. Perhaps ironically, one of the objects of prejudice among the native Guangdongese is the "Shanghainese"—a social category comprised not only of people from Shanghai proper, but from central and sometimes even northern China.[5]

Whether the ethnic function of native place identity extends beyond the treaty port cities of Shanghai and Hong Kong is impossible to determine at this point, as no studies of other cities have made it the focus of inquiry. Both David Strand's study of Beijing and William Rowe's of Hankou describe native place groups as playing an ethnic-like social role, but the data they present are insufficient to explore how native place identities inform popular culture, class structure, and social conflict. Casual conversation with Hankou residents suggests a disdain for Henan natives that is reminiscent of attitudes toward Subei people in Shanghai. Henan natives are looked down on, avoided as marriage partners, and perceived as being dirty and lacking in manners. One Wuhan native recalled visiting as a child the home of a primary school classmate from Henan who lived in the so-called Henan village and being stunned to find that his family's home was clean. At least one writer has observed a "Subei-like" phenomenon in Beijing, where natives of Sanhe *xian,* who historically filled the ranks of barbers, bathhouse attendants, and maids, are looked down on by Beijing natives.[6] In other words, further study may reveal that the role of native place identity, in Hankou and Beijing at least, may be somewhat analogous to that in Shanghai. The relative invisibility of native place ethnicity in local studies certainly does not mean that it does not exist, but rather that it may need to be more closely observed.

The application of theories of ethnicity to the experience of Subei people in Shanghai makes visible identities, social relationships, and historical processes that have been largely ignored in studies of Chinese history and society. Even if native place identity in China does not always assume—perhaps only rarely assumes—ethnic dimensions, an analysis of Subei people demonstrates the need to radically revise how native place is understood. No longer can it be interpreted as describing the literal, statically defined places that answers to questions on official documents imply. An individual's declaration of native place cannot be taken at face value.

Rather, native place identity—no matter where and when in China—must be understood as a social and historical construct.

In order to suggest new ways of analyzing native place identity in China, this history of Subei people has drawn on theories of ethnicity derived primarily from studies that concern neither China nor native place per se. Instead, they focus on immigrant and racial groups in the United States or tribal groups in Africa. Yet a study of these issues in the context of China may, in turn, highlight a form of ethnic identity—one based on native place—that is perhaps more prevalent in other historical and cultural contexts than has been previously recognized.[7] This book concerns the creation of Chinese ethnicity, but the ethnic dimensions of native place identity may prove not to be uniquely Chinese at all.

NOTES

CHAPTER 1. INTRODUCTION

1. See, e.g., Kraus; Walder; White; Davis-Friedmann.
2. See Handlin.
3. For an excellent historical analysis of the Okies, see Gregory.
4. Gregory, 102–03.
5. See, e.g., Gladney; Harrell, "Ethnicity, Local Interests, and the State." Pamela Crossley's study of the Manchus provides an excellent analysis of the way in which racial identity was a social construct, not a "thing real in itself." See Crossley, *Orphan Warriors*.
6. Cole, "Social Discrimination in Traditional China," 100–01.
7. Myron L. Cohen, 243–48. Also see Blake, 8–10, 49–50.
8. Blake, 1–2.
9. Averill.
10. Perdue, 97–112.
11. The significance of "native"/"immigrant" identities is emphasized by C. Fred Blake in his study of ethnicity in a market town in Guangdong. Blake, 12.
12. Goodman, 4.
13. Ho, "The Geographical Distribution"; Skinner, "Mobility Strategies."
14. Susan Mann Jones, "The Ningbo Pang."
15. Cole, *Shaohsing*.
16. Rawski and Naquin, 47.
17. Strand.
18. Rowe, *Hankow: Commerce and Society*, 247.
19. Ibid., 213–51, 259–67. Also see Rowe, *Hankow: Conflict and Community* for a discussion of the role of local origins.
20. Yanagisako; Blu; Clifford, esp. "Identity in Mashpee," 277–346.
21. Yancey, Ericksen, and Juliani, 400. Among the first to reject "common heri-

tage" as the basis of ethnicity was Frederik Barth, "Introduction," in Barth, 9–38.

22. For an analysis of the uses of the term *ethnic* by anthropologists, see Sollors, esp. 20–39. Also see Blu, 200–35.

23. Drummond, 354.

24. Mandel, 72.

25. Fei, *Toward a People's Anthropology,* 60–77.

26. See, for example, Lamley; Rowe, *Hankou: Commerce and Society,* 213–14, 246–47. In his study of overseas Chinese communities in Southeast Asia, Gary Hamilton wavers between calling groups defined by native place identity *ethnic* and *subethnic.* Hamilton, 338–41.

27. Crossley, "Thinking about Ethnicity in Early Modern China," 15. Crossley's critique of the term *subethnic* is echoed by Stevan Harrell, who in discussing ethnic identities in late Qing Taiwan, concludes that "so-called 'sub-ethnic' activity works exactly the same way as 'ethnic' activity." See Harrell, "From *Xiedou* to *Yijun,*" 109.

28. Skinner, "Introduction: Urban Social Structure in Ch'ing China," 544.

29. See Ownby; Harrell, "From *Xiedou* to *Yijun.*"

30. Gates.

31. See Blake.

32. As Dru Gladney points out, Blake's description of ethnic groups among the Han population of the New Territories has provoked almost no controversy, perhaps because the locale is Hong Kong, not China "proper." "What will happen to these so-called ethnic groups once Hong Kong reverts to China?" Gladney appropriately asks. "Will Blake be criticized for confusing sub-regional identity with ethnicity?" (Gladney, 306–07) Presumably the same question applies to ethnicity on Taiwan.

33. Li Weiqing, 108. This passage was originally cited in Goodman, 1.

34. From 1885 to 1935, Shanghai natives accounted for an average of only 19 percent of the population of the International Concession and 26 percent of the Chinese-owned parts of the city. Zou, 112–13.

35. Leung, "Regional Rivalry," 30–31.

36. Ibid., 29–50

CHAPTER 2. IN SEARCH OF SUBEI

1. Jin, 10–11.

2. Examples of the use of the term *Jiangbei ren* can be found in almost any issue of Shanghai's daily newspaper *Shenbao.* For some specific cases, see Mar. 7, 1872; Mar. 7, 9, 13, 1915; Apr. 24, 1915; Sept. 28, 1915.

3. For an analysis of the construction of definitions of Appalachia, see Batteau.

4. Fei, "Small Towns," 88.

5. As Wang Nanbi, in his survey of Jiangbei villages, put it, "This area, in terms of geography, history, customs, and personality, is a coherent unit." Wang Nanbi, 610.

6. Quoted in Finnane, 103.

7. Stauffer.

8. Esherick, 19.

9. Quoted in Esherick, 23.

10. Wang Peitang, 348–49.

11. Ash, 268–69.

12. Finnane, 101.

13. Ibid., 107–11.

14. Perry, *Rebels and Revolutionaries,* 10–47. The treatment of the northernmost parts of Jiangsu and southern Shandong as composing a coherent region is also depicted in *The Death of Woman Wang* by Jonathan Spence, particularly in his comparison of Tancheng (in southern Shandong) and Peixian (in northern Jiangsu). See Spence, 118.

15. Esherick, 18–19.

16. Chen Guofu, 19.

17. Fan, 1.

18. Yi, 4, 28.

19. Wang Shuhuai, 67.

20. Zhou Zhenhe and You Rujie, 25. Also see Zhao, chap. 8, pp. 192–5.

21. Jiangsusheng he Shanghaishi fangyan diaocha zhidaozu, 1–27.

22. Zhou Zhenhe and You Rujie, 44. Also see Jiang Junzhang, pt. 3, p. 2.

23. Zhou Zhenhe and You Rujie, 44.

24. Jiang Junzhang, pt. 3, p. 3.

25. Wang Peitang asserts that all Huaibei people (meaning, in his study, the part of Jiangsu north of the Huai) speak Shandong dialect. He also believes that Huaiyin and Huai'an people speak Shandong dialect. Wang Peitang, 369. Li Changfu also says that people in Huaibei speak Shandong dialect. Li Changfu, 103. Also see Jiang Junzhang, pt. 3, p. 3.

26. "Jingjiang funü shenghuo."

27. Zhou Zhenhe and You Rujie, 44.

28. Li Changfu, 23.

29. Wang Peitang, 348.

30. Wang Shuhuai, 67.

31. For an account of the origins of Huai opera, see Gao Yilong, Ji Sufan, and Zhang Chi, 27–28. Also see Zhongguo dabaike quanshu xiqu quyi bianxiezu, 130.

32. Chen Debo, 18–26; Zhongguo dabaike quanshu xiqu quyi bianxiezu, 527–28.

33. Fan, 1.

34. Feng Hefa, vol. 1, p. 341.

35. Welch, 255.

36. Fei, "Small Towns," 91.

37. Hinton, "The Grain Tribute System of the Ch'ing Dynasty," 339–54.

38. E. H. Schafer quoted in Finnane, 34.

39. See Finnane's excellent dissertation on Yangzhou and its hinterland, 2, 279–304. Also see Ho, "The Salt Merchants of Yang-chou," 156–58, and Zhu Zongshou, 13–19.

40. Shanghai tongshe, 504–07.

41. Jones and Kuhn, 119.
42. Ruan Yuan quoted in Finnane, 4–5. For a discussion of the decline of the Grand Canal, see Jameson.
43. Faure, 37.
44. Wang Shuhuai, 12–13.
45. For an excellent analysis of the economic development of Jiangnan, see Philip C. C. Huang.
46. Naquin and Rawski, 101.
47. Mann, "Women's Work and the Household Economy," 16.
48. Luo Qiong, 108.
49. Wang Shuhuai, 326.
50. Ibid., 428–29.
51. Quoted in Perry, *Rebels and Revolutionaries,* 34.
52. Li Pingheng, 2–3.
53. Bureau of Foreign Trade.
54. Wang Nanbi, 622.
55. Zhao Ruheng, chap. 8, pp. 17–22.
56. Philip C. C. Huang, 119. Also see Walker.
57. Fei, "Small Towns," 88–89.
58. For a discussion of the governing of Jiangsu during the early Qing, see Ocko, 23.
59. Hinton, *The Grain Tribute System of China,* 75. It is interesting to note that this new Jianghuai Province was to include Nanjing as well.
60. Richards, 164.
61. For a discussion of the various proposals made in the 1930s, see Jiang Junzhang, pt. 5, pp. 6–7.
62. Johnson, 149.
63. Ash, 263.

CHAPTER 3. FROM IMMIGRANTS TO ETHNICS

1. The anthropologist Frederik Barth emphasizes the articulation of cultural, social, and economic boundary markers as the essence of ethnicity. See Barth.
2. Fei, "Small Towns," 107.
3. Faure, 163.
4. Junkin, 79–80. The experience of a family like the Zhangs is the subject of Pearl Buck's classic novel *The Good Earth.* Although set in Anhui, Wang Lung's experience is a quintessential Subei one: he and his family flee their village after it is devastated by floods; they make their way to a "southern city" (which could be Shanghai, Nanjing, Wuxi, or any Jiangnan city), where they seek out soup kitchens and relief agencies. Eventually they live in a shack settlement; he makes a living by pulling a rickshaw, while his wife and children beg. They are looked down on by "southerners" both because of their northern-sounding dialect as well as for the smell of garlic on their breath.
5. Bernhardt, 130. The migrants who settled in Jiangnan in the 1880s were not

all from Subei. There were famine refugees from Hunan, Hubei, and Henan as well. Little is known about what percentage of these refugees Subei people represented.

6. Wang Shuhuai, 455. Wang observes that from 1911 to 1934, Subei was the major source of immigrants to Yixing.

7. Ibid., 454–55.

8. Fei, "Small Towns," 107.

9. Muramatsu, 581.

10. Wang Shuhuai, 454. Wang observes that during the Republican period, most of the shack dwellers (*pengmin*) in Wuxi were from such Subei areas as Yancheng, Dongtai, and Taixian. Also see Kyong, 5.

11. Wang Shuhuai, 455. Also see Wang Peitang, 363.

12. Tao Jitian, 114–15.

13. This observation was first made in Wu Shoupeng, 69. It was quoted in the following: Feng Hefa, vol. 1, pp. 361–62; Wang Peitang, 365; Luo Meihuan, 70; Jiang Junzhang, pt. 4, pp. 7–8.

14. This edict is dated July 9, 1814. *Daqing shichao shengxun*, 1820. I am grateful to Harold Kahn for calling my attention to this document.

15. Faure, 279–80.

16. *Shibao*, Aug. 3, 1911.

17. Unfortunately, data that would make possible a history of migration from northern Jiangsu to Shanghai, including the number of migrants, are not available. Nowhere is the percentage of the Shanghai population composed of northern Jiangsu migrants recorded. Only one statistic is available: in 1949, approximately 1,500,000 Subei people allegedly lived in Shanghai, representing one-fifth of the city's population at that time. Xie Junmei, 112. On the one hand, this statistic is dubious: Xie cites no source nor is it clear whether the number includes all people of Subei heritage or only first-generation immigrants. Nor is it clear how *Subei* is defined. On the other hand, however, the figure is probably roughly indicative of the percentage of the Shanghai population composed by northern Jiangsu immigrants through most of the Republican period, as immigrants from all parts of Jiangsu consistently represented close to 50 percent of the city's population. Zou Yiren, 114–5.

18. *North China Herald*, Feb. 22, 1907.

19. Tōa dobunkai, vol. 1, pp. 388–89.

20. "Flood Damage in China during 1931," 343–44.

21. Shanghai Municipal Council, *Report for the Year 1931 and Budget for the Year 1932*, 66.

22. Xu Shiying, 17–18. The statistics in this report show that of the 75,004 registered refugees, 33,053 were from Jiangsu. Map 4 shows that the overwhelming majority of those from Jiangsu were from the Subei.

23. *Da gong bao*, Sept. 20, 1947.

24. Subei nanmin jiuji huiyi Shanghai banshichu.

25. Ibid., 49.

26. Zhang Yaozhong, 82.

27. Records of the Subei Haimen liuwang nanmin jiuji xiehui, 10–11.
28. See, for example, *Shenbao*, Sept. 18, 1931.
29. *Shibao*, Jan. 8, 20, 1911.
30. *Shibao*, June 11, 1911.
31. *Shenbao*, Mar. 8, 1911.
32. Shanghai Municipal Council, *Report for the Year 1917*, 61a. I am grateful to Ruth Rogaski for bringing this report to my attention.
33. Shanghai Municipal Council, *Report for the Year 1935 and Budget for the Year 1936*, 189.
34. Shanghai Police Daily Reports, Dec. 7, 1925.
35. Clark, 67. I am grateful to James Finkle for calling attention to this passage.
36. For a description of these boats, see Xu Ke, vol. 90, p. 7. For a small number of Subei people, living in shack settlements was a step down. For example, one hut resident was a man from Funing in his fifties. When he first came to Shanghai, he had a small business selling medicine on Chaoyang Road. Eventually, as business declined, he was forced to close his shop. Unable to afford rent where he lived, he had no choice but to move to a hut settlement. *Shenbao*, Sept. 9, 1936.
37. Shanghai shehui kexueyuan, jingji yanjiusuo, *Shanghai penghuqude bianqian*, 11.
38. Ibid.; Zhang Jiaqi and Ban Zhiwen, 237.
39. Shanghai chuzu qiche gongsi, vol. 2, p. 201.
40. Shanghai shehui kexueyuan jingji yanjiusuo, *Shanghai penghuqude bianqian*, 11–12.
41. Zhang Jiaqi and Ban Zhiwen, 237.
42. Honig, 23.
43. Zhang Jiaqi and Ban Zhiwen, 237.
44. Zhu Bangxing, Hu Lin'ge, and Xu Sheng, 598.
45. Darwent.
46. Shanghai shehui kexueyuan jingji yanjiusuo, *Shanghai penghuqude bianqian*, 3.
47. Ibid., 4.
48. Ibid.
49. Ibid.
50. Ibid., 6.
51. Ibid., 6, 16.
52. Ibid., 7.
53. Ibid., 9.
54. *Shenbao*, Sept. 24, 1872.
55. Shanghai shehui kexueyuan, jingji yanjiusuo, *Shanghai penghuqude bianqian*, 28.
56. M. T. Tchou quoted in Fang Fu-an, 123–24.
57. Shanghai shehui kexueyuan, jingji yanjiusuo, *Shanghai penghuqude bianqian*, 21.
58. *Shenbao*, Mar. 14, 1937.
59. Shanghai shehui kexueyuan jingji yanjiusuo, *Shanghai penghuqude bianqian*, 21.
60. Ibid., 22.
61. Ibid., 22–3.

62. *Shenbao,* Mar. 8, 1936.

63. Shanghai shehui kexueyuan, jingji yanjiusuo, *Shanghai penghuqude bianqian,* 2.

64. *Shenbao,* Sept. 24, 1872.

65. *Shenbao,* Mar. 31, 1915, July 17, 1921.

66. Shanghai shehui kexueyuan, jingji yanjiusuo, *Shanghai penghuqude bianqian,* 28.

67. Shanghai Municipal Council, *Report for the Year 1931 and Budget for the Year 1932,* 155–56.

68. Shanghai Municipal Council, *Report for the Year 1932 and Budget for the Year 1933,* 211.

69. Ibid., 202.

70. *Shenbao,* July 12, 1936.

71. Ibid.

72. *Shenbao,* July 16, 18, 1936.

73. *Shenbao,* Sept. 3, 4, 1936.

74. *China Weekly Review,* May 8, 1937.

75. Shanghai shehui kexueyuan, jingji yanjiusuo, *Shanghai penghuqude bianqian,* 28.

76. *Shenbao,* Dec. 7, 10, 1946.

77. For an overly optimistic account of the Party's attempts to eliminate the hut districts, see Shanghai shehui kexueyuan, jingji yanjiusuo, *Shanghai penghuqude bianqian,* 53–80.

78. Luo Meihuan, 70; *Shenbao,* March 1, 6, 31, 1915.

79. Wang Dunqing, 17–18.

80. Jin Yuan, 9.

81. Cao Hui, 10.

82. Zhongguo xijujia xiehui and Shanghaishi wenhuaju, 5.

83. Zhongguo dabaike quanshu xiqu quyi bianxiezu, 130, 528.

84. Liu Peiqian, 201–02, 207–09.

85. *Shenbao,* Apr. 1, 1932.

86. Chen Debo, 22.

87. Interview with Xiao Wenyan.

88. Gao Yilong, Ji Sufan, and Zhang Chi, 29.

89. *Shenbao,* Jan. 6, 1947.

90. Gao Yilong, 17–18, 26–29.

91. Zhou Zhenhe and You Rujie, 50.

92. Liu Peiqian, 143.

93. Li Tiangang, 235.

94. Xu Ke, vol. 80, pp. 79–80. For the Yangzhou *bang* of prostitutes in Hankou, see Ceng Xianluo, 145. Yangzhou women, at least during the Qing, were particularly desirable as courtesans for the emperor. See Ko.

95. Zhu Bangxing, Hu Lin'ge, and Xu Sheng, 81–82.

96. Interview with Xu Shumei.

97. Yi Junzuo, 7.

98. See Liu Peiqian, 119–29.

99. Tu Shipin, pt. 3, p. 10. Artistic styles in Shanghai may also reflect a marginaliza-

tion of Subei tastes, although here the evidence is less clear-cut. Qing-dynasty Yangzhou had not only been the home of some of China's most famed artists (including the Yangzhou Eccentrics), but boasted its own style of painting. While nothing systematic has been written about the ways in which Yangzhou styles influenced the Shanghai school of painting that began to develop in the mid-nineteenth century, James Soong suggests that the influence was noticeable primarily by its absence. Taking issue with previous scholars who assumed that the Shanghai school was an offshoot of the prestigious Yangzhou school, Soong finds it more plausible that both drew on the same artistic sources, making Yangzhou itself largely irrelevant to Shanghai painting. In other words, in an enterprise for which Yangzhou's cultural heritage might well have been explicitly praised, it appears to have been ignored. Soong.

100. Quan Zhuanzhan, 43–44. The definition of *Jiangbei swine* (*Jiangbei zhuluo*) explains that it is a curse word describing the resemblance of Jiangbei people to pigs. It also refers to the fact that "Jiangbei coolies are illiterate and stupid. Their food is like pig slop."

CHAPTER 4. SUBEI NATIVES IN THE LABOR MARKET

1. Murphey.
2. Liu Huiwu et al., vol. 2, pp. 12–23.
3. For an analysis of the role of Irish immigrants in London's labor market, see Lees, 88–122. It should be noted that there were individuals from northern Jiangsu who worked at more prestigious jobs. For examples, see *Shanghai shirenzhi*. Also see Shanghaishi shanghui.
4. Shanghaishi chuzu qiche gongsi, 17.
5. Huang Renjing, 85.
6. Shanghaishi shehuiju, 103.
7. Ibid.
8. Shanghaishi renlicheye tongye gonghui, 3.
9. Biweng, 60–64.
10. Chen Caitu, quoted in Lei Jingdun. Courtesy of Elizabeth Perry.
11. Ibid. Also see Shanghaishi shehuiju, 54.
12. Zhu Bangxing, Hu Lin'ge, and Xu Sheng, 573. In addition to the Subei *bang* there was also a Hubei, Ningbo, and Canton *bang* at the docks. According to one study, workers from Subei did the heaviest jobs of transporting cargo on shoulder poles, while those from Canton worked aboard the boats, arranging cargo. Shanghai gangshi hua bianxiezu, 276–79.
13. Perry, *Shanghai on Strike*, chap. 3, p. 8.
14. Shanghai gangshi hua bianxiezu, 276.
15. Li Cishan, 60. Quite possibly, Subei people's domination of the transport industry was related to the demobilization of labor along the Grand Canal in the nineteenth century, and subsequent migration of former employees from Subei to Shanghai.

16. Shanghai shehui kexueyuan lishi yanjiusuo, 12. Li Cishan, 48–49. Also see *Shenbao,* Apr. 26, 1915.

17. Wei, 75–76.

18. Li Cishan, 79–80. Also see Shanghaishi renmin zhengfu gongshangju jingji jihuachu, 66.

19. For cobblers, see *Shenbao,* Apr. 26, 1915; for night soil collectors, see interview with Zhou Guozhen; for garbage collectors, see Zhu Bangxing, Hu Lin'ge, and Xu Sheng, 607.

20. Zhu Bangxing, Hu Lin'ge, and Xu Sheng, 607.

21. Interview with workers at the Shanghai Jing'an District Sanitation Bureau.

22. Li Cishan, 48–49.

23. Interview with workers at the Jing'an District Sanitation Bureau.

24. Interview with Zhou Guozhen.

25. Honig, 59–62.

26. The possibility that Subei people were latecomers to factory work, suggested by the scarce factory records that are available, is reinforced by the description of Subei people in a Japanese study written in 1909. The author observed a "class" comprising Subei people, who worked as cobblers, coolies, cart and rickshaw pullers, night soil and garbage collectors, and peddlers. No mention was made of Subei people as factory workers at that time. This does not imply that no Subei people worked in factories, but rather that their number was relatively small. See Tōa dobunkai, vol. 1, pp. 388–89.

27. Zhongguo shehui kexueyuan jingji yanjiusuo, ed., *Shanghai minzu jiqi gongye,* vol. 1, pp. 50–51, 58, 68. Also see Leung, "Regional Rivalry," 9–40.

28. Shanghai Bureau of Social Affairs, 80–81. These wage statistics serve only as a rough index of the differences in earnings of workers in Jiangnan-dominated versus Subei-dominated industries. As averages, they represent workers in all workshops of particular industries, female, male, and child workers, those employed on both time and piece rates. They do not take into account the seasonal nature of some industries.

29. The division of labor according to native place in the cotton industry is discussed more extensively in Honig, 72–74.

30. Interview with He Zhiguang.

31. Shanghai Bureau of Social Affairs, 102–03, 108–09. This represents the wage for women in the weaving department of cotton mills, whereas the $.61 listed above is for women in separate weaving mills.

32. Honig, 73.

33. Zhu Bangxing, Hu Lin'ge, and Xu Sheng, 125.

34. Deng, 9–10.

35. Perry, *Shanghai on Strike,* chap. 7, p. 9.

36. Ibid., chap. 7, p. 7.

37. Shanghai shehui kexueyuan jingji yanjiusuo, *Nanyang xiongdi yancao gongsi shiliao,* 74.

38. Shanghai shehui kexueyuan jingji yanjiusuo, *Rongjia qiye shiliao,* vol. 1, pp. 134.
39. Shanghai shehui kexueyuan jingji yanjiusuo, *Jiangnan zaochuanchang changshi, 1865–1949.5,* 155.
40. Zhu Bangxing, Hu Lin'ge, and Xu Sheng, 236, 247, 340. Xu Dejing is described in the Shanghai Municipal Police Files, Jan. 12, 1940, D4176 (reel 12).
41. *Shenbao,* Dec. 18, 1939, translated in Shanghai Municipal Police Files, D4176 (reel 12).
42. Honig, 71. Also see Huang Renjing, 127. For a far more detailed discussion of the hierarchy of prostitution, see Hershatter.
43. Hershatter, 472.
44. Interview with Zhou Guozhen.
45. Interview with retired workers at Zhongxing Street Residence Committee (Zhabei District, Shanghai).
46. Interview with Chen Dewang.
47. Tu Shipin, pt. 3, p. 90. Also see Wei, 69.
48. Xu Ke, vol. 92, pp. 1–2.
49. Wang Shuhuai, 455.
50. Zhang Jiaqi, 238.
51. Wu Yuanshu and Jiang Sitai. Courtesy of Elizabeth Perry.
52. Ibid.
53. Huang Renjing, 171.
54. Zhuan, 96–98, 122–23.
55. Xue, "Jindai Shanghaide liumang," 168.
56. Ruiz, 64.
57. Interview with Zhang Ronghua.
58. Wang Shuhuai, 466.
59. Laurie, Hershberg, and Alter.
60. Wu Liangrong, 177.
61. Yi Junzuo, 10.
62. Cao, 10–11.
63. This observation is based on interviews I conducted with retired women cotton mill workers during 1979–81 as well as on a survey of retirement cards indicating each worker's personal history.
64. Interview with He Zhenghua and Xu Liansheng. Studies of overseas Chinese communities in Southeast Asia find that although migrants from the same native place who speak the same dialect tend to concentrate in certain occupations, "the occupations monopolised by a given speech community in one place belong to others in different places and have nothing to do with regional specialisations back in China." Crissman, 186.
65. Honig, 79–93.
66. Shanghaishi shanghui.
67. Ibid.
68. Interview with Shi Xiaomei. A survey of jobs held by peasants who immigrated to Shanghai from Wuxi (1932) confirms the different opportunities for

Jiangnan peasants: most worked in cotton and silk factories, the machinery industry, noodle and food stores. Wang Shuhuai, 466.

69. Ho, "The Salt Merchants of Yang-chou," 166–67.

70. Rowe, *Hankou: Commerce and Society,* 232.

71. Leung, "Regional Rivalry," 29–30.

72. In fact, from 1730 to 1911, the number of Shanghai *daotai,* subprefects, and magistrates from Zhejiang was higher than that from any other province. Leung, *The Shanghai Taotai,* 25–26.

73. Leung, "Regional Rivalry," 43–44.

74. Xue, "Jindai Shanghaide liumang," 160–78.

75. Feng, vol. 1, pp. 359–60.

76. Zhuan Xiangyuan, 92.

77. Xue, "Wo jiechuguode Shanghai banghui renwu," 95–96.

78. Interview with Gu Shuping. Alley, 26–27.

79. Leung, "Regional Rivalry," 40. Also see Jones, "The Ningpo Pang."

80. The only study that deals extensively with guilds and native place associations in Shanghai is Tadashi Negishi, *Chūgoku no girudo.* Also see his *Shanhai no girudo.* His study makes no reference to Subei associations in Shanghai.

81. The association was the Yangzhou bashu gongsuo (Yangzhou eight-county guild) and was reported in *Shenbao,* Jan 4, 1917. A Yangzhou bayi lühu tong-xianghui (Association of sojourners in Shanghai from the eight counties of Yangzhou) was reported in *Shenbao,* Sept. 2, 1931; a Dongtai lühu tongxianghui (Association of sojourners in Shanghai from Dongtai) was reported in *Shenbao,* Sept. 8, 1931; a Xinghua tongxianghui (Association of sojourners in Shanghai from Xinghua) in *Shenbao,* Sept. 10, 1931; a Huai'an liuyi huiguan (Huai'an six-county guild) is mentioned in Shanghaishi shanghui, 17, 94. In addition there were several associations that represented larger parts of Subei. For example, there was a Jianghuai lühu tongxianghui (Association of sojourners in Shanghai from Jianghuai) that existed at least from the mid-1920s. See *Shenbao,* July 7, 1925. There was also a Subei lühu tongxianghui (Association of sojourners in Shanghai from Subei), although nothing is known about its origins or development. It is mentioned in Gu Shuping, "Wo liyong Gu Zhuxuan," 360. For a more extensive discussion of these associations, see chapter 6.

82. See *Shenbao,* Sept. 2, 8, 10, 1931.

83. On Chinese workers in California factories see Ong, 69–82. On the Irish, see Griffen, 194. The fact that blacks did not become a major component of the industrial proletariat in the United States until World War II is discussed in Baron, 201.

84. Wang Peitang, 369.

85. Lu Manyan, 389.

86. Zhao Ruheng, chap. 8, p. 189.

87. Ge, vol. 2, p. 12.

88. Interview with He Zhiguang.

89. Honig, 76–77.

90. Ibid., 30–31, 77–78.
91. Shanghai shehui kexueyuan jingji yanjiusuo, *Jiangnan zaochuanchang*, 155.
92. Li Cishan, 12.
93. Griffen, 177. Also see Ong.
94. Granovetter and Tilly, 58–59.

CHAPTER 5. THE SELF-IDENTITY OF SUBEI PEOPLE

1. Sarna, 371.
2. Wolf, 381.
3. For the Jiangbei tongxiang weichihui see *Shibao*, Apr. 11, 1919; May 13, 20, 1919; *Shenbao*, July 7, 1925. The Subei lianshanhui is referred to in *Shenbao*, Nov. 27, 1926. For the Jiangbei gexian lühu tongxianghui lianhe banshichu see *Shenbao*, Feb. 13, 1936. Another Subei-wide organization existed in 1932, the Office for the Confederation of Native Place Associations of Huai'an, Yangzhou, and Nantong (Huai-yang-tong lühu tongxianghui lianhe banshichu). See *Shenbao*, Mar. 19, 1932. Nothing is known about the membership, activities, or longevity of any of these organizations.
4. Subei nanmin shourongsuo, Shanghai Municipal Archives (6–9-223). The Subei yanglao yuan is referred to in *Shanghai shirenzhi* (Atlas of the Shanghai elite), 80. The Subei yewu xiaoxuexiao is referred to in Subei nanmin jiuji huiyi Shanghai banshichu.
5. Jiangbei lühu tongxiang fuwushe luqi.
6. Subei nanmin jiuji huiyi Shanghai banshichu.
7. *Da gong bao*, Aug. 15, 1947.
8. *Shenbao*, Feb. 13, 1936.
9. Jiangbei lühu tongxiang fuwushe luqi.
10. The Yangzhou Guild (Yangzhou bashu gongsuo) is referred to in *Shenbao*, Jan. 4, 1917. Records for the Yangzhou bashu lühu tongxianghui for 1946–47 are held at the Shanghai Municipal Archives. The association is also referred to in *Shenbao*, Sept. 2, 1931.
11. The Huaiyin association is referred to in *Shenbao*, Nov. 26, 1936; the Haimen association in *Shenbao*, Dec. 7, 1936; the Xinghua association in *Shenbao*, Dec. 10, 1931; the Dongtai association in *Shenbao*, Sept. 8, 1931.
12. Records of all these associations are held at the Shanghai Municipal Archives.
13. Yi Junzuo, 28.
14. *Shenbao*, July 12, 17, 1934.
15. The Jianghuai Primary School is referred to in *Da gong bao*, July 4, 1947.
16. Jianghuai lühu tongxianghui.
17. For the Tong-ru-chong-hai-qi lühu tongxianghui, see Subei nanmin jiujihuiyi Shanghai banshichu. The Yan-fu tongxianghui is first mentioned in *Shenbao*, Mar. 3, 1926, and also May 10, 1937. Its records for 1946–47 are held at the Shanghai Municipal Archives (6–9–956).
18. Interview with Zhou Dianyuan.
19. Interview with Xia Keyun, Aug. 4, 1988.

20. Interview with Xu Liansheng.
21. Liu Housheng, 250.
22. Interview with Zhou Dianyuan.
23. Interview with Xia Keyun, Cheng Jinfan, and Pan Jingan, Aug. 4, 1988.
24. Interview with workers at Zhabei District Sanitation Bureau.
25. Interview with Xia Keyun, Aug. 4, 1988.
26. Interview with Chen Jinfan. Interview with workers at Zhabei District Sanitation Bureau. Interview with retired people at Zhongxing Street Residence Committee.
27. See Huai-yang lühu tongxiang fulihui, 1948; Jianghuai lühu tongxianghui; Huai'an lühu tongxianghui.
28. Wu Liangrong, 177.
29. Li Cishan, 48–49.
30. Shanghaishi chuzu qiche gongsi, 127–29.
31. Interview with Zhou Guozhen.
32. Interview with Xia Keyun and Jiang Sanxiao, Aug. 27, 1988.
33. Interview with retired people at Zhongxing Street Residence Committee, Zhabei.
34. *Minguo ribao,* Aug. 11, 16, 1922. I am grateful to Elizabeth Perry for calling my attention to these reports.
35. Interview with Xia Keyun and Jiang Sanxiao.
36. Interview with Xia Keyun, Aug. 4, 1988.
37. *Minguo ribao,* July 8, 1926 (Courtesy of Elizabeth Perry).
38. These statistics are based on the membership lists of the Nantong lühu tongxianghui and the Huai'an lühu tongxianghui for 1947, both held at the Shanghai Municipal Archives.
39. These data are compiled from the membership lists of the Haimen lühu tongxianghui, the Yangzhou qixian lühu tongxianghui, and the Huai'an lühu tongxianghui. This material is held at the Shanghai Municipal Archives.
40. Ronald Cohen, 382.
41. Mandel, 61–63.
42. Gregory, 120.

CHAPTER 6. THE POLITICS OF PREJUDICE

1. Hauser, 192–93.
2. Shanghaishi mianfangzhi gongye tongye gonghui.
3. Pott, 240.
4. Hauser, 206–07.
5. Wakeman, 228–29.
6. *Shenbao,* Mar. 8, 1932; *Shibao,* Mar. 10, 1932.
7. Shanghai Municipal Police Files, D-3325: Mar. 3, 1932.
8. *Shibao,* Mar. 10, 1932.
9. *Shenbao,* Apr. 4, 1932.
10. Shanghai Municipal Police Files, D3445: Apr. 18, 1932 (reel 10).

11. Shanghai Municipal Police Files, D3445: Apr. 18, 1932 (reel 10); Shanghai Municipal Police Files, D8458: Aug. 23, 1939 (reel 50); Tao Juyin, 31.

12. Shanghai Municipal Police Files, D3445: Apr. 18, 1932; May 5, 1932 (reel 10).

13. Shanghai Municipal Police Files, D-3445: Apr. 18, 1932.

14. Shanghai Municipal Police Files, D3445: Apr. 7, 1932; Apr. 18, 1932 (reel 10).

15. Shanghai Municipal Police Files, D-3345: Apr. 18, 1932.

16. Shenbao, Apr. 16, 1932.

17. Shenbao, Mar. 11, 1932.

18. Shenbao, May 11, 1932.

19. Shibao, Mar. 12, 1932.

20. Shibao, Mar. 11, 1932.

21. Shibao, Apr. 1, 1932.

22. Shanghai Municipal Police Files, D-3660: Mar. 10, 1932.

23. Shanghai Municipal Police Files, D3255: Mar. 29, 1932; Apr. 4, 1932 (reel 8).

24. Shibao, Mar. 6, 1932.

25. Shenbao, Mar. 19, 1932; Apr. 4, 1932. Also see Cao Hui.

26. The complaint was made by the head of the Huai-yang-tong lühu tongxianghui. See Shenbao, Mar. 19, 1932.

27. Shanghai Municipal Police Files, D3325: Mar. 3, 1932 (reel 9).

28. Shanghai Municipal Police Files, D8039: Feb. 21, 1941 (reel 36).

29. Shanghai Municipal Police Files, D3445: May 2, 9, 30, 1932. Subei people were not the only ones to open these kinds of establishments. Whether or not they represented the majority is difficult to determine, as the native place origins of the proprietors is not always provided in the records. In one list of six relatively small gambling dens opened in Zhabei in 1932, three of the owners were from Subei, two from Canton, and one was not identified. Ibid., May 9, 1932.

30. Moen, 85, 88.

31. Ibid., 85–88. Also see Goris, 17–21. As in Shanghai, the line separating the perception and reality of collaboration is a blurred one. Both Goris and Moen point out that the extent of collaboration may have been exaggerated.

32. Boyle, 123–33.

33. Hale, 23.

34. Ibid.

35. Shenbao, Apr. 14, 1932. It is impossible to determine the local origins of the author of this dialogue, although given the defense of common charges against Subei people, he is most likely from Subei.

36. Yu-ji, 45.

37. Ibid.

38. Shenbao, Apr. 3, 1934.

39. Lu Manyan, 389.

40. Lu Xun, vol. 4, p. 55.

41. Yi Junzuo, 22.

42. Shanghai Municipal Police Files, D7682: Dec. 7, 1936. I am grateful to Frederic Wakeman, Jr., for calling my attention to this document.

43. Xue, "Wo jiechuguode Shanghai banghui renwu," 107; Tao Juyin, 70–71; Zhuan, 201–05.

44. The records of pro-Japanese activities in Shanghai during this period do not suggest that Subei people were particularly notorious as collaborators. See Shanghai Municipal Police Files, D8059 (reel 40). The people who ran the gambling operations in the Badlands were mostly from the Guangdong Chaozhou *bang*. Xue, "Wo jiechuguode Shanghai banghui renwu," 103–04.

45. As late as 1960, the editors of Lu Xun's works believed Subei people were collaborators: "In 1932, when the Japanese occupied Zhabei in Shanghai, they made a band of Chinese spy and loot for them. The two chief traitors were from the northern part of Jiangsu Province." Lu Xun, vol. 4, p. 55.

46. *Shenbao,* Mar. 19, 1932.

47. Bing, 311.

48. *Shenbao,* Apr. 19, 1932.

49. *Shenbao,* Mar. 19, 1932; *Shibao,* Mar. 16, 1932.

50. *Shibao,* Mar. 10, 1932.

51. *Shenbao,* Mar. 10, 1932.

52. Sarna, 372–74.

53. Politics—particularly the accusation of collaboration—has often been a factor in the creation of despised social categories in China. For example, the *duomin* (lazy people) of Zhejiang and Jiangsu were alleged to be members of a Mongol regiment that resisted the Ming conquest. According to another origin myth they were collaborators with the Japanese invaders of the Zhejiang coast in the mid-sixteenth century. See Mann, "Pariah Communities in Qing Society," 5. Also see Cole, "Social Discrimination in Traditional China," 101.

54. *Shibao,* Feb. 28, 29, 1924; Mar. 3, 1924. Also see "Kankan Jiangbei ren." I am grateful to Gail Hershatter for calling my attention to this article.

55. Another example is suggested by Chinese historian Yu Xinmin. He argues that during the suppression of the Taiping rebels in Shanghai in 1862, Shanghai people believed that the members of the Huai army guilty of the most violence and terror were from Subei and therefore began to despise Subei people (*Xinmin wanbao,* Mar. 12, 1987). Soldiers in the Huai army were indeed recruited from areas commonly thought of as Jiangbei in Shanghai: the northern Jiangsu districts from Yangzhou north to the Huai River as well as from northern Anhui, Li Hongzhang's home province (Wang Ermin, 115–30). Yet whether they were particularly noted for violence is difficult to determine, as little evidence exists that would shed light on the beliefs of Shanghai people at that time.

CHAPTER 7. SUBEI PEOPLE IN POST-1949 SHANGHAI

1. Yuan Henghui, 172.

2. For a written description of the use of some of these terms, see " 'Jiangnan' he 'Jiangbei.' " Another derogatory expression used in reference to Subei people is *liang kuai tou,* literally, a "two-pieced head." This expression derives from the

fact that in Subei dialect the words "here" and "there" are *zhekuai* and *lakuai*. Interview with Qian Nairong and Ruan Henghui.

3. "Firmly Grasp the Popularization of Standard Spoken Language and the Promotion of the Teaching of Chinese Phonetization." Courtesy of Mary Erbaugh.

4. Interview with Xiao Wenyan and Wang Jianmin. Also see Song Jingtian et al., 37.

5. Interview with Chen Zhaodi.

6. Interview with Qi Yufan.

7. Song Jingtian et al., 36–37.

8. Interview with Chen Dewang; interview with workers at Jing'an District Sanitation Bureau.

9. Zhou Erfu, 194.

10. Chen Zhongya et al., 23.

11. Wang Xiaoying.

12. Han Hufeng.

13. *Jiefang ribao,* July 23, 1989.

14. Wu Liangrong, 187–88.

15. Zhang Xinxin and Sang Ye, 537–38.

16. Interview with members of the New Fourth Army Research Institute.

17. Interview with Yang Zhangfu.

18. Personal interviews.

19. The listing of Jiangsu as one's native place is not a new phenomenon. Susan Mann's analysis of group marriages sponsored by the Ningbo Guild in the mid-1940s shows that most individuals from Subei listed "Jiangsu" as their native place (whereas those from Jiangnan identified their specific county). Mann, "The Cult of Domesticity."

20. Zhou Jian, 58.

21. Zhu Yan, 14.

22. Interview with Wang Jianmin.

23. Interview with Ma Xiuying.

24. Interview with Xiao Wenyan and Wang Jianmin.

25. Personal interview.

26. Han Hufeng.

27. Interview with Chen Dewang.

28. Wang Xiaoying.

29. Han Hufeng.

30. Interview with workers at Jing'an District Sanitation Bureau.

31. Interview with He Zhenghua.

32. Interview with Zhu Dongrun, professor, department of Chinese language and literature, Fudan University, in Wu Liangrong and Lan Chengdong, 27.

33. Interview with Mi Dianqun, in Wu Liangrong and Lan Chengdong, 28.

34. Peng Xiaoming.

35. Interview with He Zhenghua.

36. See Wu Liangrong, 180–84. The information about sanitation bureau workers

is from Chen Zhongya et al., 24; it is also based on interviews with workers
and officials at the Zhabei District Sanitation Bureau and at the Jing'an District
Sanitation Bureau.

37. Wu Liangrong, 183.

38. Ibid.

39. Chinese sociologists commonly cite the *ding ti* policy of the late 1970s to explain
the persisting patterns. Through this policy educated youth who had been sent
to the countryside during the Cultural Revolution could return to Shanghai if
one parent retired. The child would then be assigned to that parent's work unit.
This, however, does not explain the employment patterns of the 1950s, 1960s,
and most of the 1970s.

40. Some joint enterprises have been accused of refusing to hire Subei people.
Interview with Xu Ping (reporter for *Haitan*).

41. Wu Liangrong, 185. This finding is corroborated in Chen Zhongya et al., 25.
Also see *Jiefang ribao*, July 23, 1980.

42. Wang Hongguang, 56.

43. Interview with Xu Ping.

44. The number of "key schools" relative to the population of each district would
be one potential index of structural discrimination. Even this, however, is
problematic, as scattered evidence suggests that the existence of a key school in
a Subei neighborhood does not guarantee the admission of Subei natives. For
example, only 13.4 percent of the students graduating in 1981 from the Fudan
University Middle School were of Subei origins, even though this is a key
school that serves the Yangpu district, where a large number of Subei people
live. See Chen Zhongya et al., 25. Two key-point middle schools serve the
more than twenty thousand people who reside in the working-class district of
Pudong (across the Huangpu River from downtown Shanghai), yet many of
the slots are taken by children from other districts who commute to Pudong.
Interview with Zhu Shouyuan.

45. Conversations with students at Fudan University, 1979–81; interview with Zhu
Shouyuan.

46. Cheng Naishan, 6.

47. Ibid., 8.

48. Interview with members of the residence committee, Aiguo cun, Dinghai
jiedao.

49. Cheng Naishan, 5.

50. Chen Yewei, 1.

51. Chen Zhongya et al., 25.

52. The continued use of the expression *Jiangbei villages* in reference to these districts
is documented in Wang Hongguang, 56.

53. Interview with members of the New Fourth Army Research Institute, Shanghai
Academy of Social Sciences.

54. Gaan, 248–49.

55. Perry, *Shanghai on Stike,* "Conclusion," 24–25.

56. Personal communication from Edward Friedman, Jan. 30, 1990.

57. Ibid.

CHAPTER 8. THE ETHNIC DIMENSIONS OF NATIVE PLACE IDENTITY

1. Crossley, *Orphan Warriors*.

2. Comaroff, 312.

3. Williams, 420.

4. Strand, 196.

5. Guldin, 148–49.

6. *Shijie ribao*, Mar. 20, 1991. According to this article, a further analogy between Subei natives of Shanghai and Sanhe natives of Beijing exists: when Beijing was liberated in 1949 by the Eighth Route Army, most of the soldiers were from Sanhe *xian* (as most of the soldiers who liberated Shanghai were Subei natives belonging to the New Fourth Army.)

7. Indeed, the anthropologist Abner Cohen, in his classic analysis of the meaning of ethnicity, insisted that "the differences between the Chinese and the Indians, considered within their own respective countries, are national not ethnic differences." Abner Cohen, xi.

BIBLIOGRAPHY

Aiguo cun, Dinghai Street Residence Committee. Interview with members, Aug. 25, 1988.

Alley, Rewi. *Yo Banfa!* London, 1952.

Ash, Robert. "Economic Aspects of Land Reform in Kiangsu, 1949–52." *China Quarterly* 66 (June 1976): 261–92.

Averill, Stephen C. "The Shed People and the Opening of the Yangzi Highlands." *Modern China* 9, 1 (January 1983): 84–126.

Baron, Harold. "Racial Domination in Advanced Capitalism: A Theory of Nationalism and Divisions in the Labor Market." In Richard Edwards et al., eds., *Labor Market Segmentation*. Lexington, Mass.: D. C. Heath and Co., 1975.

Barth, Frederik. "Introduction." In Frederik Barth, ed., *Ethnic Groups and Boundaries*, 9–38. Boston: Little, Brown, 1969.

Batteau, Allen W. *The Invention of Appalachia*. Tucson: University of Arizona Press, 1990.

Bernhardt, Kathryn. *Rents, Taxes, and Peasant Resistance: The Lower Yangzi Region, 1840–1950*. Stanford: Stanford University Press, 1992.

Bing Qian. "Jiangbei ren sanzi" (The three words 'Jiangbei ren'). *Shenghuo zhoukan* (Life weekly) 7, 20 (May 21, 1932): 311.

Biweng. "Shanghaide renlichefu" (Rickshaw drivers in Shanghai). *Shanghai shenghuo* (Shanghai life) 4, 12 (December 1940): 60–64.

Blake, C. Fred. *Ethnic Groups and Social Change in a Chinese Market Town*. Honolulu: University Press of Hawaii, 1981.

Blu, Karen. *The Lumbee Problem: The Making of an American Indian People*. New York: Cambridge University Press, 1980.

Boyle, John Hunter. *China and Japan at War, 1937–1945*. Stanford: Stanford University Press, 1972.

Buck, Pearl. *The Good Earth*. New York: The John Day Co., 1931.

155

Bureau of Foreign Trade, Ministry of Industry. *China Industrial Handbooks: Kiangsu.* Shanghai, 1933.

Cao Hui. "Jiangbei funü shenghuo gaikuang" (The general living conditions of women in Jiangbei). *Nüsheng* (Women's voice) 2, 10 (February 1934): 10–11.

Ceng Xianluo. "Yangzhou qingqu" (Yangzhou melodies). *Jiangsu wenshi ziliao xuanji* (Selected materials on Jiangsu culture and history) 14 (1984): 118–49.

Chen Debo. "Jiangsu de kunju, xiju, he yangju" (Jiangsu's Kunshan, Wuxi, and Yangzhou operas). *Jiangsu wenshi ziliao xuanji* (Selected materials on Jiangsu culture and history) 14 (1984): 18–26.

Chen Dewang. Personal interview. Shanghai Taxicab Co., October 30, 1986.

Chen Guofu. *Suzheng huiyi* (Memories of governing Jiangsu). N.p.: Zhengzhong shuju, 1951.

Chen Jinfan. Personal interview. Shanghai Harbor Coal Handling Co., Aug. 4, 1988.

Chen Yewei. "Rang Nanshi jiuqu guanfa xinde huoli" (Let the old Nanshi district glow with new vitality). *Shanghaitan* (The bund) 8 (1988): 1.

Chen Zhaodi. Personal interview. Shanghai Number One Cotton Mill, April 11, 1981.

Chen Zhongya, Xu Zhuyuan, Ying Tingjia, and Wu Lijiang. "Guanyu qishi Subei-ren qingkuang de diaocha" (An investigation of discrimination against Subei people). *Shehui* (Society) 3 (1983): 23–26.

Cheng Naishan. "Qiong jie" (Poor street). *Xiaoshuo jia* (Writers) 2 (1984): 4–99.

China Weekly Review. Shanghai.

Clark, John C. *Sketches in and around Shanghai.* Shanghai: Shanghai Mercury and Celestial Empire, 1894.

Clifford, James. *The Predicament of Culture: Twentieth-Century Ethnography, Literature, and Art.* Cambridge: Harvard University Press, 1988.

Cohen, Abner, ed. *Urban Ethnicity.* London: Tavistock Publications, 1974.

Cohen, Myron. "The Hakka or 'Guest People': Dialect as a Sociocultural Variable in Southeastern China." *Ethnohistory* 15, 3 (1968): 237–92.

Cohen, Ronald. "Ethnicity: Problems and Focus in Anthropology." *Annual Review of Anthropology* 7 (1978): 379–403.

Cole, James H. *Shaohsing: Competition and Cooperation in Nineteenth-Century China.* Tucson: University of Arizona Press, 1986.

———. "Social Discrimination in Traditional China: The To-min of Shaohsing." *Journal of the Economic and Social History of the Orient* 25, 1 (February 1982): 100–12.

Comaroff, John. "Of Totemism and Ethnicity: Consciousness, Practice and the Signs of Inequality." *Ethnos* 52, 3–4 (1987): 301–23.

Crissman, Lawrence W. "The Segmentary Structure of Urban Overseas Chinese Communities." *Man* 2, 2 (June 1967): 183–201.

Crossley, Pamela Kyle. *Orphan Warriors: Three Manchu Generations and the End of the Qing World.* Princeton: Princeton University Press, 1990.

———. "Thinking about Ethnicity in Early Modern China." *Late Imperial China* 11, 1 (June 1990): 1–34.

Da gong bao. Shanghai.

Daqing shichao shengxun: Jiaxing (Imperial edicts of the Qing dynasty: Jiaxing reign). Taibei: Wenhai chubanshe, n.d.

Darwent, Charles Ewart. *Shanghai: A Handbook for Travellers and Residents*. Shanghai: Kelly and Walsh, 1905.

Davis-Friedmann, Deborah. "Intergenerational Inequality and the Chinese Revolution," *Modern China* (April 1985): 177–201.

Deng Yuzhi. "A Visit to a Silk Filature in Shanghai." *The Green Year Supplement* (November 1928): 9–10.

Drummond, Lee. "The Cultural Continuum: A Theory of Intersystems." *Man* 15, 2 (June 1980): 352–74.

Esherick, Joseph. *The Origins of the Boxer Uprising*. Berkeley: University of California Press, 1987.

Fan Shuping. "Jiangbei yixian" (A route through Jiangbei). *Jiangsu yuebao* (Jiangsu monthly) 4, 2 (Aug. 1, 1935): 1–5.

Fang Fu-an. *Chinese Labor*. Shanghai: Kelly and Walsh, 1931.

Faure, David. "Local Political Disturbances in Kiangsu Province, China, 1870–1911." Ph.D. dissertation, Princeton University, 1976.

Fei Hsiao Tung (Fei Xiaotong). "Small Towns in Northern Jiangsu." In Fei Hsiao Tung et al., *Small Towns in China*. Beijing: New World Press, 1986.

——— . *Toward a People's Anthropology*. Beijing: New World Press, 1991.

Feng Hefa. *Zhongguo nongcun jingji ziliao* (Materials on the Chinese rural economy). Shanghai: Liming shuju, 1933.

Finnane, Antonia. "Prosperity and Decline under the Qing: Yangzhou and Its Hinterland, 1644–1810." Ph.D. dissertation, The Australian National University, 1985.

"Firmly Grasp the Popularization of Standard Spoken Language and the Promotion of the Teaching of Chinese Phonetization." *Guangming ribao* (The Guangming daily), June 25, 1973. Translated in *Survey of the China Mainland Press*, July 9–13, 1973, 98–101.

"Flood Damage in China during 1931." *Chinese Economic Journal* 10, 4 (April 1932): 343–44.

Gaan, Margaret. *Last Moments of a World*. New York: W. W. Norton and Co., 1978.

Gao Yilong, Ji Sufan, and Zhang Chi. *Xiao Wenyan wutai shenghuo* (Xiao Wenyan's life on the stage). Shanghai: Shanghai wenyi chubanshe, 1986.

Gates, Hill. "Ethnicity and Social Class." In Emily Martin Ahern and Hill Gates, eds., *The Anthropology of Taiwanese Society*, 241–81. Stanford: Stanford University Press, 1981.

Ge Yuanxi. *Huyou zaji* (Miscellaneous records of travels in Shanghai). N.p., 1876.

Gladney, Dru C. *Muslim Chinese: Ethnic Nationalism in the People's Republic*. Cambridge: Council on East Asian Studies, Harvard University, 1991.

Goodman, Bryna. "The Native Place and the City: Immigrant Consciousness and Organization in Shanghai, 1853–1927." Ph.D. dissertation, Stanford University, 1990.

Goris, Jan-Albert. *Belgium in Bondage*. New York: L. B. Fischer, 1943.

Granovetter, Mark, and Charles Tilly. *Inequality and Labor Processes*. New York: The New School for Social Research, Working Paper Series, July 1986.

Gregory, James. *American Exodus: The Dust Bowl Migration and Okie Culture in California*. New York: Oxford University Press, 1989.

Griffen, Clyde. "The 'Old' Immigration and Industrialization: A Case Study." In Richard Ehrlich, ed., *Immigrants in Industrial America, 1850–1920*, 123–50. Charlottesville: University Press of Virginia.

Gu Shuping. Personal interview. Shanghai, Nov. 19, 1986.

———. "Wo liyong Gu Zhuxuande yanhu jinxing geming huodong" (I used the cover of Gu Zhuxuan to conduct revolutionary activities). In Zhongguo renmin zhengzhi xieshang huiyi, Shanghaishi weiyuanhui wenshi ziliao gongzuo weiyuanhui, ed., *Jiu Shanghaide banghui* (Gangs in old Shanghai), 360–66. Shanghai: Shanghai renmin chubanshe, 1986.

Guldin, Gregory. "Seven-Veiled Ethnicity: A Hong Kong Chinese Folk Model." *Journal of Chinese Studies* 1, 2 (June 1984): 139–56.

Hale, Charles. "Contradictory Consciousness: Miskitu Indians and the Nicaraguan State in Conflict and Reconciliation (1860–1987)." Ph.D. dissertation, Stanford University, 1989.

Hamilton, Gary G. "Ethnicity and Regionalism: Some Factors Influencing Chinese Identities in Southeast Asia." *Ethnicity* 4 (1977): 337–51.

Han Hufeng. "Mama shi 'Jiangbei ren' " (My mother is a Jiangbei person). *Xinmin wanbao* (New people's evening news), Nov. 30, 1986.

Handlin, Oscar. *Boston's Immigrants*. New York: Atheneum, 1972.

Harrell, Stevan. "Ethnicity, Local Interests, and the State: Yi Communities in Southwestern China," *Comparative Studies in Society and History* 32 (1980): 515–48.

———. "From *Xiedou* to *Yijun*, the Decline of Ethnicity in Northern Taiwan, 1885–1895." *Late Imperial China* 11, 1 (June 1990): 99–127.

Hauser, Ernest O. *Shanghai: City for Sale*. New York: Harcourt, Brace, and Co., 1940.

Hershatter, Gail. "The Hierarchy of Shanghai Prostitution, 1870–1949." *Modern China* 15, 4 (October 1989): 463–98.

He Zhenghua. Personal interview. Xinxin Beauty Salon, Shanghai, Nov. 12, 1986.

He Zhiguang. Personal interview. Putuo District Federation of Commerce and Industry, Shanghai, June 26, 1980.

Hinton, Harold. "The Grain Tribute System of the Ch'ing Dynasty." *Far Eastern Quarterly* 11, 3 (1952): 339–54.

———. *The Grain Tribute System of China (1845–1911)*. Cambridge: Harvard University Press, 1956.

Honig, Emily. *Sisters and Strangers: Women in the Shanghai Cotton Mills*. Stanford: Stanford University Press, 1986.

Ho Ping-ti. "The Geographical Distribution of Hui-kuan (Landsmannschaften) in Central and Upper Yangtzi Provinces." *Tsing Hua Journal of Chinese Studies* 5 (1966): 120–52.

————. "The Salt Merchants of Yang-chou: A Study of Commercial Capitalism in Eighteenth-Century China." *Harvard Journal of Asiatic Studies* 17 (June 1954): 130–68.

Huai'an lühu tongxianghui (Association of sojourners from Huai'an in Shanghai). Shanghai Municipal Archives, 6–5–993.

Huai-yang lühu tongxiang fulihui (Service society for sojourners in Shanghai from Huai'an and Yangzhou), 1948. Shanghai Municipal Archives, 6–9–246.

Huang, Philip C. C. *The Peasant Family and Rural Development in the Yangzi Delta, 1350–1988.* Stanford: Stanford University Press, 1990.

Huang Renjing. *Huren baojian* (What the Chinese in Shanghai ought to know). Shanghai: Methodist Publishing House, 1913.

Jameson, C. D. "River Systems of the Provinces of Anhui and Kiangsu North of the Yangzekiang." *Chinese Recorder and Missionary Journal* 43, 1 (January 1912): 69–75.

Jiang Junzhang. "Jiangsusheng shidi gaiyao" (An outline of the history and geography of Jiangsu province). *Jiangsu yanjiu* (Jiangsu research), pt. 1: 1, 8 (Dec. 25, 1935): 1–16; pt. 2: 2, 1 (Jan. 25, 1936): 1–9; pt. 3: 2, 2 (Feb. 25, 1936): 1–9; pt. 4: 2, 3 (Mar. 25, 1936): 1–8; pt. 5: 2, 5 (May 31, 1936): 1–7.

Jiang Sanxiao. Personal interview. Shanghai Harbor Coal Handling Co., Aug. 27, 1988.

"Jiangbei lühu tongxiang fuwushe luqi" (Record of the founding of the Service Society for Jiangbei Sojourners in Shanghai), 1946. Shanghai Municipal Archives, 6–9–228.

Jianghuai lühu tongxianghui (Association for sojourners from Jianghuai in Shanghai), 1946–47. Shanghai Municipal Archives, 6–5–954.

" 'Jiangnan' he 'Jiangbei' " (Jiangnan and Jiangbei). *Zhongguo qingnian bao* (China youth news), Mar. 30, 1982.

Jiangsusheng he Shanghaishi fangyan diaocha zhidaozu, ed., *Jiangsusheng he Shanghaishi fangyan gaikuang* (The general condition of Jiangsu province and Shanghai local dialects). N.p.: Jiangsu renmin chubanshe, 1960.

Jiefang ribao (The liberation daily). Shanghai.

Jin Yuan. "Jiangbei ren zai Shanghai" (Jiangbei people in Shanghai). *Nüsheng* (Women's voice) 4 (1934): 9–11.

Jing'an District Sanitation Bureau, Shanghai. Interview with workers, Nov. 18, 1986.

"Jingjiang funü shenghuo" (The livelihood of women in Jingjiang). In Si He, ed., *Zhongguo funü xiezhen* (A description of Chinese women), 70. Shanghai: Guangxing shuju, 1934.

Johnson, Chalmers. *Peasant Nationalism and Communist Power: The Emergence of Revolutionary China, 1937–1945.* Stanford: Stanford University Press, 1962.

Jones, Susan Mann. "The Ningbo Pang and Financial Power at Shanghai." In Mark Elvin and G. William Skinner, eds., *The Chinese City between Two Worlds*, 73–96. Stanford: Stanford University Press, 1976.

Jones, Susan Mann, and Philip Kuhn. "Dynastic Decline and the Roots of Rebellion." In John Fairbank, ed., *The Cambridge History of China*, vol. 10, pp. 107–62. Cambridge: Cambridge University Press, 1978.

Junkin, William F. "Famine Conditions in North Anhui and North Kiangsu." *Chinese Recorder* 43, 1 (January 1912): 79–80.

"Kankan Jiangbei ren" (Looking at Jiangbei people). *Jingbao* (The crystal), Mar. 1, 1924.

Ko, Dorothy Yin-yee. "Toward a Social History of Women in Seventeenth-Century China." Ph.D. dissertation, Stanford University, 1989.

Kraus, Richard. *Class Conflict in Chinese Socialism*. New York: Columbia University Press, 1981.

Kyong Bae-Tsung. "Industrial Women in Wusih: A Study of Industrial Conditions." National Committee of the YWCA of China, 1929. YWCA National Board Archives.

Lamley, Harry. "Subethnic Rivalry in the Ch'ing Period." In Emily Martin Ahern and Hill Gates, eds., *The Anthropology of Taiwanese Society, 262–318*. Stanford: Stanford University Press, 1981.

Laurie, Bruce, Theodore Hershberg, and George Alter. "Immigrants and Industry: The Philadelphia Experience, 1850–1880." In Richard L. Ehrlich, ed., *Immigrants in Industrial America, 1850–1920, 123–50*. Charlottesville: University Press of Virginia, 1977.

Lei Jingdun. "Shanghai Yangshupu renlichefu diaocha" (Survey of rickshaw pullers in Shanghai's Yangshupu). Graduation thesis, Pujiang University, Shanghai, 1930.

Lees, Lynn Hollen. *Exiles of Erin: Irish Migrants in Victorian London*. Ithaca: Cornell University Press, 1979.

Leung Yuen Sang. "Regional Rivalry in Mid-Nineteenth Century Shanghai: Cantonese vs. Ningpo Men." *Ch'ing-shih wen-t'i* 4, 8 (December 1982): 29–50.

———. *The Shanghai Taotai: Linkage Man in a Changing Society, 1843–90*. Honolulu: University of Hawaii Press, 1990.

Li Changfu. *Jiangsusheng dizhi* (Gazetteer of Jiangsu province). Shanghai: Zhonghua shuju, 1936.

Li Cishan. "Shanghai laodong qingkuang" (The condition of labor in Shanghai). *Xin qingnian* (New youth) 7, 6 (May 1920): 1–83.

Li Pingheng. *Zhongguo laodong nianjian* (The China labor yearbook). Beijing, 1932.

Li Tiangang. "Cong 'huayang fenju' dao 'huayang zachu'—Shanghai zaoqi zujie shehui xilun" (From segregation to integration of the Chinese and foreign residents of Shanghai: An analysis of the early concession society in Shanghai). In Hong Ze, ed., *Shanghai yanjiu luncong* (Papers on Shanghai studies), 225–39. Shanghai: Shanghai shehui kexueyuan chubanshe, 1989.

Li Weiqing. *Shanghai xiangtu zhi* (Shanghai local gazetteer). Shanghai, 1907. Reprinted in *Shanghaitan yu Shanghairen congshu* (Collected works on Shanghai and Shanghai people). Shanghai: Shanghai guji chubanshe, 1989.

Liu Housheng. *Zhang Jian zhuanji* (Biography of Zhang Jian). Shanghai: Kexue chubanshe, 1953.

Liu Huiwu, Zhu Hua, Su Zhiliang, Cui Meiming, Sun Guoda. *Shanghai jindaishi* (Shanghai modern history), 2 vols. Shanghai: Huadong shifan daxue chubanshe, 1987.

Liu Peiqian, ed. *Da Shanghai zhinan* (Guide to Shanghai). Shanghai: Zhonghua shuju, 1936.

Lu Manyan. "Jiangnan yu Jiangbei" (Jiangnan and Jiangbei). *Renyan zhoukan* (Hearsay weekly) 1, 9 (June 23, 1934): 389–90.

Lu Xun. "Toys." In *Lu Xun: Selected Works,* vol. 4, pp. 54–55. Beijing: Foreign Languages Press, 1960.

Luo Meihuan. "Jiangsu Jiangbei gexian de meiluo—qi yuanyin ji qi jiuji banfa" (The decline of each county in Jiangbei—its causes and methods of salvation). *Jiangsu yuebao* (Jiangsu monthly) 1, 2 (Dec. 20, 1933): 69–74.

Luo Qiong. "Jiangsu beibu nongcunzhongde laodong funü" (Working women in the villages of northern Jiangsu). *Dongfang zazhi* (The eastern miscellany) 32, 14 (1935): 107–09.

Ma Xiuying. Personal interview. Zhabei District Sanitation Bureau, Nov. 3, 1986.

Mandel, Ruth. "Ethnicity and Identity among Migrant Guestworkers in West Berlin." In Nancie L. Gonzalez and Carolyn S. McCommon, eds., *Conflict, Migration, and the Expression of Ethnicity,* 60–74. Boulder: Westview Press, 1989.

Mann, Susan. "Pariah Communities in Qing Society." Paper prepared for the Annual Meeting of the Association of Asian Studies, March 1988.

———. "The Cult of Domesticity in Shanghai's Middle Class." Paper prepared for the China Regional Seminar, University of California, Berkeley, November 1990.

———. "Women's Work and the Household Economy." Paper prepared for the Berkshire Conference on the History of Women, Rutgers University, June 1990.

Minguo ribao (Republican daily).

Moen, Lars. *Under the Heel*. Philadelphia: J. B. Lippincott Co., 1941.

Muramatsu, Yuji. "A Documentary Study of Chinese Landlordism in the Late Ch'ing and Early Republican Kiangnan." *Bulletin of the School of Oriental and African Studies* 29, 3 (1966): 566–99.

Murphey, Rhoads. *Shanghai: Key to Modern China*. Cambridge: Harvard University Press, 1953.

Nantong lühu tongxianghui (Association for sojourners from Nantong in Shanghai). Shanghai Municipal Archives, 6–5-978.

Naquin, Susan, and Evelyn S. Rawski. *Chinese Society in the Eighteenth Century*. New Haven: Yale University Press, 1987.

Negishi, Tadashi. *Chūgoku no girudo* (The guilds of China). Tokyo, 1953.

———. *Shanhai no girudo* (The guilds of Shanghai). Tokyo, 1951.

New Fourth Army Research Institute, Shanghai Academy of Social Sciences. Interview with members, Nov. 13, 1987.

North China Herald. Shanghai.

Ocko, Jonathan. *Bureaucratic Reform in Provincial China: Ting Jih-ch'ang in Restora-*

tion Kiangsu, 1867–1870. Cambridge: Council on East Asian Studies, Harvard University, 1983.

O'Keefe, Thomas Andrew. "Consider the Racism in the Term 'Hispanic.'" *The New York Times,* Oct. 10, 1989.

Ong, Paul. "Chinese Labor in Early San Francisco: Racial Segmentation and Industrial Expansion." *Amerasia* 8, 1 (1981): 69–82.

Ownby, David. "The Ethnic Feud in Qing Taiwan: What Is This Violence Business, Anyway? An Interpretation of the 1782 Zhang-Quan *Xiedou.*" *Late Imperial China* 11, 1 (June 1990): 75–98.

Pan Jingan. Personal interview. Shanghai Harbor Coal Handling Co., Aug. 4, 1988.

Peng Xiaoming. "Shanghaihua yu Subeihua" (Shanghai dialect and Subei dialect). *Xinmin wanbao* (New people's evening news), Aug. 2, 1985.

Perdue, Peter. *Exhausting the Earth: State and Peasant in Hunan, 1500–1850.* Cambridge: Council on East Asian Studies, Harvard University, 1987.

Perry, Elizabeth. *Rebels and Revolutionaries in North China, 1845–1945.* Stanford: Stanford University Press, 1980.

———. "Shanghai on Strike: The Politics of Chinese Labor." Unpublished manuscript, 1989.

Pott, F. L. Hawks. *A Short History of Shanghai.* Shanghai: Kelly and Walsh, 1928.

Qi Yufan. Personal interview. Shanghai Huai Opera Troupe, Oct. 30, 1986.

Qian Nairong. Personal interview. Shanghai University, Nov. 1986.

Quan Zhuanzhan. *Shanghai suyu da zidian* (A dictionary of Shanghai slang). N.p.: Yunxuan chubanbu, 1924.

Richards, L. *Comprehensive Geography of the Chinese Empire and Dependencies.* Shanghai: T'usewei Press, 1908.

Rowe, William. *Hankow: Commerce and Society in a Chinese City, 1796–1889.* Stanford: Stanford University Press, 1984.

———. *Hankow: Conflict and Community in a Chinese City, 1796–1895.* Stanford: Stanford University Press, 1989.

Ruan Henghui. Personal interview. Shanghai University, Nov. 1986.

Ruiz, Vicki L. "By the Day or the Week: Mexicana Domestic Workers in El Paso." In Vicki L. Ruiz and Susan Tiano, eds., *Women on the U.S.-Mexico Border: Responses to Change,* 61–76. Boston: Allen and Unwin, 1987.

Sarna, Jonathan. "From Immigrants to Ethnics: Toward a New Theory of 'Ethnicization.'" *Ethnicity* 5 (1978): 370–78.

Shanghai Bureau of Social Affairs. *Wage Rates in Shanghai.* Shanghai: Commercial Press, 1935.

Shanghai chuzu qiche gongsi (Shanghai taxicab company). *Shanghai jiedao he gonglu yingye keyun shiliao jiangji* (Compendium of historical materials on the Shanghai street and road business and public transport). Shanghai, 1982.

Shanghai gangshi hua bianxiezu (Editorial committee for stories of the history of the Shanghai docks). *Shanghai gangshi hua* (Stories of the history of the Shanghai docks). Shanghai: Shanghai renmin chubanshe, 1979.

Shanghai Municipal Council. *Report for the Year 1917 and Budget for the Year 1918.* Shanghai: Kelly and Walsh, 1918.

———. *Report for the Year 1931 and Budget for the Year 1932.* Shanghai: Kelly and Walsh, 1932.

———. *Report for the Year 1932 and Budget for the Year 1933.* Shanghai: Kelly and Walsh, 1933.

———. *Report for the Year 1935 and Budget for the Year 1936.* Shanghai: Kelly and Walsh, 1936.

Shanghai Municipal Police Files. Microfilm (67 reels).

Shanghai Police Daily Reports, 1925. Shanghai Municipal Archives.

Shanghai shehui kexueyuan jingji yanjiusuo (Institute of economics, Shanghai Academy of Social Sciences). *Jiangnan zaochuanchang changshi, 1865–1949.5* (History of the Jiangnan arsenal). Yancheng: Jiangsu renmin chubanshe, 1983.

———. *Nanyang xiongdi yancao gongsi shiliao* (Historical materials of the Nanyang Brothers' Tobacco Co.). Shanghai: Shanghai renmin chubanshe, 1958.

———. *Rongjia qiye shiliao* (Historical materials of the Rong family enterprises). Shanghai: Shanghai renmin chubanshe, 1980.

———. *Shanghai penghuqude bianqian* (Changes in the squatter settlements of Shanghai). Shanghai: Shanghai renmin chubanshe, 1965.

Shanghai shehui kexueyuan lishi yanjiusuo (Institute of history, Shanghai Academy of Social Sciences). *Wusi yundong zai Shanghai shiliao xuanji* (Selected historical materials on the May Fourth Movement in Shanghai). Shanghai: Shanghai renmin chubanshe, 1980.

Shanghai shirenzhi (Atlas of the Shanghai elite). Shanghai, 1947.

Shanghaishi chuzu qiche gongsi (Shanghai taxicab company). *Shanghai jiedao he gonglu yingye shiliao jiangji* (Compendium of historical materials on the Shanghai street and road business and public transport). Shanghai, 1982.

Shanghaishi mianfangzhi gongye tongye gonghui (Bureau of statistics on the Shanghai textile industry). *Zhongguo mianfang tongji shiliao* (Statistics on the history of the cotton industry in China). Shanghai, 1950.

Shanghaishi renlicheye tongye gonghui (Shanghai rickshaw enterprise union). *Shanghai gongbuju gaige renliche jiufen zhenxiang* (The true nature of disputes about reforming rickshaws in the Shanghai Municipal Council). Shanghai, 1934.

Shanghaishi renmin zhengfu gongshangju jingji jihuachu (Economic planning office of the Bureau of Industry and Commerce of the Shanghai People's Government). *Shanghai siying gongshangye fenye gaikuang* (The general condition of each privately owned business and industrial enterprise in Shanghai). Shanghai, 1951.

Shanghaishi shanghui (Shanghai Chamber of Commerce). *Shanghaishi geye tongye gonghui lilingshi minglu* (Directory of board members of business federations of each enterprise in Shanghai). Shanghai, n.d.

Shanghaishi shehuiju (Shanghai Bureau of Social Afairs). "Shanghaishi renlichefu shenghuo zhuangkuang diaocha baogaoshu" (Report on the general living conditions of Shanghai's rickshaw pullers). *Shehui banyue kan* (Society bimonthly) 1, 1 (Sept. 10, 1934): 99–113; 1, 4 (Oct. 25, 1934): 45–57.

Shanghai tongshe. *Shanghai yanjiu ziliao* (Research materials on Shanghai). Taibei: Zhongguo chubanshe, 1973.

Shenbao (The Huangpu daily). Shanghai.

Shi Xiaomei. Personal interview. Shanghai Number One Textile Mill, Mar. 11, 1980.

Shibao (The eastern times). Shanghai.

Shijie ribao (The world daily). New York.

Skinner, G. William. "Introduction: Urban Social Structure in Ch'ing China." In G. William Skinner, ed., *The City in Late Imperial China,* 521–54. Stanford: Stanford University Press, 1977.

———. "Mobility Strategies in Late Imperial China: A Regional Analysis." In Carol A. Smith, ed., *Regional Analysis,* 327–64. New York, 1976.

Sollors, Werner. *Beyond Ethnicity: Consent and Descent in American Culture.* New York: Oxford University Press, 1986.

Song Jingtian, Lu Fangping, Zhang Xinghua, Huang Peiqing, Huang Zhenying, Li Lei. "Shanghai qunzhong wenhua shenghuo zhuangkuang diaocha" (Investigation of the cultural life of the Shanghai masses). *Xiju yishu* (Drama technique) 4 (1984): 31–38.

Soong, James Han-hsi. "A Visual Experience in Nineteenth-Century China: Jen Po-nien (1840–1895)." Ph.D. dissertation, Stanford University, 1977.

Spence, Jonathan. *The Death of Woman Wang.* New York: Penguin, 1978.

Stauffer, Milton T., ed. *The Christian Occupation of China: A General Survey of the Numerical Strength and Geographical Distribution of the Christian Forces in China Made By the Special Committee on Survey and Occupation, China Construction Committee, 1918–1921.* Shanghai: China Construction Committee, 1922.

Strand, David. *Rickshaw Beijing: City People and Politics in the 1920s.* Berkeley: University of California Press, 1989.

Subei Haimen liuwang jiuji xiehui (Association for the salvation of refugees from the Subei district of Haimen). 1946. Shanghai Municipal Archives, 6–9–219.

Subei nanmin jiuji huiyi Shanghai banshichu (Shanghai office for the salvation committee for Subei refugees). "Shanghai Subei nanmin jiuji baogao" (Report on the salvation of Subei refugees in Shanghai). 1946. Shanghai Municipal Archives, 6–9–225.

Subei nanmin shourongsuo (Subei refugee center). Shanghai Municipal Archives, 6–9–223.

Tao Jitian. "Wu-hu-hang nügong shenghuo gaikuang" (The general condition of women workers in Wuxi, Shanghai, and Hangzhou). *Minzhong yundong yuekan* (Popular movement monthly) 1, 3 (Oct. 1, 1932): 111–21.

Tao Juyin. *Gudu jianwen: kangzhan shiqide Shanghai.* (Sights and sounds of a lonely island: Shanghai during the Anti-Japanese War). Shanghai: Shanghai renmin chubanshe, 1979.

Tōa dobunkai (The East Asia Culture Association). *Shina keizai zensho* (The complete book of the Chinese economy). Osaka, 1908.

Tu Shipin. *Shanghai chunqiu* (Shanghai annals). Hong Kong: Zhongguo tushu bianjiguan, 1968.

Walder, Andrew. *Communist Neo-traditionalism*. Berkeley: University of California Press, 1986.

Wakeman, Frederic, Jr. *The Shanghai Public Security Bureau, 1927–1932*. Unpublished manuscript, 1989.

Walker, Kathy. "Merchants, Peasants and Industry: The Political Economy of the Cotton Textile Industry, Nantong County, 1895–1935." Ph.D. dissertation, University of California, Los Angeles, 1986.

Wang Dunqing. "You Jiangbei zhimindi ji" (Record of a Jiangbei colony). *Shanghai shenghuo* (Shanghai life) 8, 3 (April 1934): 17–18.

Wang Ermin. *Huaijun zhi* (Record of the Huai army). Taibei: Zhongguo xueshu zhuzuo jiangzhu weiyuanhui, 1967.

Wang Hongguang. "Laizi Shanghai 'xiaozhijiao' de baogao" (A report from the lower quarters of Shanghai). *Qingnian yidai* (The young generation) 4 (1985): 56–57.

Wang Jianmin. Personal interview. Shanghai Huai Opera Troupe, Oct. 30, 1986.

Wang Nanbi. "Jiangbei nongcun shikuang" (The actual condition of Jiangbei villages). In Qian Jiazhu, ed., *Zhongguo nongcun jingji lunwenji* (Collected essays on the Chinese rural economy). Shanghai, 1936.

Wang Peitang. *Jiangsusheng xiangtu zhi* (Local records of Jiangsu province). Changsha: Commercial Press, 1938.

Wang Shuhuai. *Zhongguo xiandaihua de qucheng yanjiu: Jiangsusheng, 1860–1916* (Modernization in China, 1860–1916: A regional study of social, political, and economic change in Kiangsu province). Taibei: Institute of Modern History, Academia Sinica, 1984.

Wang Xiaoying. "Subei guniang" (The Subei girl). *Xinmin wanbao* (New people's evening news).

Wei Hui. "Jiu Shanghai jietou de lutian zhiye" (Outdoor street enterprises in old Shanghai). In Chai Geng, ed., *Shanghai zhanggu* (Shanghai anecdotes), 69–76. Shanghai: Shanghai wenhua chubanshe, 1982.

Welch, Holmes. *The Practice of Chinese Buddhism, 1900–1950*. Cambridge: Harvard University Press, 1967.

White, Lynn T., III. *Policies of Chaos: The Organizational Causes of Violence in China's Cultural Revolution*. Princeton: Princeton University Press, 1989.

Williams, Brackette F. "A Class Act: Anthropology and the Race to Nation across Ethnic Terrain." *Annual Review of Anthropology* 18 (1989): 401–44.

Wolf, Eric. *Europe and the People without History*. Berkeley: University of California Press, 1982.

Wu Liangrong. "Shanghaishi Subeiji jumin shehui biandong fenxi" (An analysis of social mobility among Subei natives in Shanghai). In Shanghai shehuixue xuehui (Shanghai sociology association), ed., *Shehuixue wenji,* 170–90. (Collected essays on sociology). Shanghai, 1984.

Wu Liangrong and Lan Chengdong. "Zheshi jianli xinxing shehui guanxi de banjiaoshi: guanyu qishi Subeirende caifang yiyao" (This is the cornerstone of building new social relations: Interviews regarding discrimination against Subei people). *Shehui* (Society) 3 (1983): 27–31.

Wu Shoupeng. "Douliu yu nongcun jingji shidai de Xuhai geshu" (Stopping over in the agrarian age of Xuzhou and Haizhou districts). *Dongfang zazhi* (The eastern miscellany) 27, 7 (Apr. 10, 1930): 59–70.

Wu Yuanshu and Jiang Sitai. *Shanghai qibaige qigaide shehui diaocha* (A social survey of seven hundred beggars in Shanghai). Graduation thesis, Pujiang University, Shanghai, 1933.

Xia Keyun. Personal interview. Shanghai Coal Handling Co., Aug. 4, 1988; Aug. 27, 1988.

Xiao Wenyan. Personal interview. Shanghai Huai Opera Troupe, Oct. 10, 1986.

Xie Junmei. "Shanghai lishi shang renkou de bianqian" (Historical changes in the population of Shanghai). *Shehui kexue* (Social science) 3 (1980): 107–13, 124.

Xu Ke. *Qingbai leichao.* Shanghai: Shangwu shudian, 1920.

Xu Liansheng. Personal interview. Yudechi Bath House, Shanghai, Nov. 12, 1986.

Xu Ping. Personal interview. Shanghai, Sept. 1, 1988.

Xu Shimei. Personal interview. Shanghai Number One Textile Mill, Oct. 10, 1982.

Xu Shiying. *Shanghai zhanqu nanmin linshi jiujihui gongzuo baogaoshu* (Report on the work of the temporary relief efforts for refugees in Shanghai's war zones). N.p., n.d.

Xue Gengxin. "Jindai Shanghaide liumang" (Gangsters in modern Shanghai). *Shanghai wenshi ziliao* (Materials on Shanghai culture and history) 3 (1980): 160–78.

———. "Wo jiechuguode Shanghai banghui renwu" (Individuals in the Shanghai gangs with whom I had contact). In Zhongguo renmin zhengzhi xueshang huiyi Shanghaishi weiyuanhui wenshi ziliao gongzuo weiyuanhui, ed., *Jiu Shanghai de banghui* (Gangs in old Shanghai), 87–107. Shanghai: Shanghai renmin chubanshe, 1986.

Yan-fu lühu tongxianghui (Association for sojourners in Shanghai from Yancheng and Funing), 1946–47. Shanghai Municipal Archives, 6–9–956.

Yanagisako, Sylvia Junko. *Transforming the Past: Tradition and Kinship among Japanese Americans.* Stanford: Stanford University Press, 1985.

Yancey, William, Eugene Ericksen, and Richard Juliani. "Emergent Ethnicity: A Review and Reformulation." *American Sociological Review* 41, 3 (June 1976): 391–402.

Yang Zhangfu. Personal interview. Cultural Affairs Bureau, Zhongxing Street Residence Committee, Shanghai, Nov. 4, 1986.

Yangzhou bashu lühu tongxianghui (Association of sojourners in Shanghai from the eight counties of Yangzhou), 1946–47. Shanghai Municipal Archives. Yangzhou qixian lühu tongxianghui (Association of sojourners in Shanghai from the seven counties of Yangzhou). Shanghai Municipal Archives, 6–5–949.

Yi Junzuo. *Xianhua Yangzhou* (Musings of Yangzhou). Shanghai: Zhonghua shuju, 1934.

Yu-ji. "Guanyu Shanghaide shiye gongren" (Regarding unemployed workers in Shanghai). *Nü qingnian yuekan* (The YWCA monthly) 11, 4 (April 1932): 45.

Yuan Henghui. "Yangzhoudiao Shanghaihuade yuyin tezheng" (Sound characteristics of Yangzhou-accented Shanghai dialect). In Fudan daxue zhongguo yuyan wenxue yanjiusuo wuyu yanjiushi (Wu dialect research group of the Chinese language research institute at Fudan University), ed., *Wuyu luncong* (Collected essays on Wu dialect), 172–74. Shanghai: Shanghai jiaoyu chubanshe, 1988.

Zhabei District Sanitation Bureau, Shanghai. Interview with workers and officials, Nov. 3, 1986.

Zhang Jiaqi and Ban Zhiwen. "Shanghaishi penghuqu gaikuang diaocha baogao" (Report of a survey of the general condition of shack settlements in Shanghai). In Chen Renbing. *Youguan Shanghai ertong fulide shehui diaocha* (Investigation of social services for youth in Shanghai). Shanghai: Shanghai ertong fuli cujinhui, 1948.

Zhang Ronghua. Personal interview. Zhabei District Sanitation Bureau, Shanghai, Nov. 3, 1986.

Zhang Xinxin and Sang Ye. *Beijing ren: yibaige putong ren de zishu* (Chinese lives: Oral histories of one hundred ordinary people). Shanghai: Shanghai wenyi chubanshe, 1986.

Zhang Yaozhong. "Shanghai Zhabei pinminqude dixia douzhong" (The underground struggle in the Zhabei slum in Shanghai). *Shanghai wenshi ziliao* 2 (1980): 82–93.

Zhao Ruheng. *Jiangsusheng jian* (Jiangsu yearbook). Shanghai: Xin Zhongguo jianshe xuehui, 1935.

Zhongguo dabaike quanshu xiqu quyi bianxiezu, ed. *Zhongguo dabaike quanshu xiqu quyi* (Encyclopedia of Chinese opera and story-telling). Shanghai: Zhongguo dabaike quanshu chubanshe, 1983.

Zhongguo shehui kexueyuan jingji yanjiusuo (Institute of economics, Chinese Academy of Social Sciences), ed. *Shanghai minzu jiqi gongye* (The national machine industry in Shanghai). Beijing: Zhonghua shuju, 1966.

Zhongguo xijujia xiehui and Shanghaishi wenhuaju, ed. *Zhongguo difang siqu jicheng: Shanghaishi juan* (Compendium on Chinese local opera: Shanghai). Beijing: Zhongguo xiju chubanshe, 1959.

Zhongxing Street Residence Committee, Zhabei District, Shanghai. Interview with retired workers, Nov. 4, 1986.

Zhou Dianyuan. Personal interview. Yangzhou Restaurant, Shanghai, Aug. 24, 1988.

Zhou Erfu. *Morning in Shanghai*. Beijing: Foreign Languages Press, 1981.

Zhou Guozhen. Personal interview. Zhabei Sanitation Bureau. Shanghai, Nov. 3, 1986.

Zhou Jian. "Buxiang dang guanggun, Shanghai Subeiren gai jiguan" (Not wanting to be single: Subei people in Shanghai change their native place). *Chaoliu yuekan* (Tide monthly), March 15, 1989, p. 58.

Zhou Zhenhe and You Rujie. *Fangyan yu Zhongguo wenhua* (Local dialects and Chinese culture). Shanghai: Shanghai renmin chubanshe, 1986.

Zhu Bangxing, Hu Lin'ge, and Xu Sheng. *Shanghai chanye yu Shanghai zhigong* (Enterprises and workers in Shanghai). Hong Kong: Yuandong chubanshe, 1936.

Zhu Shouyuan (Union head, Shanghai Harbor Coal Handling Co.). Personal interview, Sept. 1, 1988.

Zhu Yan. *Xiaoyou waizhuan* (The unauthorized history of Lucky Little Rich). Zhengzhou, Henan: Huanghe wenyi chubanshe, 1986.

Zhu Zongshou. "Qingdai qianqi Yangzhou yanshang yu difang wenhua shiye" (Yangzhou salt merchants and local cultural affairs during the early Qing dynasty). *Yangzhou shiyuan xuebao* (Journal of Yangzhou Normal University) 4 (1984): 13–19.

Zhuan Xiangyuan. *Qingbang daheng: Huang Jinrong, Du Yuesheng, Zhang Xiaolin waizhuan* (Green Gang bosses: Biographies of Huang Jinrong, Du Yuesheng, and Zhang Xiaolin). Hong Kong: Zhongyuan chubanshe, 1987.

Zou Yiren. *Jiu Shanghai renkou bianqian de yanjiu* (Research on changes in the population of old Shanghai). Shanghai: Shanghai renmin chubanshe, 1980.

INDEX